Lecture Notes in Computer Science

Edited by G. Goos, J. Hartmanis and J. van I

Advisory Board: W. Brauer   D. Gries   J. Stoer

Josyula Ramachandra Rao

Extensions of the UNITY Methodology

Compositionality, Fairness and Probability in Parallelism

 Springer

Series Editors

Gerhard Goos
Universität Karlsruhe
Vincenz-Priessnitz-Straße 3, D-76128 Karlsruhe, Germany

Juris Hartmanis
Department of Computer Science, Cornell University
4130 Upson Hall, Ithaca, NY 14853, USA

Jan van Leeuwen
Department of Computer Science, Utrecht University
Padualaan 14, 3584 CH Utrecht, The Netherlands

Author

Josyula Ramachandra Rao
IBM Thomas J. Watson Research Center
P. O. Box 704, Yorktown Heights, NY 10598, USA

CR Subject Classification (1991): D.1.3, D.2.2, D.3, F.3, G.3

ISBN 3-540-59173-7 Springer-Verlag Berlin Heidelberg New York

CIP data applied for

© Springer-Verlag Berlin Heidelberg 1995
Printed in Germany

Typesetting: Camera-ready by author
SPIN: 10485587   06/3142-543210 - Printed on acid-free paper

Dedicated

to my parents,

Srimati Josyula Ratna and Sri Josyula Venkata Sastry.

Preface

The UNITY methodology marks an important milestone in research on program verification. The methodology shows how a simple programming notation and a small set of carefully engineered operators can be used to reason effectively about a wide variety of parallel programs. The goal of this treatise is to push these ideas further in order to explore and understand the limitations of this approach. We attempt to do this in three ways. First, we apply UNITY to formulate and tackle problems in parallelism such as compositionality. Second, we extend and generalize the notation and logic of UNITY in an attempt to increase its range of applicability. Finally, we develop paradigms and abstractions useful for algorithm design. We summarize our contributions below.

In designing a system of processes, it is desirable to have a guarantee that the progress made by each individual process is inherited by the system as a whole. Such a guarantee would aid in developing parallel programs in a compositional way. We use UNITY logic to formulate such a guarantee and use formal methods to derive sufficient (and yet practical) conditions for the guarantee to hold. These conditions require process interactions to obey certain commutativity conditions. Our restrictions permit compositional reasoning about progress properties of parallel programs and provide a rigorous justification for including certain syntactic features in parallel programming languages.

The nature of fairness assumed in executing a UNITY program determines the progress properties that can be proven of the program. Our second contribution is a uniform framework for the *systematic* design of proof rules for proving progress under a spectrum of fairness assumptions ranging from pure nondeterminism to strong fairness. Proofs of soundness and relative completeness of the synthesized rules follow by checking a set of simple conditions. Unlike existing work in this area, our proofs do not use ordinals.

One special notion of fairness that is being increasingly used by algorithm designers is that associated with tossing a coin. Of late, programmers have started using probabilistic transitions in designing simple and efficient algorithms for problems that may not have a deterministic solution. We generalize UNITY program to permit probabilistic transitions and develop a UNITY–like theory to design and prove the correctness of probabilistic parallel programs. We illustrate our theory with examples from random walks and mutual exclusion.

Finally, we propose a new paradigm for the design of probabilistic parallel programs called *eventual determinism*. The paradigm provides a means of combining probabilistic and deterministic algorithms to take advantage of both. The proofs of such algorithms use the probabilistic generalization of UNITY. We illustrate the paradigm with examples from conflict–resolution and self–stabilization.

Our investigations and results reaffirm the promise of UNITY: we conclude that it provides a versatile medium for posing and solving many of the diverse problems of parallelism.

Acknowledgements: This book is based on my doctoral dissertation which was completed at the University of Texas at Austin in August 1992. The work reported here has been deeply influenced by discussions with several people and I would like to take this opportunity to thank some of them.

I owe an enormous debt of gratitude to my supervisor, Professor J. Misra and to Professor Edsger W. Dijkstra. I have been greatly influenced by their taste in research topics and their clarity of thought. In writing this book, I have tried to achieve their conception of simplicity and elegance while aspiring for their high standards of rigor and excellence. I have also had the privilege of improving my work through discussions with Professor C. A. R. Hoare. I will remain indebted to him for his valuable criticisms and timely words of encouragement.

Chapters 4 and 5 of this thesis represent collaborative work with two of my colleagues, Ernie Cohen and Charanjit Jutla respectively: it has been a pleasure to work with them. I would also like to thank my colleagues in the UNITY group and the Distributed Systems Discussion Group at Austin especially Mike Barnett, Ken Calvert, Ted Herman, and Dave Naumann.

I gratefully acknowledge the financial support that I received from the Office of Naval Research, the Texas Advanced Research Program, the National Science Foundation, and the University of Texas at Austin.

I have been extremely fortunate to have enjoyed the company of good friends at all stages of my life. In particular, I would like to thank Asoke Chattopadhyaya, Vipin Chaudhary, Leena and Manoj Dharwadkar, T. Krishnaprasad, Lyn and David Loewi, Linda Mohusky, Vijaya and K. Muthukumar and Bikash Sabata. Finally, I will remain indebted to my parents, my sisters, Surya and Sundari, and my wife, Sailaja, for their love and emotional support.

Yorktown Heights, New York
December 1994

Josyula R. Rao

Table of Contents

यस्मिन सर्वाणि भूतान्यात्मैवाभूद्विजानतः ।
तत्र को मोहः कः शोक एकत्वमनुपश्यतः ॥

— ईशावास्योपनिषत्

For him who see unity in everything,
Where is the delusion, where is the grief ?

— Iśāvāsyopanishad
(circa 1000 BC)

1. Prologue

1.1 Background and Motivation

The problem of developing correct and reliable software has assumed the proportions of a crisis in the field of software development. The problem is not a new one: its debilitating grip on the software industry was felt as early as the sixties, when it was termed a *software crisis*. Three decades later, the crisis is still with us. Current approaches to software development are primitive and ad hoc at best. Programs are developed by a process of trial and error. Given a problem, the programmer uses his/her intuition to develop a program that purports to solve the problem. To increase his confidence in its correct functioning, the programmer executes the program on a representative sample of the expected inputs: the testing is restricted to a sample as it is impossible to test the program exhaustively on the potentially infinite set of inputs that might arise in practice. The programmer deems his job done when the program executes correctly on the subset of inputs that he considers typical. This, however, does not constitute a guarantee that the program is correct as it is well–known that "program testing can be used to show the presence of errors but never their absence"[1]. In a large software system, several such (possibly erroneous) programs interact and when they do, their errors get compounded by interacting in insidious and subtle ways. Locating errors in such a software system is akin to looking for needle in a haystack: it is a long, costly and time–consuming process.

This ad hoc approach to developing software has several undesirable consequences. First, due to the unpredictable nature of debugging, software managers find it difficult (if not impossible) to estimate and set project deadlines. Second, the absence of a convincing argument for correctness is reflected by the conspicuous absence of a warranty on the software product being delivered to the customer. What is surprising is that the customer is willing to invest large sums of money in a product in which, sooner or later, previously undetected errors begin to surface. Worse still, the process of correcting detected errors introduces more errors. In this sense, this is a costly proposition both for the customer and the vendor. Third, the approach does not scale up as the cost of applying it to large–scale systems is prohibitive. Finally, such an approach is completely unacceptable when developing programs whose performance is critical to human life and safety.

---

[1] This quote has been attributed to Edsger W. Dijkstra.

Even in the sixties, scientists such as Robert Floyd, C.A.R. Hoare and Edsger W. Dijkstra recognized the unprecedented scope and magnitude of the problem that confronted software development. They realised that what was needed was a new and radical approach to developing programs. Their equally revolutionary proposal was to *formally verify* the functionality of a program from the text of the program before ever executing it. The process of designing a program was elevated to the level of proving a theorem of mathematics. It was envisaged that such proofs would dramatically increase the programmer's confidence in the correct functioning of the software while completely eliminating the debugging phase in software development. With this aim in mind, Floyd [1967] introduced the idea of inductive assertions for proving the correctness of sequential programs. In his approach, programs were specified as flowcharts and the task of verifying them was reduced to proving two kinds of properties about them — *invariance* (or partial correctness) assertions and *termination* (or total correctness) assertions about them. This was followed by several theories for developing sequential programs, notably the partial correctness triples of Hoare [1969] and the weakest precondition theory of Dijkstra [1975].

The initial proposals for program verification were *a–posteriori*. The program came first and then one set about the task of constructing a proof of its correctness. This was a difficult task as one still had to guess at a program *before* verifying it. It was soon realised that a much more meaningful effort was to develop a program and its proof of correctness "hand in hand". In this approach, one begins with an abstract specification of the problem to be solved and *refines* it to obtain a new specification. The new specification has two properties: (a) any program that satisfies it, satisfies the original specification, and (b) it is easier to implement than the original specification. Refinement is an iterative process: at each step, the specification of the previous step is refined. The process terminates when one obtains a specification from which one can extract a program. Refinement has three advantages. First, a programmer does not guess at a program: it is suggested by the final specification. Second, the process of refinement automatically guarantees that a program that satisfies the final specification also satisfies the specification that one begins with. Lastly, the process of program design is transformed from a miraculous conception of a program to a sequence of well–justified steps. This activity, also termed as *program derivation*, has been used quite effectively in Dijkstra [1976] and Gries [1981] to develop a wide range of programs.

In the seventies, the realization of the importance of nondeterminism and the emergence of parallelism prompted researchers to try to extend verification techniques to cover programs incorporating these features as well. While sequential programs are *transformational* in that they transform a given input to an output and terminate, most parallel programs are ongoing and non-terminating. They are said to be *reactive*, in the sense that they continue to react to inputs from the environment. Preliminary efforts for verifying properties of reactive programs (Keller [1976], Lamport [1977], Owicki and Gries [1976], Owicki and Gries [1976]) concentrated on proving partial correctness or the so-called *safety* properties. While they were successful in this respect, their achievements with regard to proving general progress properties (like reachability) were modest.

In the early eighties, it was recognized that an essential ingredient of proofs of progress for parallel programs is *fairness*. Simply put, an assumption of fairness guarantees that every process is scheduled for execution *sufficiently often*, regardless of the state of the other processes. *Sufficiently often* was variously defined giving rise to differing notions of fairness, the simplest being *eventually*. While it is uncertain as to who originated the concept of fairness, the move stirred a lot of debate and controversy in the community. Critiques of fairness ranged from the linguistic ("the term proposes moral connotations where none exist") to the semantic ("the semantic functions of fair constructs are not ω-continuous Dijkstra [1976] and are thus non–computable and require the use of higher countable ordinals "). It was recognized that reasoning with fairness assumptions was akin to reasoning about unbounded non–determinism and this meant that the standard techniques of induction with natural numbers would not work in proving termination properties (Apt and Plotkin [1986], Lehmann et al. [1981]). In fact, Emerson and Clarke [1981] show that termination under fairness assumptions is not definable in the first–order theory of arithmetic. In an eloquent critique (Dijkstra [1987]), Edsger W. Dijkstra wrote, "... fairness, being an unworkable notion, can be ignored with impunity."

The notion of fairness opened a fertile research area and several papers proposing proof rules based on a variety of fairness notions (such as unconditional fairness, weak fairness, strong fairness, and extreme fairness) appeared in the literature (Apt et al [1984], Gabbay et al. [1980], Grumberg et al. [1981], Lehmann et al. [1981], Owicki and Lamport [1982], Park [1981], Pnueli [1983], Queille and Sifakis [1983], Stomp et al. [1989]). Occupying the middle ground were proponents of fairness, who insisted that programmer be required to encode the notion of fairness required by the application into the program (Apt and Olderog [1983], Olderog and Apt [1986]). In an effort to bring a semblance of coherence to the vast proliferation of formalisms and proof theories for fairness, Nissim Francez compiled them into a book (Francez [1986]). While this succeeded in creating a valuable sourcebook for the theoreticians practicing in this area, it was not as successful in simplifying and unifying the presentation of the material.

In the late eighties, K. Mani Chandy and Jayadev Misra introduced UNITY (Chandy and Misra [1988]), a formalism to aid in the specification and verification of parallel programs. By relentlessly using Occam's razor, Chandy and Misra stripped the treatment of parallelism down to its bare essentials. They started out by ignoring all aspects of programming language and architecture. A UNITY program is simply, a set of conditional multiple assignment statements. The equally minimal UNITY logic is very powerful: it consists of three operators — one for proving safety properties (**unless**) and two for proving progress properties (**ensures**, *leads–to*). These operators are used to develop a powerful set of theorems that can be used for program design. In spite of its extreme simplicity, UNITY has been used to derive a number of algorithms for a wide range of problems encountered in parallel programming.

1.2 Contributions of this Treatise

The goal of this treatise is explore the full potential of the UNITY style of program verification. Our aim is to understand, extend and generalize some of the choices made by the designers of UNITY. In an effort to push the boundaries, we raise several questions. Can UNITY programs contain statements more general than the multiple assignment? What properties of the multiple assignment are essential to the use of UNITY logic? How does one justify the format of the proof rules for progress? Are the proof rules sound and complete? In particular, can the relation **ensures** be substituted by some other relation without jeopardizing soundness and completeness? Does the relation *leads-to* compose? How essential is the UNITY assumption of unconditional fairness? How would the proof rule for progress change with a different assumption of fairness? Can one synthesize sound and complete proof rules for different fairness notions? How would one express probabilistic algorithms in UNITY? What changes are needed to reason about properties of probabilistic programs? Our contributions open up into four categories. We describe them below.

1.2.1 The Role of Commutativity in Parallel Program Design

Our first contribution is in the development of techniques that aid a programmer in implementing a given specification in compositional fashion. Existing techniques are helpful if the specification consists of safety properties alone and the actions of the different processes of the program satisfy a commutativity condition introduced by Richard Lipton (Lipton [1975]). A different commutativity condition proposed recently by Jayadev Misra (Misra [1991]) goes further in allowing progress properties in the specification provided the process implementing the progress property does so in a *wait–free* manner.

In this chapter, we integrate existing work on commutativity with research in compositional methodologies. We begin by presenting two relations on programs: *decoupling* and *weak decoupling*. These relations were first introduced in Cohen [1993]. The importance of these relations is justified by the observation that in a system of processes, if a process is decoupled (or weakly decoupled) from the rest of the system then the progress properties that it exhibits when executed in isolation, are also inherited by the system of processes. We refine these relations to obtain two new definitions of commutativity of programs. Our definitions are weaker than existing definitions and combine elements of Lipton and Misra commutativity in varying proportions.

Our definitions have two important consequences. First, they form the basis of a simple theorem for compositional reasoning about parallel program design. This methodology is better than Lipton's, in that *both* safety and progress properties are permitted in the specification of a parallel program. It improves on the methodology proposed by Misra by removing the constraint of *wait–freedom* on processes implementing progress properties. Second, from the perspective of a programming language designer, these definitions suggest constraints on the variables that can be shared between programs.

1.2.2 On the Design of Proof Rules for Fair Parallel Programs

Our second contribution is an attempt to simplify and unify existing work on fairness. To this end, we combine ideas from UNITY, the theory of predicate transformers, temporal logic and the μ–calculus to propose a framework for the systematic design of UNITY–style proof rules for progress for a range of fairness assumptions including pure nondeterminism, unconditional fairness, minimal progress, weak fairness and strong fairness.

Beginning with an intuitive branching time temporal logic ($CTL^\star$) formula characterizing progress for the fairness notion being considered, we obtain simple fixpoint characterizations of a predicate transformer called the weakest predicate that leads–to (denoted, **wlt**). We show that the fixpoint characterizations of a range of fairness assumptions share a common structure – they are all expressed in terms of a simpler predicate transformer, called the generalized weakest precondition (denoted, **gwp**). Using the definition of **gwp** as a guide, we extract simple UNITY–like proof rules for proving progress under the aforementioned fairness constraints. A key feature of our framework is that by merely checking a set of simple conditions, the soundness and completeness of the proof rules is easily guaranteed. Since one of the fairness assumptions is UNITY's notion of fairness, we prove the soundness and completeness of the progress fragment of UNITY logic. It is to be noted that unlike previous work on proof rules for fairness, our meta–theoretic arguments are conducted without resorting to any complicated machinery such as ordinals. Further, the UNITY–like formulation of the proof–rule enables one to use the UNITY theory of progress when designing programs based on different notions of fairness.

In many treatments of meta–theoretic arguments about fairness, the assumptions underlying the meta–theoretic result are not completely explicated. By drawing comparisons to Hoare triples, we show that a notion of completeness of a proof rule is subject to the same constraint of *relative completeness in the sense of Cook* as Hoare triples.

1.2.3 Reasoning About Probabilistic Parallel Programs

In the last decade, algorithm designers have used probabilistic transitions in algorithms to obtain simple and efficient algorithms to problems which at times have no deterministic solution. For the gain in simplicity and efficiency, one has to trade the notion of absolute correctness of algorithms for a probabilistic notion of correctness. Using ideas based on existing proof-systems for probabilistic algorithms, we develop a UNITY-like theory which can be used to specify and derive properties of probabilistic parallel programs that either hold deterministically or with probability one.

To this end, we generalize UNITY's notion of a program from a set of deterministic statements to a set of probabilistic statements. While we retain UNITY's notion of unconditional fairness in the selection of statements, we require *extreme fairness* (Pnueli [1983]) in executing a probabilistic statement. We show that one can continue using the theory of UNITY to prove deterministic safety and progress properties of probabilistic parallel programs. To prove progress properties that hold with probability one, we generalize UNITY's operators **unless**, **ensures** and *leads–to* to corresponding probabilistic versions **upto**, **entails** and *probabilistically leads–to*. We illustrate our theory by proving examples from random walk problems and mutual exclusion. Finally, we show that our theory is sound and complete for proving properties of finite state programs.

Although the proofs of probabilistic programs are tortuous at best, we show that they can be derived with the same rigor and elegance that we have seen in Dijkstra's derivation of sequential programs (Dijkstra [1976]) and Chandy and Misra's derivation of parallel programs (Chandy and Misra [1988]).

1.2.4 Eventual Determinism: Using Probabilistic Means to Achieve Deterministic Ends

We introduce a new paradigm for the design of parallel algorithms called *eventual determinism*. In an *eventually–determinizing* algorithm, all processes execute identical programs from identical starting states. A program has two parts (also called *modes*) — *probabilistic* and *deterministic*. A process begins execution in the probabilistic mode and eventually (with probability one) switches to a deterministic mode. The decision to switch is taken *independently* by each process. This means that it is possible for different processes to be executing in different modes at the same time. It is possible that a process may change back to the probabilistic mode but it is required that eventually, each process should switch and stay in the deterministic mode. Thus determinacy pervades the system.

Eventually–determinizing algorithms are designed to combine the advantages of probabilistic and deterministic algorithms. Probabilistic algorithms typically use randomization in a limited way. Typically, the probabilistic mode is used for a task that either can be done more efficiently probabilistically or cannot be accomplished deterministically (e.g. breaking symmetry). Once this has been accomplished, a process can switch modes to take advantage of determinacy (e.g. the worst case complexities are bounded). We emphasize two features of our method: first, the switchover point is *not* a bottleneck for the system; second, the specification of the component modes can be used to construct a compositional proof of the specification of the eventually–determinizing algorithm.

We illustrate the design of eventually–determinizing algorithms with two examples. First, we address the problem of conflict–resolution for distributed systems. We construct an algorithm for a ring of dining philosophers by combining a modified version of the probabilistic Lehmann–Rabin's Free Philosopher algorithm (which only ensures deadlock–freedom) with the deterministic Chandy–Misra algorithm. The resulting system is proved to be starvation–free. Our second example is drawn from the field of self–stabilization. We construct a simple probabilistic algorithm for a ring containing an odd number of processes. Using this algorithm as a basis, we develop an eventually–determinizing algorithm for self–stabilization. This algorithm has the pleasing property that only deterministic transitions are used in its normal mode of operation. When faults occur, probabilisitic transitions are used to bring the system back to a legal state. Compared to deterministic algorithms which require a minimum number of three shared states per process, the eventually determinizing algorithm uses only two states per process.

The paradigm of eventual determinism has been designed to take advantage of the proof system for probabilistic programs developed earlier. One of the features of the proof system is that it allows the manipulation of probabilistic and deterministic properties within one unified framework. Our hope was to take existing proofs of component algorithms along with a proof of correctness of their interaction to construct a compositional proof of the eventually determinizing algorithm as a whole. In the interests of brevity, we only present proof sketches of the algorithms in this thesis.

1.3 Overview of this Treatise

We begin, in Chapter 2, with a brief overview of the notation used, useful results about predicate transformers and the format in which our proofs are presented. In Chapter 3, we introduce the UNITY programming notation and logic. The next four chapters contain our contributions. Chapter 4 presents our results on compositional reasoning about parallel programs. In Chapter 5, we develop a framework for designing UNITY–style proof rules based on a range of fairness assumptions. We apply our framework to design proof rules for pure nondeterminism, minimal progress, unconditional fairness, weak fairness and strong fairness. In Chapter 6, we generalize the deterministic transitions of UNITY programs to probabilistic transitions and develop a logic to reason about program properties that either hold deterministically or with probability one. We illustrate the use of our logic by proving programs from random walk problems and mutual exclusion. Chapter 7 introduces a new paradigm called *eventual determinism* for the design of probabilistic parallel programs. We illustrate the paradigm by designing eventually–determinizing algorithms for conflict resolution and self–stabilization. Finally, in Chapter 8, we summarize our research and suggest some topics for future research.

2. Preliminaries

In the first section of this chapter, we introduce the notation used in this book. The notions of a predicate transformer and their junctivity properties are introduced in section 2.2. In the third section, we define three well–known predicate transformers and summarize their junctivity properties. In section 2.4, we introduce the concept of an extremal solution of an equation and state some useful theorems about such solutions. We conclude with a brief description of the proof format used in this book.

2.1 Notation and Terminology

We assume that the reader is familiar with the concepts of the state space of a program (defined as the cross–product of the domains of the program variables). We also assume the existence of an assertion language (corresponding to $L_{\infty\omega}$) for expressing predicates on program states. The set of such state predicates will be denoted by **Pred**. Universal quantification over all program variables (that is, the state space of the program) is denoted by surrounding a predicate by square brackets ([], read: *everywhere*). This unary operator has all the properties of universal quantification over a non–empty range. For a detailed discussion of this notation the reader is referred to Dijkstra and Scholten [1990].

We write X, Y, Z to denote predicates on program states and $\mapsto$, $\rightsquigarrow$ etc. to denote relations on predicates. For binary relations **R, S** on predicates, we say that **R** is *stronger* than **S** (in formulae **R** $\Rightarrow$ **S**), if and only if $\langle \forall X, Y :: X \, \mathbf{R} \, Y \Rightarrow X \, \mathbf{S} \, Y \rangle$.

We will use the following notational conventions: the expression

$$\langle \underline{Q}x : r.x : t.x \rangle$$

where $Q \in \{\forall, \exists\}$, denotes quantification over all $t.x$ for which x satisfies $r.x$. We call x the **dummy**, $r.x$ the **range** and $t.x$ the **term** of the quantification. When the range $r.x$ is understood from the context, we will omit it and write the same quantified expression as

$$\langle \underline{Q}x :: t.x \rangle$$

We adopt the convention that all formulae are universally quantified over all free variables occurring in them (these are variables that are neither dummies nor program variables).

For an assignment statement of the form $x := e$, and a state predicate X, we denote the predicate obtained by substituting all free occurrences of variable x in X with e by $\{x := e\}X$.

To summarize, angle brackets ($\langle\ \rangle$) denote the scope of quantification, square brackets ($[\ ]$) denote quantification over an anonymous state space and curly brackets ($\{\ \}$) are reserved for the operation of substitution.

The other operators we use are summarized below, ordered by increasing binding powers.

$$\equiv, \not\equiv$$
$$\Leftarrow, \Rightarrow$$
$$\Longmapsto, \mapsto, \rightsquigarrow, \text{ etc.}$$
$$\wedge, \vee$$
$$\neg$$
$$=, \neq, \leq, <, \geq, >$$
$$+, -$$
$$\text{``.''} \text{ (function application)}$$

Note that *dot* (".") is used to denote function application. All boolean and arithmetic operators have their usual meanings.

2.2 Predicate Transformers and Their Junctivity Properties

Informally, a *predicate transformer* can be described as a mapping which takes a finite list of predicates as an argument and yields a predicate as its result. Formally, a *predicate transformer* is a function from **Pred**^{n} to **Pred**, where **Pred** is the set of predicates. In this book, we will only consider unary predicate transformers (that is, $n = 1$).

We use the letters f, g and h to denote predicate transformers. For predicate transformers f, g, we say that f is *stronger* than g if and only if

$$\langle \forall X :: [f.X \Rightarrow g.X] \rangle.$$

In this section, we define a number of junctivity[1] properties for our predicate transformers. The following definitions and theorems have been taken from Dijkstra and Scholten [1990] (particularly chap. 6).

Definition 2.2.1. *A predicate transformer f is said to be* conjunctive *over a bag of predicates V if and only if*

$$[f.\langle \forall X : X \in V : X \rangle \equiv \langle \forall X : X \in V : f.X \rangle]$$

Definition 2.2.2. *A predicate transformer f is said to be* disjunctive *over a bag of predicates V if and only if*

$$[f.\langle \exists X : X \in V : X \rangle \equiv \langle \exists X : X \in V : f.X \rangle]$$

---

[1] We use the term *junctive* and its noun form to stand for either *conjunctive* or *disjunctive*.

In other words, the conjunctivity of f describes the extent to which f distributes over universal quantification and its disjunctivity describes how it distributes over existential quantification. The less restricted the bag of predicates V, the stronger the type of junctivity. Accordingly, we can distinguish the following types of junctivity:

- *universally junctive* : junctive over all V.
- *positively junctive* : junctive over all non–empty V.
- *denumerably junctive* : junctive over all non–empty V with denumerably many distinct predicates.
- *finitely junctive* : junctive over all non–empty V with a finite number of distinct predicates.
- *and-continuous* : conjunctive over all non–empty V, the distinct predicates of which can be ordered as a monotonic sequence.
- *or-continuous* : disjunctive over all non–empty V, the distinct predicates of which can be ordered as a monotonic sequence.
- *monotonic* : junctive over all non–empty V, the distinct predicates of which can be ordered as a monotonic sequence of finite length.

The various types of junctivity are related by the following theorem.

Theorem 2.2.1. *Relating Junctivity Properties :*

- *(universally junctive $\Rightarrow$ positively junctive)*
- *(positively junctive $\Rightarrow$ denumerably junctive)*
- *(denumerably conjunctive $\Rightarrow$ finitely conjunctive and and-continuous)*
- *(denumerably disjunctive $\Rightarrow$ finitely disjunctive and or-continuous)*
- *Both finitely conjunctive and and-continuity $\Rightarrow$ monotonicity*
- *Both finitely disjunctive and or-continuity $\Rightarrow$ monotonicity*

2.3 Some Useful Predicate Transformers

In this thesis, we will make extensive use of three predicate transformers introduced in Dijkstra [1975]. These are

1. **Weakest Liberal Precondition (wlp):** For a statement s and a state predicate X, the *weakest liberal precondition* of s with respect to X is denoted by $\mathbf{wlp}.s.X$. It characterizes precisely those initial states beginning in which each execution of statement s *either* fails to terminate *or* terminates in a state satisfying predicate X.
2. **Weakest Precondition (wp):** For a statement s and a state predicate X, the *weakest precondition* of s with respect to X is denoted by $\mathbf{wp}.s.X$. It characterizes precisely those initial states beginning in which each execution of statement s is guaranteed to terminate in a state satisfying predicate X.
3. **Strongest Postcondition (sp):** For a statement s and a state predicate X, the *strongest postcondition* of s with respect to X is denoted by $\mathbf{sp}.s.X$. It characterizes precisely those final states for which there exists an execution

of statement s beginning in a state satisfying X and terminating in that final state.

For the statements that we consider, these predicate transformers satisfy the following "healthiness" conditions. The reader is referred to chap. 7, 11 and 12 of Dijkstra and Scholten [1990] for proofs of these theorems.

1. *Conjunctivity of* **wlp**.s *and* **wp**.s: For every statement s, the predicate transformer **wlp**.s is universally conjunctive and the predicate transformer **wp**.s is positively conjunctive.

2. *Disjunctivity of* **wlp**.s *and* **wp**.s: For every *deterministic* statement s, the predicate transformer **wlp**.s is positively disjunctive and the predicate transformer **wp**.s is universally disjunctive.

3. *Law of the Excluded Miracle*: For every statement s,

$$[\mathbf{wp}.s.false \equiv false]$$

We can shown that for every statement, the predicate transformers **wlp**.s and **sp**.s are converse predicate transformers in the following sense.

$$[X \Rightarrow \mathbf{wlp}.s.Y] \equiv [\mathbf{sp}.s.X \Rightarrow Y].$$

This means that the predicate transformer **sp**.s is as disjunctive as **wp**.s is conjunctive. Equivalently, the predicate transformer **sp**.s is universally disjunctive.

The weakest preconditions of a number of program statements (such as skip, assignment, conditional, iteration, recursion) have been defined in the literature (Dijkstra [1975], Dijkstra and Scholten [1990]).

2.4 Extremal Solutions of Equations

For a set of equations E in the unknown x, we write $x : E$ to explicate the dependence of the equations E on the unknown x. Given an ordering $\Rightarrow$ on the solutions of E, y is the *strongest solution* (*or the least fixpoint of E*) if and only if

1. y solves E
2. $\langle \forall z : z \, \text{solves} \, E : y \Rightarrow z \rangle$

The *weakest solution* (*or the greatest fixpoint*) of E can be defined in a similiar manner.

We extend the notation for quantification, introduced earlier, to cover extremal solutions as well. We allow expressions of the form

$$\langle \underline{Q}x :: E \rangle$$

where Q can be one of μ and ν to denote the strongest and weakest solution of $x : \bar{E}$ respectively. Notice that in this case, we leave the range empty. In the case where E is of the form $[X \equiv f.X]$, we write $\langle \underline{Q}X :: f.X \rangle$ to mean $\langle \underline{Q}X :: [X \equiv f.X] \rangle$.

Finally, we will use the following form of the Theorem of Knaster–Tarski (see p. 154, 158–159, chap. 8 in Dijkstra and Scholten [1990]) to prove properties of extremal solutions.

Theorem 2.4.1 (Knaster–Tarski). *For monotonic f, the equation*

$$Y : [f.Y \equiv Y]$$

has a strongest and a weakest solution. Furthermore, it has the same strongest solution as

$$Y : [f.Y \Rightarrow Y]$$

and the same weakest solution as

$$Y : [f.Y \Leftarrow Y].$$

Theorem 2.4.2. *For monotonic f, let g.X be the strongest solution and h.X the weakest solution of*

$$Y : [f.X.Y \equiv Y].$$

Then both g and h are monotonic. Furthermore, h inherits the conjunctivity type of f and g inherits the disjunctivity type of f.

2.5 Proof Format

Most of our proofs will be purely calculational in the sense that they will consist of a number of syntactic transformations instead of semantic reasoning steps. For manipulating formulae of predicate calculus, we use a proof format that was proposed by Feijen, Dijkstra and others, and that greatly facilitates this kind of reasoning.

For instance, a proof that $[A \equiv D]$ could be rendered in our format as

$$
\begin{array}{ll}
& A \\
= & \{\text{hint why } [A \equiv B]\} \\
& B \\
= & \{\text{hint why } [B \equiv C]\} \\
& C \\
= & \{\text{hint why } [C \equiv D]\} \\
& D
\end{array}
$$

We also allow other transitive operators in the leftmost column. Among these are the more traditional *implies* ($\Rightarrow$) but also for reasons of symmetry, *follows-from* ($\Leftarrow$). For a more thorough treatment of this subject the reader is referred to Dijkstra and Scholten [1990] (chap. 4).

For manipulating formulae that may depend on several hypotheses, we retain the same calculational style but introduce a different format. Each row of the proof format looks as follows

                        ,hint why the formula holds

The advantage of this format is that if a particular step depends on several preceding proof steps rather than just the immediate predecessor then this dependence can be explicated in the hint by indicating the step numbers of the hypotheses. This will be particularly useful for proving temporal properties of programs.

3. An Introduction to UNITY

In this chapter, we give an overview of the UNITY programming methodology. The reader is referred to Chandy and Misra [1988] for a more thorough and detailed introduction to the subject.

3.1 The Programming Notation

A UNITY program consists of four parts: a collection of variable declarations, a set of abbreviations used to write programs succinctly, a set of initial conditions and a *finite* set of statements. These sections are called **declare, always, initially** and **assign** respectively. Thus a UNITY program may be seen as having the following form:

Program   *program-name*
    declare   *declare-section*
    always   *always-section*
    initially   *initially-section*
    assign   *assign-section*
end

The following UNITY program encodes Euclid's algorithm for finding the greatest common divisor of the numbers X and Y. It will be used to illustrate the various concepts of UNITY that we summarize in this chapter.

Program   *GCD*
    declare $x, y : natural$
    initially $x, y = X, Y$
    assign $x := x - y$ **if** $x > y$
        $\parallel$ $y := y - x$ **if** $y > x$
end

3.1.1 The Declare Section

The **declare** section of a UNITY program contains the names of the variables used in the program and their associated types. In program *GCD*, there are two variables, x and y, of type *natural*.

3.1.2 The Always Section

The **always** section defines abbreviations that can be used to write programs succinctly. It contains a set of equations that define certain program variables, known as *transparent variables*, as functions of other program variables. Transparent variables provide a convenient way of abbreviating expressions that occur frequently in specifications and programs. It is assumed that the set of equations is *proper*, that is, circular definitions of abbreviations are ruled out. Individual equations are separated using the symbol ⫿.

For instance, in program GCD, we could define transparent variables $decx$ and $decy$ as

$$decx \;=\; x > y$$
$$⫿$$
$$decy \;=\; y > x$$

and use them as abbreviations in the **assign** section. Since, the definitions of $decx$ and $decy$ don't depend upon one another, we could also define them simultaneously as

$$decx, decy \;=\; x > y, \; y > x$$

Equivalently, we can express simultaneous definition of transparent variables by using $\|$ as follows:

$$decx \;=\; x > y$$
$$\|$$
$$decy \;=\; y > x$$

If we wished to define a third transparent variable *equal* as

$$equal \;=\; \neg decx \wedge \neg decy$$

we cannot define it simultaneously with $decx$ and $decy$ as these variables have to be defined for the definition of *equal* to be meaningful.

3.1.3 The Initially Section

The **initially** section is a set of equations that define initial values for some program variables: uninitialized variables have arbitrary initial values. Just as in the **always** section, it is assumed that the set of equation is *proper*, that is, circular initializations of variables are ruled out. The equations in the **initially** section define a predicate on the program variables: we refer to this predicate as the *initial condition* of the program.

In program GCD, variables x and y are *simultaneously* initialized to the values X and Y respectively. The two equations

$$x \;=\; X$$
$$⫿$$
$$y \;=\; Y$$

would have performed the same initialization, albeit not simultaneously. The single equation

$$x = y$$

by itself would be meaningless since y would not have an initial value. The initial condition of program GCD is

$$(x = X) \wedge (y = Y)$$

3.1.4 The Assign Section

The **assign** section is a finite and non–empty set of statements. Instead of giving an explicit syntactic characterization of the statements allowed in a UNITY program, we give an alternate characterization using predicate transformers. We permit any statement, s, which is *deterministic* and *terminating*. We can use Dijkstra's predicate transformers (Dijkstra and Scholten [1990]), *weakest precondition* (**wp**) and the *weakest liberal precondition* (**wlp**), to express these conditions.

The determinacy of a statement s is captured by postulating

(S0) $[\textbf{wp}.s.(\neg X) \equiv \neg(\textbf{wlp}.s.X)].$

Similarly, termination of a statement s is given by,

(S1) $[\textbf{wp}.s.true \equiv true]$

or equivalently,

$$[\textbf{wp}.s.X \equiv \textbf{wlp}.s.X].$$

That is, the assumption of terminating statements permits us to dispense with one of the predicate transformers **wp**.s or **wlp**.s. In the sequel, we will restrict ourselves to **wp**.s.

Recall that in introducing the **wp** predicate transformer in Section 2.3, we outlined a list of "healthiness" conditions for the predicate transformers **wp**.s, **wlp**.s and **sp**.s. The first "healthiness" condition requires **wp**.s to be *universally conjunctive*. The requirement of universal conjunctivity is expressed by

(S2) $[\textbf{wp}.s.\langle \forall X : X \in W : X \rangle \equiv \langle \forall X : X \in W : \textbf{wp}.s.X \rangle].$

Since our statements are deterministic and terminating, the second "healthiness" condition when considered with property S1 requires **wp**.s to be universally disjunctive. That is,

(S3) $[\textbf{wp}.s.\langle \exists X : X \in W : X \rangle \equiv \langle \exists X : X \in W : \textbf{wp}.s.X \rangle].$

The third "healthiness" condition (Law of the Excluded Miracle) requires **wp**.s to be strict. That is,

$$[\textbf{wp}.s.false \equiv false].$$

Strictness also follows from the universal disjunctivity of **wp**.s and the fact the existential quantification over an empty set of predicates is equivalent to *false*.

In summary, conditions S0, S1, S2 and S3 constitute a specification of the statements that are allowed in UNITY programs.

An example of a statement satisfying conditions S0, S1, S2 and S3 is the *multiple assignment* (MA).

$$x := e$$

where x is a list of program variables and e is a list of expressions. Operationally, such a statement is executed by evaluating all the expressions and assigning them to the corresponding program variables. It is required that the number and type of expressions match the number and type of variables and further that the expressions be deterministic, that is, they should be well–defined functions of the state.

Remark: Note that, without loss of generality, an expression can be a *conditional* expression. That is, a statement can be a *conditional multiple assignment* (CMA) of the form

$$
\begin{aligned}
x \quad := \quad & e.0 \quad \text{if} \quad b.0 \sim \\
& e.1 \quad \text{if} \quad b.1 \sim \\
& \quad \vdots \\
& e.k \quad \text{if} \quad b.k
\end{aligned}
$$

where x is a list of variables, each $e.i$ $(0 \leq i \leq k)$ is a list of expressions and each $b.i$ is a boolean condition. A conditional multiple assignment is executed by assigning any $e.i$ to x, if the corresponding $b.i$ is true. If none of the boolean conditions is true, then the value of x is left unchanged. If more than one of the boolean conditions is true, then it is required that the corresponding expressions have the same value. This requirement guarantees that the statement is deterministic. (*End of Remark*).

Formally, the weakest precondition of a multiple assignment is given by,

$$[\textbf{wp}.MA.X \equiv \{x := e\}X]$$

where $\{x := e\}X$ is the predicate obtained by substituting all free occurrences of x in X by e.

Remark : Similarly, the weakest precondition of a conditional multiple assignment is given by,

$$[\textbf{wp}.CMA.X \equiv \langle \forall i : 0 \leq i \leq k : b.i \Rightarrow \{x := e.i\}X \rangle$$

$$\wedge \left(\langle \forall i : 0 \leq i \leq k : \neg b.i \rangle \Rightarrow X \right)].$$

(*End of Remark*).

Next, we explore the junctivity properties of $\textbf{wp}.MA.X$ (and $\textbf{wp}.CMA.X$): thanks to the restriction to terminating statements, it is universally conjunctive and thanks to the restriction to deterministic expressions, it is universally disjunctive as well.

Theorem 3.1.1. *The predicate transformer* **wp** *.MA is universally conjunctive.*

Proof. The universal conjunctivity of **wp** *.MA* follows from the universal conjunctivity of the operation of substitution. The interested reader is referred to Dijkstra and Scholten [1990](p. 117, chap. 6). We will now illustrate the universal conjunctivity of **wp** *.CMA*.

$$\text{wp}.CMA.\langle\forall X : X \in W : X\rangle$$

$= \quad$ {definition of **wp** *.CMA*; omitting ranges}

$$\langle\forall i :: b.i \Rightarrow \{x := e.i\}\langle\forall X :: X\rangle\rangle \land (\langle\forall i :: \neg b.i\rangle \Rightarrow \langle\forall X :: X\rangle)$$

$= \quad$ {universal conjunctivity of multiple assignment}

$$\langle\forall i :: b.i \Rightarrow \langle\forall X :: \{x := e.i\}X\rangle\rangle \land (\langle\forall i :: \neg b.i\rangle \Rightarrow \langle\forall X :: X\rangle)$$

$= \quad$ { $\Rightarrow$ over $\forall$ twice}

$$\langle\forall i :: \langle\forall X :: b.i \Rightarrow \{x := e.i\}X\rangle\rangle \land (\langle\forall X :: \langle\forall i :: \neg b.i\rangle \Rightarrow X\rangle)$$

$= \quad$ {interchange quantification}

$$\langle\forall X :: \langle\forall i :: b.i \Rightarrow \{x := e.i\}X\rangle\rangle \land (\langle\forall X :: \langle\forall i :: \neg b.i\rangle \Rightarrow X\rangle)$$

$= \quad$ {$\forall$ distributes over $\land$}

$$\langle\forall X :: \langle\forall i :: b.i \Rightarrow \{x := e.i\}X\rangle \land (\langle\forall i :: \neg b.i\rangle \Rightarrow X)\rangle$$

$= \quad$ {definition of **wp** *.CMA*}

$$\langle\forall X :: \text{wp}.CMA.X\rangle$$

$\square$

The universal disjunctivity of **wp** *.MA* follows from the universal disjunctivity of the operation of substitution. The reader is referred to Dijkstra and Scholten [1990] (see p. 117, chap. 6).

To prove the universal disjunctivity of **wp** *.CMA*, under the assumption of disjoint guards needs more work. The following theorems are modelled after similiar theorems about the alternative construct with disjoint guards in Dijkstra and Scholten [1990] (p. 142–144, chap. 7). Lemmas 3.1.2 and 3.1.3 have been generalized slightly.

Lemma 3.1.1. *We have for any b and R,*

$$[\langle\exists i :: b.i\rangle \equiv (\langle\forall i : b.i : R.i\rangle \Rightarrow \langle\exists i : b.i : R.i\rangle)]$$

Proof. We observe for any b and R,

$$\langle\forall i : b.i : R.i\rangle \Rightarrow \langle\exists i : b.i : R.i\rangle$$

$= \quad$ {predicate calculus and de Morgan}

$$\langle\exists i : b.i : \neg R.i\rangle \lor \langle\exists i : b.i : R.i\rangle$$

$= \quad$ {combine the terms}

$$\langle\exists i : b.i : \neg R.i \lor R.i\rangle$$

$= \quad$ {Excluded Middle and trading}

$$\langle\exists i :: b.i\rangle$$

$\square$

Lemma 3.1.2. *We have for any b and R,*

$$[\langle \forall i,j : b.i \wedge b.j : R.i \equiv R.j \rangle \Rightarrow (\langle \exists i : b.i : R.i \rangle \Rightarrow \langle \forall j : b.j : R.j \rangle)]$$

Proof. We observe for any b and R,

$\qquad \langle \exists i : b.i : R.i \rangle \Rightarrow \langle \forall j : b.j : R.j \rangle$
$= \quad \{\text{predicate calculus}\}$
$\qquad \langle \forall i : b.i : \neg R.i \rangle \vee \langle \forall j : b.j : R.j \rangle$
$= \quad \{\vee \text{ distributes over } \forall; \text{ unnesting}\}$
$\qquad \langle \forall i,j : b.i \wedge b.j : \neg R.i \vee R.j \rangle$
$\Leftarrow \quad \{\text{Excluded Middle}\}$
$\qquad \langle \forall i,j : b.i \wedge b.j : R.i \equiv R.j \rangle$

$\qquad\qquad\qquad\qquad\qquad\qquad\qquad\qquad\qquad\qquad\qquad\qquad\qquad\quad \square$

Lemma 3.1.3. *We have for any b and R,*

$$[\langle \forall i,j : b.i \wedge b.j : R.i \equiv R.j \rangle] \quad \Rightarrow \quad \begin{array}{l} [\langle \exists i :: b.i \rangle \wedge \langle \forall i : b.i : R.i \rangle \equiv \langle \exists i : b.i : R.i \rangle] \wedge \\ [\neg \langle \exists i :: b.i \rangle \vee \langle \exists i : b.i : R.i \rangle \equiv \langle \forall i : b.i : R.i \rangle] \end{array}$$

Proof. We observe for any b and R,

$\qquad [\langle \exists i :: b.i \rangle \wedge \langle \forall i : b.i : R.i \rangle \equiv \langle \exists i : b.i : R.i \rangle]$
$= \quad \{\text{Lemma 3.1.1 and predicate calculus}\}$
$\qquad [\langle \exists i : b.i : R.i \rangle \wedge \langle \forall i : b.i : R.i \rangle \equiv \langle \exists i : b.i : R.i \rangle]$
$\Leftarrow \quad \{\text{Lemma 3.1.2 and predicate calculus}\}$
$\qquad [\langle \forall i,j : b.i \wedge b.j : R.i \equiv R.j \rangle]$

This gives us the first conjunct on the right. Substitution of $\neg R$ for R in the first conjunct and negating both sides yields the second conjunct. $\qquad \square$

Lemma 3.1.4.

$$[\mathbf{wp}.CMA.X \equiv \langle \exists i : b.i : \{x := e.i\}X \rangle \vee (\langle \forall i :: \neg b.i \rangle \wedge X)]$$

Proof.

$\qquad \mathbf{wp}.CMA.X$
$= \quad \{\text{definition of } \mathbf{wp}.CMA\}$
$\qquad \langle \forall i : b.i : \{x := e.i\}X \rangle \wedge (\langle \forall i :: \neg b.i \rangle \Rightarrow X)$
$= \quad \{\text{predicate calculus}\}$
$\qquad (\langle \forall i : b.i : \{x := e.i\}X \rangle \wedge \langle \exists i :: b.i \rangle) \vee (\langle \forall i : b.i : \{x := e.i\}X \rangle \wedge X)$
$= \quad \{\text{first conjunct of Lemma 3.1.3 with } R.i := \{x := e.i\}X\}$
$\qquad \langle \exists i : b.i : \{x := e.i\}X \rangle \vee (\langle \forall i : b.i : \{x := e.i\}X \rangle \wedge X)$
$= \quad \{\text{second conjunct of Lemma 3.1.3 with } R.i := \{x := e.i\}X\}$
$\qquad \langle \exists i : b.i : \{x := e.i\}X \rangle \vee (\langle \forall i :: \neg b.i \rangle \wedge X)$

$\qquad\qquad\qquad\qquad\qquad\qquad\qquad\qquad\qquad\qquad\qquad\qquad\qquad\quad \square$

Theorem 3.1.2. *The predicate transformer* **wp** *.CMA is universally disjunctive.*

Proof.

$\quad$ **wp** $.CMA.\langle \exists X : X \in W : X \rangle$

$= \quad$ {Lemma 3.1.4 with $X := \langle \exists X :: X \rangle$; omitting ranges}

$\quad \langle \exists i : b.i : \{x := e.i\} \langle \exists X :: X \rangle \rangle \vee ((\forall i :: \neg b.i) \wedge \langle \exists X :: X \rangle)$

$= \quad$ {universal disjunctivity of multiple assignment; $\wedge$ over $\exists$}

$\quad \langle \exists i : b.i : \langle \exists X :: \{x := e.i\} X \rangle \rangle \vee (\langle \exists X :: \langle \forall i :: \neg b.i \rangle \wedge X \rangle)$

$= \quad$ {interchange of quantification}

$\quad \langle \exists X :: \langle \exists i : b.i : \{x := e.i\} X \rangle \rangle \vee (\langle \exists X :: \langle \forall i :: \neg b.i \rangle \wedge X \rangle)$

$= \quad$ {$\exists$ distributes over $\vee$}

$\quad \langle \exists X :: \langle \exists i : b.i : \{x := e.i\} X \rangle \vee (\langle \forall i :: \neg b.i \rangle \wedge X) \rangle$

$= \quad$ {definition **wp** $.CMA$}

$\quad \langle \exists X :: \mathbf{wp}.CMA.X \rangle$

$\hfill \square$

This means that the weakest precondition of a multiple assignment and a conditional multiple assignment satisfy conditions S2 and S3. Since both these statements are deterministic and terminating, they satisfy conditions S0 and S1 as well. Thus the **assign** section of a UNITY program can contain multiple assignment statements. For instance, the **assign** section of the *GCD* program contains two assignment statements.

We use the symbol "$[\![$" to separate assignment statements (in the **assign** section). For example, the **assign** section of program *GCD* has a set of two assignment statements: the statements in the set are separated by $[\![$. When used with assignment statements, $[\![$ captures *asynchronous* composition of statements in parallel. The operator $[\![$ is symmetric, associative and idempotent. The identity element of the operation is the empty assignment or the **skip** statement.

We use the symbol "$\|$" as a means of rewriting an assignment to a long list of variables (in the **assign** section) in terms of simpler components. A mutiple assignment of the form

$$x, y := y, x$$

may be rewritten as

$$x := y \| y := x.$$

When used with equations $\|$ denotes *simultaneous* definition or initialization. When used with assignments, $\|$ captures *synchronous* composition of statements in parallel. For example, if each of the assignments, $x := y$ and $y := x$ is implemented as a process, then

$$x := y \| y := x$$

represents synchronized assignment to x and y in parallel, in a single step.

Since $\|$ and $[\![$ are symmetric, associative and idempotent operations, they can be used to write quantified expressions of the form

$$\langle\| \; i : 0 \leq i \leq N : A[i] := max(A[i], B[i])\rangle$$

and

$$\langle[\!]\; i : 0 \leq i \leq N : A[i] := A[i] - 1\rangle$$

with the constraint that the range of the quantification be statically fixed: this is required to ensure that the text of the program does not change during the course of program execution: for instance, creation or deletion of new components of assignments and assignment statements is prohibited.

3.2 Executing a UNITY Program

A *state* of a UNITY program is an assignment of values to the variables of the program. It is assumed that these variables have been declared in the **declare** section of the program and that the values assigned to the variables are consistent with the type associated with the variables in the **declare** section.

An *execution* of a UNITY program begins in a state that satisfies the initial condition. It proceeds by repeatedly selecting a statement from the **assign** section and executing it with the selection being subject to a *fairness* constraint: in an infinite execution, each statement is selected infinitely often. Such a fairness constraint is termed *unconditional fairness*. In other words, an execution of a UNITY program is a sequence of states, beginning in a state that satisfies the initial condition. Thus, in the UNITY model of computation, parallelism is captured by a fair, interleaved execution of the statements of the program with each statement being executed atomically. In this sense, a UNITY program may be looked upon as a set of unconditionally fair execution sequences.

In the sequel, we will sometimes refer to a UNITY program as a set of processes. By this we mean that the set of statements in the **assign** section is arbitrarily partitioned and that a process has been assigned to execute statements in each element of the partition. Thus, a process executes a subset of the statements of a given UNITY program. In the extreme case, there can be one process for each statement of the UNITY program. Two processes synchronize if they have statements that access (either read or write) common variables. This synchronization can be either by means of shared variables or by message communication over channels.

3.3 The UNITY Programming Theory

Traditionally, research in program specification and verification has focussed attention on two classes of program properties: *safety* and *progress*. The designers of UNITY followed the same approach and provided three operators in their logic: one to reason about safety and two to reason about progress. Unlike state-based computational models that reason about properties of individual execution sequences, UNITY operators capture properties of programs, that is, the set of all unconditionally–fair execution sequences.

One of the important contributions of UNITY is a set of powerful rules about program properties. These rules serve two purposes: first, given that a program satisfies some safety and progress properties, the rules can be used to conclude new properties of the program: in this sense, the rules enable one to replace common patterns of tedious (and often error–prone) operational reasoning by the invocation of specific rules, that is, calculational reasoning. Provided the hypothesis and the conclusion of the rule have been correctly instantiated, considerable time and effort is saved. Second, given a specification, the rules can be used "in reverse" to refine a specification, bringing it "closer" to an implementable specification.

In the rest of this section, we introduce the UNITY operators and reproduce rules that are useful in reasoning about them. The proofs of the rules are straight–forward and can be found in Chandy and Misra [1988].

3.3.1 Reasoning About Safety

In UNITY, safety properties are expressed using the **unless** operator. The **unless** relation is a binary relation on state predicates and is formally defined as follows:

$$\frac{\langle \forall s : s \, in \, F : [X \wedge \neg Y \Rightarrow \mathbf{wp} \, .s.(X \vee Y)] \rangle}{(X \textbf{ unless } Y)}$$

where the dummy s quantifies over the statements of a UNITY program F and where X and Y are state predicates.

Intuitively, X **unless** Y means that in all executions, if X holds in some state of the execution, X continues to hold in succeeding states as long as Y does not hold: if Y never holds, then X holds forever.

For instance, consider the following UNITY program.

$$
\begin{array}{ll}
\textbf{declare} & x, y : integer \\
\textbf{initially} & x, y = 0, 1 \\
\textbf{assign} & x, y := x + 1, y + 1 \ \ \textbf{if} \ \ prime.y \\
\ [\![\ & y := y + 1 \ \ \textbf{if} \ \ \neg prime.y \\
\textbf{end} &
\end{array}
$$

This program has the safety property, for all k, ($x = k$ **unless** $prime.y$). Other examples of **unless** properties include assertions such as "a message is not received unless it is sent" and "a philosopher is hungry unless it eats."

Two special cases of **unless** are *stability* and *invariance*:

– *Stability*: A state predicate is said to be *stable* if once it becomes true, it remains true forever. In terms of **unless**,

$$\textbf{stable } X \ \equiv \ X \textbf{ unless } false$$

Since the predicate *false* never holds, the above ensures that X holds forever. For instance, the property $(x \geq 0) \wedge (y \geq 0)$ is a stable property of program *GCD*. The assertions "the value of program variable x is nondecreasing" and "the system is deadlocked" are other examples of stable properties.

- *Invariance*: A state predicate X is said to be *invariant* if it holds in every reachable program state. Invariance requires that X hold initially and that X be stable. That is,

$$\text{invariant} \quad X \equiv [\textit{initial condition} \Rightarrow X] \wedge \text{stable } X.$$

where the *initial condition* refers to the predicate asserted in the *initally* section of the UNITY program. For instance, the assertion $gcd(x, y) = gcd(X, Y)$ is an invariant property of program *GCD*. The assertion of mutual exclusion, that is, "two processes are never in the critical section at the same time", is another example of a program invariant.

The relation **unless** is a useful operator as it can be used to specify many safety properties succinctly. One of the contributions of UNITY is a rich theory to combine **unless** properties. The theory is based on the following four postulates.

1. Reflexivity and anti-reflexivity:

$$X \text{ unless } X$$

$$X \text{ unless } \neg X.$$

2. Consequence weakening:

$$\frac{X \text{ unless } Y, [Y \Rightarrow Z]}{X \text{ unless } Z}$$

3. General conjunction and disjunction: For i ranging over an arbitrary set I,

$$\frac{\langle \forall i :: X.i \text{ unless } Y.i \rangle}{\begin{array}{l} \langle \forall i :: X.i \rangle \text{ unless } \langle \forall i :: X.i \vee Y.i \rangle \wedge \langle \exists i :: Y.i \rangle \quad \text{(general conjunction)} \\ \langle \exists i :: X.i \rangle \text{ unless } \langle \forall i :: \neg X.i \vee Y.i \rangle \wedge \langle \exists i :: Y.i \rangle \quad \text{(general disjunction)} \end{array}}$$

Using the rule of consequence weakening, the following are special cases of general conjunction and disjunction:

Simple conjunction and simple disjunction:

$$\frac{\begin{array}{c} X \text{ unless } Y \\ U \text{ unless } V \end{array}}{\begin{array}{l} (X \wedge U) \text{ unless } (Y \vee V) \quad \text{(simple conjunction)} \\ (X \vee U) \text{ unless } (Y \vee V) \quad \text{(simple disjunction)} \end{array}}$$

4. Cancellation:

$$\frac{X \text{ unless } Y, \quad Y \text{ unless } Z}{(X \vee Y) \text{ unless } Z}$$

3.3.2 Reasoning About Progress

Typically, safety properties rule out undesirable states and transitions. A specification consisting of safety properties alone is easily satisfied by a program that starts in a state satisfying the specification and then does nothing. Such trivial implementations are ruled out by including progress properties in the specification. Typically, progress properties require a program to do some useful work.

The basis of the definition of progress in UNITY is the **ensures** operator. The **ensures** operator is a binary relation on state predicates and is formally defined as

$$\frac{X \text{ unless } Y, \ \langle \exists s : s \text{ in } F : [X \wedge \neg Y \Rightarrow \mathbf{wp} . s . Y] \rangle}{X \text{ ensures } Y}$$

where s ranges over the statements of the UNITY program F and where X and Y are state predicates.

Intuitively, an **ensures** property strengthens an **unless** property by ruling out the possibility that a program remains in a state satisfying X forever. It does so by postulating the existence of a statement s, which when executed in a state satisfying $X \wedge \neg Y$ is guaranteed to terminate in a state satisfying Y. So, if the program is in a state satisfying X, the **unless** part of the proof obligation guarantees that the only way that a program leaves such a state (if ever) is by transiting to a state satisfying Y. The existence of statement s and the requirement of unconditional fairness guarantee that eventually statement s is executed and the program transits to a state satisfying Y.

There are two important things to note about an **ensures** property: first, X ensures Y means that, if X holds in a state, then X *continues* to hold in all succeeding states until a state satisfying Y is reached. Further, it is guaranteed that a state satisfying Y will be reached. Second, an **ensures** property roughly corresponds to a single statement in the **assign** section of the program, namely, the statement that is guaranteed to take the program from *all* states satisfying $X \wedge \neg Y$ to a state satisfying Y. This means that, if we are given a specification consisting of **ensures** properties only, we can extract a program that satisfies the specification: one statement for each **ensures** property.

For instance, consider the following UNITY program.

$$
\begin{array}{ll}
\textbf{declare} & x : integer \\
\textbf{assign} & x := 0 \ \ \textbf{if} \ \ even.x \\
\text{[\hspace{-1pt}]} & x := 0 \ \ \textbf{if} \ \ odd.x \\
\textbf{end} &
\end{array}
$$

This program satisfies both properties $even.x$ **ensures** $(x = 0)$ and $odd.x$ **ensures** $(x = 0)$. While this can be shown formally by applying the definition of **ensures** given above, it suffices to see that there exists a single statement in the program that can take the program from *all* states in which $even.x$ holds to a state in which $(x = 0)$ holds. The property *true* **ensures** $(x = 0)$ does not hold for this program, as there is no single statement that works for *all* states.

In UNITY, general progress properties are expressed using the *leads–to* operator (denoted, $\mapsto$). The $\mapsto$ operator is a binary relation on state predicates and is formally defined as the strongest relation that satisfies the following three conditions:

1. *Base case:*

$$\frac{X \text{ ensures } Y}{X \mapsto Y}$$

2. *Transitivity:*

$$\frac{X \mapsto Y, \ Y \mapsto Z}{X \mapsto Z}$$

3. *Disjunctivity:* For an arbitrary set of predicates, W:

$$\frac{\langle \forall X : X \in W : X \mapsto Y \rangle}{\langle \exists X : X \in W : X \rangle \mapsto Y}$$

That is, the relation $\mapsto$ is the transitive, disjunctive closure of the **ensures** relation. Intuitively, the property $X \mapsto Y$ means that if X holds in a state of an unconditionally fair execution sequence, then Y holds either in that state or in a later state.

For instance, the UNITY program given above satisfies the progress property $true \mapsto (x = 0)$. This can be seen by the following.

0. *even.x* **ensures** $(x = 0)$
        ,From above
1. *even.x* $\mapsto (x = 0)$
        ,Base Case of $\mapsto$ applied to 1
2. *odd.x* **ensures** $(x = 0)$
        ,From above
3. *odd.x* $\mapsto (x = 0)$
        ,Base Case of $\mapsto$ applied to 2
4. *true* $\mapsto (x = 0)$
        ,Disjunctivity of $\mapsto$ applied to 1 and 3

Just as in the case of the **unless** relation, one of the important contributions of UNITY is a powerful theory to manipulate progress properties.

The basic postulates underlying the theory of **ensures** are the following.

1. Reflexivity:

$$X \text{ ensures } X$$

2. Consequence weakening:

$$\frac{X \text{ ensures } Y, \ [Y \Rightarrow Z]}{X \text{ ensures } Z}$$

3. Impossibility:

$$\frac{X \text{ ensures } false}{[\neg X]}$$

4. Conjunction:

$$\frac{U \textbf{ ensures } V, \quad X \textbf{ unless } Y}{(U \wedge X) \textbf{ ensures } (U \wedge Y) \vee (X \wedge V) \vee (V \wedge Y)}$$

5. Disjunction:

$$\frac{X \textbf{ ensures } Y}{(X \vee Z) \textbf{ ensures } (Y \vee Z)}$$

6. E–continuity: For a weakening sequence of predicates $X.i$,

$$\frac{\langle \forall i :: X.i \textbf{ ensures } Y \rangle}{\langle \exists i :: X.i \rangle \textbf{ ensures } Y}$$

The E–continuity property of **ensures** is due to Ernie Cohen and a proof can be found in Cohen [1993].

The important postulates about the $\mapsto$ are the following:

1. Implication:

$$\frac{[X \Rightarrow Y]}{X \mapsto Y}$$

2. Impossibility:

$$\frac{X \mapsto \textit{false}}{[\neg X]}$$

3. Disjunction: For i ranging over an arbitrary set I,

$$\frac{\langle \forall i :: X.i \mapsto Y.i \rangle}{\langle \exists i :: X.i \rangle \mapsto \langle \exists i :: Y.i \rangle}$$

4. Cancellation:

$$\frac{W \mapsto (X \vee Y), \ Y \mapsto Z}{W \mapsto (X \vee Z)}$$

5. Progress–Safety–Progress (PSP):

$$\frac{X \mapsto Y, \ U \textbf{ unless } V}{(X \wedge U) \mapsto (Y \wedge U) \vee V}$$

6. Completion: For i ranging over any finite set I,

$$\frac{\langle \forall i :: X.i \mapsto Y.i \rangle, \ \langle \forall i :: X.i \textbf{ unless } Z \rangle}{\langle \forall i :: X.i \rangle \mapsto \langle \forall i :: Y.i \rangle \vee Z}$$

7. Induction principle: Let $(W, \prec)$ be a well–founded set. Let M be a metric mapping program states to W. Then

$$\frac{\langle \forall m : m \in W : (X \wedge M = m) \mapsto (X \wedge M \prec m) \vee Y \rangle}{X \mapsto Y}$$

3.3.3 Remark on Presentation

We began this section by introducing a definition for the **unless** operator in terms of the weakest preconditions of the statements of a program. We then introduced a set of useful proof–rules about **unless**, which the given definition satisfied.

Alternately, we could have started by proposing a set of proof–rules (an axiomatization, if you will) for **unless**: this could have been the properties that we expected an operator for safety to obey. The axiomatization would have served as the basis of soundness and completeness arguments for a proof system for safety. The given definition of **unless** would have been just *one* relation that would have satisfied the axiomatization: there could be many more.

Our presentation here models the development of the theory as given in Chandy and Misra [1988] and so we have not adopted the second approach. Similiar considerations apply to the presentation of the **ensures** and $\mapsto$.

3.3.4 Substitution Axiom

Recall that an **invariant** of a program is a program property that holds in all the states of the program. Thus, in the context of a program, an invariant is logically equivalent to *true*. The *Substitution Axiom* exploits this fact by allowing us to replace an invariant by *true* and vice versa in any program property. For instance, using the fact that I is an invariant, we can use the substitution axiom to infer $X \mapsto Y$ from $(X \wedge I) \mapsto Y$. Using the substitution axiom once again, we can infer $X \mapsto (Y \wedge I)$ from $X \mapsto Y$.

3.3.5 Program Composition in UNITY

The definitions and the proof–rules that we have introduced so far enable one to prove properties of a *single* UNITY program. In practice, it is desirable to have a methodology using which one can decompose a large program into a number of small components, prove properties of the components independently, compose the components to get back the original program and deduce the properties of the original program from the properties already proven of its components. A methodology that has these features is said to be *compositional*.

In UNITY, there are two ways of composing program components to obtain larger programs: *union* and *superposition*.

The *union* of two UNITY programs F and G is denoted by $F \parallel G$ where F and G are the *component* programs and $F \parallel G$ is the *composite* program. The composite program is obtained by appending the corresponding sections of the two component programs: it is assumed that there are no inconsistencies in the definitions of the variables, **always**–sections or initializations of the two programs F and G.

How can one deduce properties of the composite program from the properties of the components? A partial answer is provided by the *union* theorem which states:

Theorem 3.3.1 (Union Theorem for unless). *For state predicates X and Y and programs F and G,*

$$(X \text{ unless } Y \text{ in } F \parallel G) \equiv (X \text{ unless } Y \text{ in } F) \land (X \text{ unless } Y \text{ in } G)$$

Theorem 3.3.2 (Union Theorem for ensures). *For state predicates X and Y and programs F and G,*

$$(X \text{ ensures } Y \text{ in } F \parallel G) \equiv (X \text{ unless } Y \text{ in } F \parallel G) \land \\ ((X \text{ ensures } Y \text{ in } F) \lor (X \text{ ensures } Y \text{ in } G))$$

The union theorem does not apply to general progress properties: it is possible for a progress property $X \mapsto Y$ to hold in both component programs and not hold in the composite program (see Section 4.1). Reasoning about progress properties in a compositional manner is a tricky issue and one that will be postponed to the next chapter.

Technical Remark on the use of the Substitution Axiom: When reasoning about the properties of a composite program $F \parallel G$, it is required that all applications of the substitution axiom use invariants of the composite program and not the components. This is required to ensure the soundness of the UNITY proof system. The reader interested in the rationale for this is referred to Misra [1990] and Sanders [1990]. (*End of Technical Remark*).

The second structuring operator that we employ in our proofs is the *superposition* operator. We recapitulate the salient details.

Unlike program union, program superposition is an *asymmetric* operator. Given an *underlying program* (whose variables will be called *underlying variables*), superposition allows it to be transformed by the application of the following two rules.

1. Augmentation Rule. A statement s in the underlying program may be transformed to the statement $s \| r$ where r is a statement that does not assign to the underlying variables and is executed *in synchrony* with s.
2. Restricted Union Rule. A statement r may be added to the underlying program provided that r does not assign to the underlying variables.

By adhering to the discipline of superposition, it is ensured that every property of the underlying program is a property of the transformed program. This is also called the superposition theorem.

can propose an asynchronous scheme to the problem of cache–coherence which enables the scaling up of shared–memory multiprocessors.

In this chapter, we attempt to answer the following question: *how can ideas of commutativity be used to develop a theory for composing progress properties?* Unlike the approaches due to Lipton and Misra, we work backwards: we identify a crucial paradigm that seems instrumental in compositionality results and then use formal techniques to derive the commutativity conditions that are needed.

In the first part of this chapter, we use the intuition underlying the idea of *loose–coupling* proposed in Misra [1991] and the concept of the *closure of a program* to introduce a binary relation on programs called *decoupling*. This relation was first proposed in Cohen [1993]. Beginning with a definition of *decoupling* of programs expressed in terms of progress properties ($\mathbf{dec}_{prog}$), we progressively strengthen the definition to obtain definitions in terms of **ensures** properties ($\mathbf{dec}_{ens}$) and finally in terms of **stable** properties ($\mathbf{dec}_{safe}$). The process of strengthening yields the following relationship between the three definitions:

$$\mathbf{dec}_{safe} \implies \mathbf{dec}_{ens} \implies \mathbf{dec}_{prog} .$$

A special instance of decoupling is *weak decoupling*. While decoupling is a relation between two arbitrary programs F and G, weak decoupling is decoupling between program F and $F \parallel G$. In a manner analogous to our study of decoupling, we introduce the corresponding definitions of weak decoupling in terms of progress properties ($\mathbf{wdec}_{prog}$), ensures properties ($\mathbf{wdec}_{ens}$) and stable properties ($\mathbf{wdec}_{safe}$). The process of strengthening yields the following relationship between the three definitions:

$$\mathbf{wdec}_{safe} \implies \mathbf{wdec}_{ens} \implies \mathbf{wdec}_{prog} .$$

While $\mathbf{wdec}_{ens}$ and $\mathbf{wdec}_{prog}$ are weaker than $\mathbf{dec}_{ens}$ and $\mathbf{wdec}_{prog}$ respectively, it turns out that $\mathbf{dec}_{safe}$ and $\mathbf{wdec}_{safe}$ are incomparable. These relationships can be summarized by the following figure. The importance of these

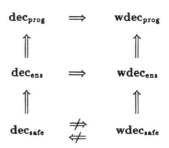

Fig. 4.1. Relating the definitions of decoupling and weak decoupling

definitions is justified by the following theorem: for two programs F and G, if

(F **wdec**$_{prog}$ G) holds, then the progress properties of F are preserved in the composite program $F \parallel G$.

Cautionary Remark: We suggest that the reader familiarize himself with this figure and use it as a roadmap as he/she makes his/her way through the profusion of commutativity definitions in this chapter. Of the six relations, we consider **dec**$_{safe}$ and **wdec**$_{safe}$ to be the most important. (*End of Cautionary Remark*).

In the second part of this chapter, we introduce two notions of commutativity. The first notion is due to Lipton: *Lipton left commutativity* (**lco**$_l$) and *Lipton right commutativity* (**rco**$_l$) and the second notion due to Misra: *Misra commutativity* (**co**$_m$). We show that each of these notions captures a fundamental aspect of asynchrony that is different from the other. While Lipton commutativity captures the fact that the environment of a process cannot *enable* the actions of a process, Misra commutativity imposes the requirement that the environment of a process cannot *disable* the actions of a process.

We show that our definitions of commutativity derived from considerations of *decoupling* and *weak decoupling* combine elements of Lipton and Misra commutativity. Specifically, we show that

$$(F \, \text{lco}_l \, G) \wedge (F \, \text{co}_m \, G) \Rightarrow (F \ \text{dec}_{safe} \ G)$$

and

$$(F \, \text{co}_m \, (F \parallel G)) \Rightarrow (F \ \text{wdec}_{safe} \ G).$$

The second theorem justifies the special consideration that we give to **wdec**$_{prog}$ even though it is a weakening of **dec**$_{prog}$.

Remark: Notice that Misra commutativity (**co**$_m$) occurs as a hypothesis for proving both decoupling (**dec**$_{safe}$) and weak decoupling (**wdec**$_{safe}$). Keeping in mind that decoupling and weak decoupling were instrumental in obtaining a compositional theory for progress, we do not find it very surprising that Lipton's work (Lipton [1975]) and subsequent works based on his notion of commutativity (Doeppner [1977], Lamport and Schneider [1989]) were constrained to results about safety properties. (*End of Remark*).

We conclude by showing the implications of these results for the design of parallel programming languages. In particular, we show that if the variables shared by two programs are restricted to be logic variables (Chandy and Taylor [1990]), then the programs satisfy Misra commutativity, that is, their progress properties compose.

In summary, this chapter attempts to integrate the research in the commutativity of programs with the research in developing a compositional theory for program design. In particular, the contributions of this chapter are two new definitions of commutativity (**dec**$_{safe}$ and **wdec**$_{safe}$) that generalize existing definitions of commutativity. Our definitions have two important consequences. First, they form the basis of a simple compositional methodology for parallel

program design. This methodology is better than Lipton's, in that *both* safety
and progress properties are permitted in the specification of a parallel program.
It improves on the methodology proposed by Misra by removing the constraint
of *wait–freedom* on processes implementing progress properties. Second, from the
perspective of a designer of a parallel programming language, these definitions
suggest constraints on the variables that can be shared between programs.

The work in this chapter has been done in collaboration with Ernie Cohen.
I am indebted to him for sharing his many insights with me.

4.1 The Problem with Composing Progress Properties

In the last chapter (see Section 3.3.5) we introduced the union theorem to relate
the **unless** and **ensures** properties of a composite program to the corresponding
properties of its components. For a long time, a corresponding result for composing general progress properties (such as, the $\mapsto$ operator) was not known.

For example, consider the following UNITY program.

Program   F
    declare $x : integer$
    initially $x = 0$
    assign $x := x + 1$
end

It is easy to see that program F satisfies the progress property

$$true \mapsto (|x| = 2).$$

Now consider the following UNITY program G.

Program   G
    declare $x : integer$
    initially $x = 0$
    assign $x := x - 1$
end

Since there is no conflict in the **declare**, **always** and **initially** sections of the
two programs, their union, $F \parallel G$ is defined (see Section 3.3.5) and given by

Program $F \parallel G$
    declare $x : integer$
    initially $x = 0$
    assign $x := x + 1$
        $\parallel$ $x := x - 1$
end

Consider the following execution of program $F \parallel G$: the execution begins in a state in which the value of x is 0 and proceeds by selecting each of the statements alternately. Executing the first statement (from F) would increase the value of x to 1. Executing the second statement (from G) in the very next step, would decrease the value x to 0. By repeatedly executing the two statements alternately, we get a *fair* execution sequence in which there is no state in which the value of x is 2. That is, the progress property

$$true \mapsto (|x| = 2)$$

does not hold for the composite program $F \parallel G$. Notice that this is the case even though the property holds in program G when it is executed in isolation.

Our example proves that, in general, a composite program does not inherit the progress properties of its components. A closer look at program $F \parallel G$ reveals that the problem lies with the interaction of the programs F and G. When started in a state in which the value of x is 0, program F has a strategy of attaining a state in which the value of x is 2: to wit, by incrementing x by 1. However program G defeats F's strategy by *undoing* any progress that F may have made: to wit, by decrementing x by 1. Intuitively speaking, a process (such as F) in a system of processes can make progress only if the other processes in the system (such as G) do not destroy the progress made by the process. A compositional theorem for progress properties should prohibit such destructive interference.

Our conclusions suggest that for a composite program (such as $F \parallel G$) to inherit the progress properties of a component (such as F), there should be restrictions on how the other components that execute in parallel (such as G) access shared variables (such as x). Such restrictions, when formally derived, can be used to justify important features of a parallel programming language. Ideally, we would like such restrictions to be as *weak* as possible so as to grant maximum flexibility and leeway to the designer and the user of the programming language. Restrictions, motivated by similiar concerns, were developed in the theory of loose–coupling: in the next section, we review this theory briefly.

4.2 Loose Coupling

A first step towards developing a compositional theory for progress properties was taken in Misra [1991] when Jayadev Misra introduced the concept of *loose coupling*. It is important to isolate and understand the essence of loose coupling. In a loosely coupled system, the only form of communication between processes is by message passing. The interaction between two processes can therefore be viewed as an instance of the producer–consumer paradigm where the sender of the message is the producer and the recipient of the message is the consumer. Such message–passing systems have three important characteristics. First, since message–passing is the only form of interaction between processes, the processes in the system can execute at arbitrary speeds. A sender can execute arbitrarily fast and produce an arbitrary number of messages. It only waits if the channel is full. Similarly, as long as the channel is non-empty, the receiver can execute arbitrarily fast and consume messages from the channel. Second, since a message can take an arbitrary (but finite) amount of time to travel from the sender to the receiver, the message can arrive at the receiver after an inordinate amount of time. The data in the message may be old and may not reflect the current values of the variables at the sender. The beauty of a loosely–coupled system is that in spite of this, the receiver is able to utilise the message and the system functions correctly. Third, a sender can execute arbitrarily fast without the danger of overwriting values not yet read (as opposed to a process that writes to a shared variable) and a receiver can execute arbitrarily fast without the danger of reading the same value again (as opposed to a process that reads from a shared variable). There is an implicit guarantee that each "write" of the sender will eventually be "read" by the receiver.

In the paper, Misra makes the important observation that a loosely–coupled system is easier to program than a system in which processes communicate by shared variables (also known as *tightly coupled* systems). This observation seems to be borne out by practice as well. Programming a tightly–coupled system requires an intricate analysis of all possible execution sequences to guarantee the absence of *race conditions*. Roughly speaking, there seems to be a compositional theory underlying the design of loosely–coupled systems which designers seem to use consciously or otherwise. In fact, Misra is able to show a *preliminary* theory for composing progress properties for loosely–coupled systems. Specifically, Misra proves that if a progress property is implemented in a *wait-free* manner by a component process, then the property holds in any loosely–coupled collection of processes that contains the component process and satisfies a simple stability property. It is for this reason that we consider loose–coupling to be a crucial insight in the development of a compositional theory for progress. In the next section, we will rely on the intuitions developed in this section to define a phenomenon similiar to loose–coupling, called *decoupling*.

4.3 Towards a Theory of Decoupling

4.3.1 The Closure of a Program

In order for us to introduce the concept of *decoupling*, we need to introduce one more concept: the notion of a *closure of a program*.

In our study of decoupling, we will use the UNITY programming model with one modification. We will assume that the initial condition of a program is true: or equivalently, the **initially** section of the program is empty. It is easy to translate any UNITY program with an **initially** section to an equivalent one in which the **initially** section is empty: one leaves the **initially section** empty and introduces assignment statements in the **assign** section that explicitly initialize the variables to the desired values. These statements are suitably guarded so that they are the first statements selected for execution and then they disable themselves. Thus the suggested modification does not over–simplify the problem.

Given such a UNITY program, it makes sense to ask the following question: if program execution is begun in a state satisfying state predicate P, what is the predicate that characterizes the *smallest* set of states in which this program will remain? Clearly, such a set would contain any state that satisfies P. Further, such a set would be stable for the program. That is, executing the program in any state in the set would result in a state that is already in the set. For a given UNITY program H (without an **initially** section), we capture this notion by means of a predicate transformer h that takes the predicate P as an argument. We call h the *closure* of program H.

Formally, given a program H and a state predicate P, consider the set CL of equations CL0–CL1 in the unknown predicate Z:

(CL0) $\qquad\qquad\qquad [P \;\Rightarrow\; Z]$
(CL1) $\qquad\qquad\qquad (Z \text{ unless } false \text{ in } H)$

Condition CL0 states that P is contained in Z. Condition CL1 states that Z is stable in program H.

The *strongest* solution of equations CL would characterize the smallest set of states that can be reached by executing program H in any state satisfying predicate P. However, it is not clear whether such a strongest solution exists. Recall that to apply the Theorem of Knaster–Tarski (see Theorem 2.4.1 in Section 2.4) the predicate transformer defining the equation has to be monotonic and it is not clear whether conditions CL0 and CL1 define a predicate transformer monotonic in Z. To show that this is indeed the case, we prove the following theorem.

Lemma 4.3.1. *For a program H and a state predicate P, the equations CL can be equivalently rewritten as,*

$$\langle \mu Z :: [P \vee \langle \exists s : s \in H : \text{sp}.s.Z \rangle \equiv Z] \rangle$$

Proof.

$\qquad \langle \mu Z :: [P \Rightarrow Z] \wedge (Z \text{ unless } false \text{ in } H) \rangle$
$= \quad \{\text{definition of } \textbf{unless}\}$
$\qquad \langle \mu Z :: [P \Rightarrow Z] \wedge \langle \forall s : s \in H : [Z \Rightarrow \textbf{wp}.s.Z] \rangle \rangle$
$= \quad \{\text{property S1; } \textbf{wlp}.s \text{ and } \textbf{sp}.s \text{ are converses}\}$
$\qquad \langle \mu Z :: [P \Rightarrow Z] \wedge \langle \forall s : s \in H : [\textbf{sp}.s.Z \Rightarrow Z] \rangle \rangle$
$= \quad \{\text{interchange quantification}\}$
$\qquad \langle \mu Z :: [P \Rightarrow Z] \wedge [\langle \forall s : s \in H : \textbf{sp}.s.Z \Rightarrow Z \rangle] \rangle$
$= \quad \{\text{predicate calculus}\}$
$\qquad \langle \mu Z :: [P \Rightarrow Z] \wedge [\langle \exists s : s \in H : \textbf{sp}.s.Z \rangle \Rightarrow Z] \rangle$
$= \quad \{\text{predicate calculus}\}$
$\qquad \langle \mu Z :: [P \vee \langle \exists s : s \in H : \textbf{sp}.s.Z \rangle \Rightarrow Z] \rangle$
$= \quad \{\text{Theorem 2.4.1}\}$
$\qquad \langle \mu Z :: [P \vee \langle \exists s : s \in H : \textbf{sp}.s.Z \rangle \equiv Z] \rangle$

$\qquad\qquad\qquad\qquad\qquad\qquad\qquad\qquad\qquad\qquad\qquad\qquad\qquad\qquad\qquad\quad \square$

The proof of Lemma 4.3.1 shows how the equations CL can be rewritten in a more familiar "equational" form. Since $\mathbf{sp}.s$, $\exists$ and $\vee$ used in defining the left hand side of the equation are all universally disjunctive, the predicate transformer $P \vee \langle \exists s : s \in H : \mathbf{sp}.s.Z \rangle$ itself is universally disjunctive and by Theorem 2.2.1 is monotonic in Z. Thus we can apply the Theorem of Knaster–Tarski to conclude that a strongest solution of equations CL0 and CL1 exists.

Definition 4.3.1 (closure). *For a given program H, the strongest solution of equations CL will be denoted as $h.P$. We call the predicate transformer, h, the closure of program H.*

Remark: Alternately, one can observe that the *conjunction* of all the solutions of equations CL is a solution of the equation CL. Clearly, this is the strongest solution, since it implies all solutions. (*End of Remark*).

We can assert the following properties of the closure.

(H0) $$[P \Rightarrow h.P]$$
(H1) $$(h.P \text{ unless } false \text{ in } H)$$
(H2) $$[P \Rightarrow Z] \wedge (Z \text{ unless } false \text{ in } H) \Rightarrow [h.P \Rightarrow Z]$$

H0 and H1 follow from the fact that the closure, $h.P$, solves equations CL. From the fact that the closure is the strongest solution, we get H2.

The alternate characterization of the closure of a program, as the least fixpoint of a predicate calculus expression, gives us the following properties.

(H3) $$[h.P \equiv P \vee \langle \exists s : s \in H : \mathbf{sp}.s.(h.P) \rangle]$$
(H4) $$[Z \Leftarrow P \vee \langle \exists s : s \in H : \mathbf{sp}.s.Z \rangle] \Rightarrow [h.P \Rightarrow Z]$$
(H5) $$[h.(h.P) \equiv h.P]$$
(H6) $$[h.\langle \exists X : X \in W : X \rangle \equiv \langle \exists X : X \in W : h.X \rangle]$$

H3 states that the closure is a solution of the fixpoint expression and H4 that it is the strongest solution. H5 states the idempotence of the closure which follows from its definition as a fixpoint. H6 states that the closure of a program is universally disjunctive. This follows from Theorem 2.4.2 which states that the strongest solution inherits the disjunctivity type of the predicate transformer that defines it.

We will make use of the following properties of closures in our theorems.

Lemma 4.3.2. *For a program H with closure h and a state predicate Z,*

$$\mathbf{stable} \, Z \, \mathbf{in} \, H \equiv [h.Z \equiv Z]$$

Proof. The proof will be by mutual implication.

($\Rightarrow$)

$\quad$ **stable** Z **in** H
$=$ {predicate calculus}
$\quad$ $[Z \Rightarrow Z] \wedge (Z$ **unless** *false* **in** $H)$
$\Rightarrow$ {property H2}
$\quad$ $[h.Z \Rightarrow Z]$
$=$ {property H0}
$\quad$ $[h.Z \equiv Z]$

$(\Leftarrow)$

$\quad$ *true*
$=$ {property H1; definition **stable**}
$\quad$ **stable** $h.Z$ **in** H
$=$ {hypothesis $[h.Z \equiv Z]$; substituion axiom}
$\quad$ **stable** Z **in** H

$\square$

Lemma 4.3.3. *Given a program* F,

$$X \text{ unless } Y \text{ in } F \Rightarrow [f.(X \vee Y) \equiv X \vee f.Y]$$

where f *is the closure of program* F.

Proof. The proof is by mutual implication.
$(\Rightarrow)$

$\quad$ $[f.(X \vee Y) \Rightarrow X \vee f.Y]$
$\Leftarrow$ {property H2}
$\quad$ $[X \vee Y \Rightarrow X \vee f.Y] \wedge$ **stable** $(X \vee f.Y)$ **in** F
$=$ {predicate calculus}
$\quad$ $[X \Rightarrow X \vee f.Y] \wedge [Y \Rightarrow X \vee f.Y] \wedge$ **stable** $(X \vee f.Y)$ **in** F
$=$ {predicate calculus; property H0}
$\quad$ **stable** $(X \vee f.Y)$ **in** F
$\Leftarrow$ {general disjunction property of **unless**}
$\quad$ $(X$ **unless** Y **in** $F) \wedge$ (**stable** $f.Y$ **in** $F)$
$=$ {hypothesis; property H1}
$\quad$ *true*

$(\Leftarrow)$

$\quad$ $X \vee f.Y$
$\Rightarrow$ {property H0}
$\quad$ $f.X \vee f.Y$
$=$ {property H6}
$\quad$ $f.(X \vee Y)$

$\square$

Lemma 4.3.4. *Given programs F and G, let f be the closure of F and h be the closure of $F \parallel G$. Then,*

$$\langle \forall X :: [h.(f.X) \equiv h.X] \rangle.$$

Proof. The proof is by mutual implication.

($\Rightarrow$)

$\qquad [h.(f.X) \Rightarrow h.X]$
$\Leftarrow \quad$ {property H2}
$\qquad [f.X \Rightarrow h.X] \wedge$ **stable** $h.X$ **in** $(F \parallel G)$
$\Leftarrow \quad$ {property H1}
$\qquad [f.X \Rightarrow h.X]$
$\Leftarrow \quad$ {property H2}
$\qquad [X \Rightarrow h.X] \wedge$ **stable** $h.X$ **in** F
$\Leftarrow \quad$ {property H0}
$\qquad$ **stable** $h.X$ **in** F
$\Leftarrow \quad$ {union theorem for **unless**}
$\qquad$ **stable** $h.X$ **in** $(F \parallel G)$
$= \quad$ {property H1}
$\qquad true$

($\Leftarrow$)

$\qquad [h.X \Rightarrow h.(f.X)]$
$\Leftarrow \quad$ {monotonicity of h from property H6 and Theorem 2.2.1}
$\qquad [X \Rightarrow f.X]$
$\qquad$ {property H1}
$\qquad true$

$\qquad\qquad\qquad\qquad\qquad\qquad\qquad\qquad\qquad\qquad\qquad\qquad\qquad\qquad \square$

4.3.2 Decoupling in Terms of Progress

We begin with a detailed consideration of the *producer–consumer* paradigm. Recall that message–passing, which is the crux of loose–coupling, is an instance of this paradigm.

Assume that we are given a *producer* program and a *consumer* program that communicate by means of an infinite buffer. Let M denote the number of (unconsumed) items in the buffer and let N denote the number of items consumed by the *consumer*. It is clear that the progress property

$$(M = 1) \wedge (N = 0) \longmapsto (M = 0) \wedge (N = 1)$$

holds of the *consumer* program when it is executed in isolation. What happens when the *producer* and *consumer* are composed and executed in parallel?

Suppose the (UNITY–style) execution of the composite program is begun in a state satisfying predicate $(M = 1) \wedge (N = 0)$. It is conceivable that the *producer* executes arbitrarily faster than the *consumer* filling the buffer with items. In logical terms, instead of $(M = 1) \wedge (N = 0)$, $(M \geq 1) \wedge (N = 0)$ holds: that is, a predicate obtained by applying the closure of the *producer* program to the predicate $(M = 1) \wedge (N = 0)$ holds. By the fairness requirement on the execution of the composite program, actions of the *consumer* will eventually be selected and executed. While this will decrease the number of items in the buffer, one cannot guarantee that a state in which $(M = 0) \wedge (N = 1)$ holds will be reached. However, a little thinking reveals that the composite program will reach a state in which $(M \geq 0) \wedge (N = 1)$ holds: that is, a predicate obtained by applying the closure of the *producer* program to the predicate $(M = 0) \wedge (N = 1)$. Therefore, the composite program satisfies the property

$$(M \geq 1) \wedge (N = 0) \mapsto (M \geq 0) \wedge (N = 1).$$

We use this idea as a basis of a definition of *decoupling*. We say that a program F is *decoupled* from a program H, if for each progress property $X \mapsto Y$ of program F, the *relativized* property $h.X \mapsto h.Y$ holds in the parallel composition, $F \parallel H$, where h is the closure of program H. Formally,

Definition 4.3.2 (decoupling using progress). *Given programs F and H, let h be the closure of program H. Then*

$$F \ \mathbf{dec}_{prog} \ H \equiv \langle \forall X, Y : X \mapsto Y \ \text{in} \ F : h.X \mapsto h.Y \ \text{in} \ F \parallel H \rangle$$

One of the nice properties of $\mathbf{dec}_{prog}$ is that it is reflexive. That is,

Lemma 4.3.5. *For all programs F,*

$$F \ \mathbf{dec}_{prog} \ F.$$

Proof. Our proof obligation is to show that for all progress properties of F of the form $X \mapsto Y$,

$$X \mapsto Y \ \text{in} \ F \ \Rightarrow \ f.X \mapsto f.Y \ \text{in} \ F$$

where f is the closure of F. The proof will be by induction on the structure of the proof of $X \mapsto Y$ in F.

Base case: Assume X **ensures** Y in F. From the definition of **ensures**, X **unless** Y in F holds. This justifies the use of Lemma 4.3.3 as a hint in the proof.

$\quad$ *true*
$\Rightarrow$ {property H1}
$\quad$ **stable** $f.X$ in F
$\Rightarrow$ {definition of **stable** and consequence weakening}
$\quad$ $f.X$ **unless** $f.Y$ in F
$\Rightarrow$ {hypothesis X **ensures** Y}
$\quad$ $f.X$ **unless** $f.Y$ in F $\wedge$ $\langle \exists s :: [X \wedge \neg Y \Rightarrow \mathbf{wp}.s.Y] \rangle$
$=$ {predicate calculus}

0. $X \mapsto Y$ in F
     ,hypothesis
1. $F \ dec_{prog} \ H$
     ,hypothesis
2. $h.X \mapsto h.Y$ in $F \parallel H$
     ,0,1 and definition 4.3.2
3. $[X \Rightarrow h.X]$
     ,property H0
4. $X \mapsto h.X$ in $F \parallel H$
     ,3 and Implication Theorem of $\mapsto$
5. $X \mapsto h.Y$ in $F \parallel H$
     ,4,2 and transitivity of $\mapsto$
6. $[h.Y \equiv Y]$
     ,hypothesis and Lemma 4.3.2
7. $X \mapsto Y$ in $F \parallel H$
     ,6 and substitution of equals

$\square$

The theorem gives conditions under which progress properties of a component program are maintained in the composite program. The second condition requires the stability of a predicate in the remaining system. The reader may feel that requiring the stability of Y rather than X runs counter to intuition but we will defer an explanation to later. The third condition requires decoupling of programs.

Now definition 4.3.2 is universally quantified over all progress properties. Such a condition is very difficult to check. In the rest of this section, we will simplify this definition, *in stages*, to obtain more tractable conditions of decoupling.

4.3.3 Decoupling in Terms of Ensures

The first step in our investigation is to strengthen Definition 4.3.2 and restate it in terms of **ensures** properties.

Definition 4.3.3 (decoupling using ensures). *Given programs F and G, let g be the closure of program G. Then*

$$F \ dec_{ens} \ G \equiv \langle \forall X, Y : X \ ensures \ Y \ in \ F : g.X \ ensures \ g.Y \ in \ F \parallel G \rangle$$

The following theorem shows that definition 4.3.3 strengthens definition 4.3.2.

Theorem 4.3.2. *Given programs F and G,*

$$(F \ dec_{ens} \ G) \Rightarrow (F \ dec_{prog} \ G).$$

Proof. Let X and Y be state predicates. Given that $X \mapsto Y$ in F, our proof obligation is to show that $g.X \mapsto g.Y$ in $F \parallel G$. The proof will be by induction on the structure of the proof of $X \mapsto Y$ in F.

Base Case : Assume that X ensures Y in F. Then,

$\qquad X$ ensures Y in F
$\Rightarrow \quad \{F \text{ dec}_{ens} G\}$
$\qquad g.X$ ensures $g.Y$ in $F \parallel G$
$\Rightarrow \quad \{\text{definition of } \mapsto\}$
$\qquad g.X \mapsto g.Y$ in $F \parallel G$

Induction Step (transitivity) : Assume that $X \mapsto Z$ in F and $Z \mapsto Y$ in F. Then,

$\qquad (X \mapsto Z \text{ in } F) \wedge (Z \mapsto Y \text{ in } F)$
$\Rightarrow \quad \{\text{induction hypothesis, twice}\}$
$\qquad (g.X \mapsto g.Z \text{ in } F \parallel G) \wedge (g.Z \mapsto g.Y \text{ in } F \parallel G)$
$\Rightarrow \quad \{\text{transitivity of } \mapsto\}$
$\qquad (g.X \mapsto g.Y \text{ in } F \parallel G)$

Induction Step (disjunctivity) : Assume that $\langle \forall Z : Z \in W : Z \mapsto Y \text{ in } F \rangle$. Then,

$\qquad \langle \forall Z : Z \in W : Z \mapsto Y \text{ in } F \rangle$
$\Rightarrow \quad \{\text{induction hypothesis}\}$
$\qquad \langle \forall Z : Z \in W : g.Z \mapsto g.Y \text{ in } F \parallel G \rangle$
$\Rightarrow \quad \{\text{disjunctivity of } \mapsto\}$
$\qquad \langle \exists Z : Z \in W : g.Z \rangle \mapsto g.Y \text{ in } F \parallel G$
$= \quad \{\text{property H6}\}$
$\qquad g.\langle \exists Z : Z \in W : Z \rangle \mapsto g.Y \text{ in } F \parallel G$

$\hfill \square$

4.3.4 Decoupling in Terms of Stability

The second step in our investigation is to strengthen definition 4.3.3 further to obtain a definition of decoupling in terms of stability.

Definition 4.3.4 (decoupling using stability). *Given programs F and G, let g be the closure of program G. Then*

$$F \text{ dec}_{safe} G \equiv \langle \forall s, Z : s \in F \wedge \text{stable } Z \text{ in } G : \text{stable wp}.s.Z \text{ in } G \rangle$$

At first sight, this definition might appear rather uninituitive. We will first show that this definitions is sufficient to discharge our proof obligation and then explain its intuitive significance.

Lemma 4.3.6. *Given programs F and G such that F dec$_{safe}$ G. Let g be the closure of G and let X and Y be state predicates. Then,*

$$(X \text{ unless } Y \text{ in } F) \Rightarrow (g.X \text{ unless } g.Y \text{ in } F \parallel G).$$

Proof.

$\quad$ $g.X$ **unless** $g.Y$ in $F \parallel G$

$=$ {union theorem for safety}

$\quad$ $g.X$ **unless** $g.Y$ in $F \wedge g.X$ **unless** $g.Y$ in G

$\Leftarrow$ {consequence weakening for **unless**}

$\quad$ $g.X$ **unless** $g.Y$ in $F \wedge g.X$ **unless** $false$ in G

$=$ {property H1}

$\quad$ $g.X$ **unless** $g.Y$ in F

$=$ {definition of **unless**}

$\quad$ $\langle \forall s : s \in F : [g.X \wedge \neg g.Y \Rightarrow \text{wp}.s.(g.X \vee g.Y)] \rangle$

$=$ {predicate calculus; omitting range of F}

$\quad$ $\langle \forall s :: [g.X \Rightarrow g.Y \vee \text{wp}.s.(g.X \vee g.Y)] \rangle$

$\Leftarrow$ {property H2}

$\quad$ $\langle \forall s :: [X \Rightarrow g.Y \vee \text{wp}.s.(g.X \vee g.Y)] \wedge$
$\quad$ $(g.Y \vee \text{wp}.s.(g.X \vee g.Y))$ **unless** $false$ in $G \rangle$

$\Leftarrow$ {property H0}

$\quad$ $\langle \forall s :: [X \Rightarrow Y \vee \text{wp}.s.(g.X \vee g.Y)] \wedge$
$\quad$ $(g.Y \vee \text{wp}.s.(g.X \vee g.Y))$ **unless** $false$ in $G \rangle$

$\Leftarrow$ {property H0 and monotonicity of **wp**.s}

$\quad$ $\langle \forall s :: [X \Rightarrow Y \vee \text{wp}.s.(X \vee Y)] \wedge$
$\quad$ $(g.Y \vee \text{wp}.s.(g.X \vee g.Y))$ **unless** $false$ in $G \rangle$

$=$ {predicate calculus}

$\quad$ $\langle \forall s :: [X \wedge \neg Y \Rightarrow \text{wp}.s.(X \vee Y)] \wedge$
$\quad$ $(g.Y \vee \text{wp}.s.(g.X \vee g.Y))$ **unless** $false$ in $G \rangle$

$=$ {assumption and definition of X **unless** Y}

$\quad$ $\langle \forall s :: (g.Y \vee \text{wp}.s.(g.X \vee g.Y))$ **unless** $false$ in $G \rangle$

$\Leftarrow$ {simple disjunction property of **unless**}

$\quad$ $\langle \forall s :: \text{stable } g.Y \text{ in } G \wedge \text{stable wp}.s.(g.(X \vee Y)) \text{ in } G \rangle$

$=$ {property H1}

$\quad$ $\langle \forall s :: \text{stable wp}.s.(g.(X \vee Y)) \text{ in } G \rangle$

$\Leftarrow$ {F dec$_{safe}$ G with $Z := g.(X \vee Y)$}

$\quad$ **stable** $g.(X \vee Y)$ in G

$=$ {property H1}

$\quad$ $true$

$\hfill \square$

Lemma 4.3.7. *Given programs F and G,*

$$(F \text{ dec}_{safe} G) \Rightarrow (F \text{ dec}_{ens} G)$$

Proof. Let g be the closure of program G and let X and Y be state predicates. Then our proof obligation is to show that if X ensures Y in F then $g.X$ ensures $g.Y$ in $F \parallel G$

$\qquad$ $g.X$ ensures $g.Y$ in $F \parallel G$

$\Leftarrow$ {union theorem for ensures}

$\qquad$ $(g.X$ ensures $g.Y$ in $F) \wedge (g.X$ unless $g.Y$ in $G)$

$\Leftarrow$ {consequence weakening}

$\qquad$ $(g.X$ ensures $g.Y$ in $F) \wedge (g.X$ unless $false$ in $G)$

$=$ {property H1}

$\qquad$ $g.X$ ensures $g.Y$ in F

$=$ {definition of ensures}

$\qquad$ $(g.X$ unless $g.Y$ in $F) \wedge \langle \exists s : s \in F : [g.X \wedge \neg g.Y \Rightarrow \mathbf{wp}.s.(g.Y)] \rangle$

$\Leftarrow$ {Lemma 4.3.6, X ensures Y in F, F $\mathbf{dec}_{safe}$ G}

$\qquad$ $\langle \exists s : s \in F : [g.X \wedge \neg g.Y \Rightarrow \mathbf{wp}.s.(g.Y)] \rangle$

$=$ {omitting range, predicate calculus}

$\qquad$ $\langle \exists s :: [g.X \Rightarrow g.Y \vee \mathbf{wp}.s.(g.Y)] \rangle$

$\Leftarrow$ {property H2}

$\qquad$ $\langle \exists s :: [X \Rightarrow g.Y \vee \mathbf{wp}.s.(g.Y)] \wedge (g.Y \vee \mathbf{wp}.s.(g.Y))$ unless $false$ in $G \rangle$

$\Leftarrow$ {property H0}

$\qquad$ $\langle \exists s :: [X \Rightarrow Y \vee \mathbf{wp}.s.(g.Y)] \wedge (g.Y \vee \mathbf{wp}.s.(g.Y))$ unless $false$ in $G \rangle$

$\Leftarrow$ {property H0 and monotonicity of $\mathbf{wp}.s$}

$\qquad$ $\langle \exists s :: [X \Rightarrow Y \vee \mathbf{wp}.s.Y] \wedge (g.Y \vee \mathbf{wp}.s.(g.Y))$ unless $false$ in $G \rangle$

$=$ {predicate calculus}

$\qquad$ $\langle \exists s :: [X \wedge \neg Y \Rightarrow \mathbf{wp}.s.Y] \wedge (g.Y \vee \mathbf{wp}.s.(g.Y))$ unless $false$ in $G \rangle$

$\Leftarrow$ {predicate calculus}

$\qquad$ $\langle \exists s :: [X \wedge \neg Y \Rightarrow \mathbf{wp}.s.Y] \wedge$

$\qquad$ $\langle \forall u : u \in F : (g.Y \vee \mathbf{wp}.u.(g.Y))$ unless $false$ in $G \rangle \rangle$

$=$ {predicate calculus}

$\qquad$ $\langle \exists s :: [X \wedge \neg Y \Rightarrow \mathbf{wp}.s.Y] \rangle \wedge$

$\qquad$ $\langle \forall u : u \in F : (g.Y \vee \mathbf{wp}.u.(g.Y))$ unless $false$ in $G \rangle$

$\Leftarrow$ {assumption and definition X ensures Y}

$\qquad$ $\langle \forall u : u \in F : (g.Y \vee \mathbf{wp}.u.(g.Y))$ unless $false$ in $G \rangle$

$\Leftarrow$ {definition of stable}

$\qquad$ $\langle \forall u :: $ stable $g.Y$ in $G \wedge$ stable $\mathbf{wp}.u.(g.Y)$ in $G \rangle$

$=$ {property H1}

$\qquad$ $\langle \forall u :: $ stable $\mathbf{wp}.u.(g.Y)$ in $G \rangle$

$\Leftarrow$ {F $\mathbf{dec}_{safe}$ G}

$\qquad$ stable $g.Y$ in G

$=$ {property H1}

$\qquad$ *true*

$\qquad\qquad\qquad\qquad\qquad\qquad\qquad\qquad\qquad\qquad\qquad\qquad\qquad\qquad$ $\square$

Important Remark: We now explain the intuitive significance of the definition of $\mathbf{dec}_{safe}$. Recall the form of the theorem (Theorem 4.3.1) for preserving progress properties. The assertion $X \mapsto Y$ in F means that F has a strategy for going from a state in which predicate X holds to a state in which predicate Y holds. Roughly speaking, F's strategy may be to traverse a sequence of states satisfying the predicates $X_0, X_1 \ldots X_{(n-1)}, X_n$, where $X = X_0$ and $Y = X_n$ and the transition from X_i to $X_{(i+1)}$ is made by some *helpful* statement of F. Now, one of the hypotheses of Theorem 4.3.1 is that Y is stable in G. From this and the definition of $\mathbf{dec}_{safe}$, we conclude that $\mathbf{wp}.s.Y$ is stable in G, for all statements s in F. Thus, if the statement of F that was helpful in going from $X_{(n-1)}$ to Y was t, then $\mathbf{wp}.t.Y$ would be stable in G and $[X_{(n-1)} \Rightarrow \mathbf{wp}.t.Y]$. So, if the execution of $F \parallel G$ ever reaches a state satisfying $X_{(n-1)}$, executing statements of G would keep the system in a state satisfying $\mathbf{wp}.t.Y$. Executing statements of F does not affect the strategy of F. Eventually, by unconditional fairness, t will be executed and the system will transit to a state in which Y holds. Since $\mathbf{wp}.t.Y$ is stable in G, one can repeat this procedure and apply the definition of $\mathbf{dec}_{safe}$ again to conclude that $X_{(n-2)}$ is part of a stable set of G and the whole argument can be repeated to conclude that any statement of F, whose execution is instrumental in achieving part of F's strategy for progress, will still remain helpful when F and G are executed in parallel. To coin an anthropomorphism, G *respects* F's strategy for making progress. This also explains why it is important for Y to be stable in G and not for X, as intuition might erroneously suggest. A similiar explanation can be given for $\mathbf{wdec}_{safe}$. This is one more case where the clue to solving a difficult problem lies in reasoning "backwards". (*End of Important Remark*).

4.3.5 A Special Case of Decoupling: Weak Decoupling

For reasons that will become clear later, we are interested in a special instance of decoupling of programs F and G: namely where $F \; \mathbf{dec}_{prog} \; (F \parallel G)$. We term this *weak decoupling*. Formally,

Definition 4.3.5 (weak decoupling using progress). *Given programs F and G,*

$$F \; \mathbf{wdec}_{prog} \; G \equiv F \; \mathbf{dec}_{prog} \; (F \parallel G).$$

With h be the closure of program $F \parallel G$ this means,

$$F \; \mathbf{wdec}_{prog} \; G \equiv \langle \forall X, Y : X \mapsto Y \text{ in } F : h.X \mapsto h.Y \text{ in } F \parallel G \rangle$$

The corresponding version of Theorem 4.3.1 for weak decoupling is obtained by instantiating H with $F \parallel G$:

$$\frac{\begin{array}{c} X \mapsto Y \text{ in } F \\ \text{stable } Y \text{ in } (F \parallel G) \\ F \; \mathbf{wdec}_{prog} \; G \end{array}}{X \mapsto Y \text{ in } (F \parallel G)}$$

Weak decoupling is weaker than decoupling, in the sense that if two programs F and G are decoupled then they are weakly decoupled. Formally,

Theorem 4.3.3. *Given programs F and G,*

$$(F \ \mathbf{dec}_{prog} \ G) \Rightarrow (F \ \mathbf{wdec}_{prog} \ G).$$

Proof. Assume $X \mapsto Y$ in F. Assume that g is the closure of G and h is the closure of $F \parallel G$.

$\quad X \mapsto Y$ in F
$\Rightarrow \quad$ {definition of $F \ \mathbf{dec}_{prog} \ G$}
$\quad g.X \mapsto g.Y$ in $(F \parallel G)$
$\Rightarrow \quad$ {Lemma 4.3.5}
$\quad h.(g.X) \mapsto h.(g.Y)$ in $(F \parallel G)$
$\Rightarrow \quad$ {Lemma 4.3.4}
$\quad h.X \mapsto h.Y$ in $(F \parallel G)$

The derivation shows that $F \ \mathbf{wdec}_{prog} \ G$.   □

In a similiar fashion, one can give definitions of weak decoupling in terms of **ensures** and **stable** properties.

Definition 4.3.6 (weak decoupling using ensures). *Given programs F and G,*

$$F \ \mathbf{wdec}_{ens} \ G \equiv F \ \mathbf{dec}_{ens} \ (F \parallel G).$$

Note that by substituting $\mathbf{wdec}_{ens}$ for $\mathbf{dec}_{ens}$, $\mathbf{wdec}_{prog}$ for $\mathbf{dec}_{prog}$, h (the closure of $F \parallel G$) for g, and $F \parallel G$ for G, in Theorem 4.3.2 and its proof, we can show that $\mathbf{wdec}_{ens}$ strengthens $\mathbf{wdec}_{prog}$.
The analog of Theorem 4.3.3 holds here as well.

Theorem 4.3.4. *Given programs F and G,*

$$(F \ \mathbf{dec}_{ens} \ G) \Rightarrow (F \ \mathbf{wdec}_{ens} \ G).$$

Proof. Assume that $X \mapsto Y$ in F. Assume that g is the closure of G and h is the closure of $F \parallel G$.

$\quad X$ ensures Y in F
$\Rightarrow \quad$ {definition of $F \ \mathbf{dec}_{ens} \ G$}
$\quad g.X$ ensures $g.Y$ in $(F \parallel G)$
$\Rightarrow \quad$ {Base case of Lemma 4.3.5}
$\quad h.(g.X)$ ensures $h.(g.Y)$ in $(F \parallel G)$
$\Rightarrow \quad$ {Lemma 4.3.4}
$\quad h.X$ ensures $h.Y$ in $(F \parallel G)$

The derivation shows that $F \ \mathbf{wdec}_{ens} \ G$.   □

The definition of weak decoupling in terms of **stable** properties is given by

Definition 4.3.7 (weak decoupling using stability). *Given programs F and G,*

$$F \ \mathbf{wdec}_{safe} \ G \equiv F \ \mathbf{dec}_{safe} \ (F \parallel G).$$

That is, (F $\mathbf{wdec}_{safe}$ *G) holds if and only if*

$$\langle \forall s, Z : s \in F \ \wedge \ \mathbf{stable} \, Z \ \mathbf{in} \ (F \parallel G) : \mathbf{stable} \, wp \, .s. Z \ \mathbf{in} \ (F \parallel G) \rangle$$

Lemmas 4.3.6 and 4.3.7 with $\mathbf{wdec}_{safe}$ substituted for $\mathbf{dec}_{safe}$, h (the closure of $F \parallel G$) substituted for g and $F \parallel G$ substituted for G prove that $\mathbf{wdec}_{safe}$ strengthens $\mathbf{wdec}_{ens}$.

The analog of Theorem 4.3.3 does not hold for $\mathbf{dec}_{safe}$ and $\mathbf{wdec}_{safe}$. In fact, the two definitions are incomparable.

Theorem 4.3.5. *Given programs F and G,*

$$(F \ \mathbf{dec}_{safe} \ G) \nRightarrow (F \ \mathbf{wdec}_{safe} \ G)$$

and

$$(F \ \mathbf{wdec}_{safe} \ G) \nRightarrow (F \ \mathbf{dec}_{safe} \ G).$$

Proof.

0. Let the programs F and G be as follows.

```
Program    F
    declare      x : (-1, 0, 1)
    assign       x :=   1 if (x = 0)
           ∥     x := -1 if (x = 0)
end
```

```
Program    G
    declare      x : (-1, 0, 1)
    assign       x := x
end
```

Clearly all properties are stable in G. Therefore $\mathbf{dec}_{safe}$ is trivially satisfied. It is easy to see that $\mathbf{stable}\,(x = 1)$ $\mathbf{in}$ $(F \parallel G)$ holds. However, wp ."$x := 1$ $\mathbf{if}$ $(x = 0)$".$(x = 1)$ is $(x = 0 \vee x = 1)$ and this predicate is not stable in $F \parallel G$, violating $\mathbf{wdec}_{safe}$.

1. Let the programs F and G be as follows.

```
Program    F
    declare      x : (-1, 0, 1)
    assign       x :=   0 if (x = 1)
           ∥     x := -1 if (x = 0)
end
```

Program   G
  declare $x : (-1, 0, 1)$
  assign $x := -1 \text{ if } (x = 1)$
end

The stable predicates, Z, of $F \parallel G$ are $(x = -1)$, $(x = 0 \vee x = -1)$ and $(x = -1 \vee x = 0 \vee x = 1)$. One can check that, for all statements s of F, **wp**$.s.Z$ is also stable in $F \parallel G$. Therefore **wdec**$_{safe}$ is satisfied. It is easy to see that **stable**$(x = 0)$ in G holds. However, **wp**$.\text{"}x := 0 \text{ if } (x = 1)\text{"}.(x = 0)$ is $(x = 0 \vee x = 1)$ and this predicate is not stable in G, violating **dec**$_{safe}$. $\square$

4.3.6 Summary

In this section, we introduced the concepts of *decoupling* and *weak decoupling* of programs. These concepts enabled us to derive a theorem for composing progress properties. Using formal manipulations, we derived a number of sufficient conditions for decoupling, namely, **dec**$_{prog}$, **dec**$_{ens}$ and **dec**$_{safe}$; the corresponding conditions for weak decoupling were **wdec**$_{prog}$, **wdec**$_{ens}$ and **wdec**$_{safe}$. All these conditions enforce some form of commutativity restrictions on the programs that they relate. Of these conditions, we adopt **dec**$_{safe}$ and **wdec**$_{safe}$ as our working conditions of commutativity. In the next section, we review existing definitions of commutativity with the aim of eventually integrating them with our work.

4.4 Existing Definitions of Commutativity

In this section, we give an overview of two definitions of commutativity of program actions due to Richard Lipton and Jayadev Misra. We show that the key idea underlying Lipton's definition of commutativity is that the environment of a process cannot *enable* the actions of the process. In contrast, we show that Misra's definition of commutativity entails that the environment of a process cannot *disable* the actions of a process. We conclude by showing that the two definitions are incomparable.

For the purposes of this and the next section, we will consider a statement of a UNITY program to be a *guarded* statement of the form

$$s :: grd.s \rightarrow S.$$

The *guard* of statement s is denoted by $grd.s$. Operationally, executing s in a state requires that the guard be evaluated first: if the guard is true, then the *body* of the statement, S, is executed. If the guard is false, the state is left unchanged. Formally, the *weakest precondition* semantics of a guarded statement is defined as

$$[\textbf{wp}.s.Z \equiv (grd.s \wedge \textbf{wp}.S.Z) \vee (\neg grd.s \wedge Z)].$$

4.4.1 Lipton's Definition

In Lipton [1975], Richard Lipton introduced the idea of *left movers* and *right movers* to simplify the task of proving partial correctness properties of parallel programs. Motivated by his ideas, we introduce the operators *left-commutes* (lco_l), *right-commutes* (rco_l) and *commutes* (co_l).

Definition 4.4.1 (Lipton). *Let s and t be two guarded statements of the form $grd.s \to S$ and $grd.t \to T$ respectively. Then $(s\,\text{lco}_l\,t)$ if and only if*

$$[grd.t \wedge \mathbf{wp}.T.(grd.s) \Rightarrow grd.s \wedge \mathbf{wp}.S.(grd.t)] \qquad \wedge$$
$$\langle \forall Z :: [grd.t \wedge \mathbf{wp}.T.(grd.s \wedge \mathbf{wp}.S.Z) \Rightarrow \mathbf{wp}.S.(\mathbf{wp}.T.Z)] \rangle$$

Further,

$$(s\,\text{rco}_l\,t) \equiv (t\,\text{lco}_l\,s).$$
$$(s\,\text{co}_l\,t) \equiv (s\,\text{lco}_l\,t) \wedge (s\,\text{rco}_l\,t).$$

Intuitively, if $s\,\text{lco}_l\,t$ holds then t cannot *enable* s. To see this, note that the first conjunct in the definition of $s\,\text{lco}_l\,t$ implies:

$$[grd.t \wedge \mathbf{wp}.T.(grd.s) \Rightarrow grd.s \wedge \mathbf{wp}.S.(grd.t)]$$
$\Rightarrow$ {predicate calculus}
$$[grd.t \wedge \mathbf{wp}.T.(grd.s) \Rightarrow grd.s]$$
$=$ {contrapositive}
$$[(\neg grd.s) \Rightarrow (\neg grd.t \vee \neg\,\mathbf{wp}.T.(grd.s))]$$
$\Rightarrow$ {predicate calculus}
$$[(\neg grd.s) \wedge grd.t \Rightarrow \neg\,\mathbf{wp}.T.(grd.s)]$$
$=$ {property S0 and S1 of $\mathbf{wp}$; definition of $\mathbf{wp}.t$}
$$[(\neg grd.s) \Rightarrow \mathbf{wp}.t.(\neg grd.s)]$$

If in a state, $grd.s$ is false then $grd.s$ is still false after executing t in the same state. That is, t cannot enable s. The three operators, lco_l, rco_l and co_l can be naturally extended to programs as follows.

Definition 4.4.2. *For any two programs F and G,*

$$(F\,\text{lco}_l\,G) \equiv \langle \forall s,t : s \in F \wedge t \in G : s\,\text{lco}_l\,t \rangle.$$
$$(F\,\text{rco}_l\,G) \equiv (G\,\text{lco}_l\,F).$$
$$(F\,\text{co}_l\,G) \equiv (F\,\text{lco}_l\,G) \wedge (F\,\text{rco}_l\,G).$$

4.4.2 Misra's Definition

In Misra [1991], Jayadev Misra introduced the idea of *loose-coupling*. An integral part of his work was a commutativity relation between functions of different processes comprising the program. Motivated by his ideas, we introduce the operator *commutes* (co_m).

Definition 4.4.3 (Misra). *Let s and t be two guarded statements of the form $grd.s \to S$ and $grd.t \to T$ respectively. Then $(s\,\text{co}_m\,t)$ if and only if*

$$[grd.s \wedge grd.t \Rightarrow \mathbf{wp}.S.(grd.t) \wedge \mathbf{wp}.T.(grd.s)] \qquad \wedge$$
$$\langle \forall Z :: [grd.s \wedge grd.t \wedge \mathbf{wp}.(S;T).Z \Rightarrow \mathbf{wp}.(T;S).Z] \rangle.$$

Intuitively, if $s \, \mathbf{co}_m \, t$ then t cannot *disable* s. To see this, note that the definition of $s \, \mathbf{co}_m \, t$ requires

$$[grd.s \land grd.t \Rightarrow \mathbf{wp} \, .T.(grd.s)]$$

If in a state, both $grd.s$ and $grd.t$ are true, then $grd.s$ is still defined after executing T in the same state. In other words, t cannot disable s.

The operator, $\mathbf{co}_m$ can be naturally extended to programs as follows.

Definition 4.4.4. *For any two programs, F and G,*

$$(F \, \mathbf{co}_m \, G) \equiv \langle \forall s, t : s \in F \land t \in G : s \, \mathbf{co}_m \, t \rangle.$$

4.4.3 Incomparability of Lipton and Misra Commutativity

In the previous sections, we introduced two notions of commutativity due to Lipton and Misra. While it might appear that Lipton commutativity ($\mathbf{co}_l$) is stronger than Misra commutativity ($\mathbf{co}_m$), the two notions of commutativity are actually incomparable.

Theorem 4.4.1. *There exist functions s and t such that,*

$$(s \, \mathbf{co}_l \, t) \land \neg(s \, \mathbf{co}_m \, t)$$

and

$$\neg(s \, \mathbf{co}_l \, t) \land (s \, \mathbf{co}_m \, t).$$

Proof. The first assertion follows by choosing s and t to be P operations on a semaphore. The second assertion follows by choosing s to be a P operation and t to be a V operation on a semaphore. $\qquad\qquad\square$

4.5 Putting it All Together

In this section, we will relate the relations $\mathbf{dec}_{safe}$ and $\mathbf{wdec}_{safe}$ to Lipton and Misra commutativity.

In our calculations, we will need to manipulate the expression $\mathbf{wp} \, .t.(\mathbf{wp} \, .s.Z)$ where s and t are guarded statements. Using the definition of the weakest precondition of a guarded statement, we expand this expression to a form that we will use.

$\quad \mathbf{wp} \, .t.(\mathbf{wp} \, .s.Z)$
$= \quad \{\text{definition of } \mathbf{wp} \, .t\}$
$\quad (grd.t \land \mathbf{wp} \, .T.(\mathbf{wp} \, .s.Z)) \lor (\neg grd.t \land \mathbf{wp} \, .s.Z)$
$= \quad \{\text{definition of } \mathbf{wp} \, .s\}$
$\quad (grd.t \land \mathbf{wp} \, .T.((grd.s \land \mathbf{wp} \, .S.Z) \lor (\neg grd.s \land Z))) \lor$
$\quad (\neg grd.t \land grd.s \land \mathbf{wp} \, .S.Z) \lor$
$\quad (\neg grd.t \land \neg grd.s \land Z)$

We are now ready to present our first Theorem.

Theorem 4.5.1. *Given programs F and G,*

$$(F \operatorname{lco}_l G) \wedge (F \operatorname{co}_m G) \Rightarrow (F \operatorname{dec}_{safe} G)$$

Proof. We first rewrite $F \operatorname{dec}_{safe} G$ in a more convenient form.

$F \operatorname{dec}_{safe} G$
= {definition of $\operatorname{dec}_{safe}$ }
$\langle \forall s, Z : s \in F : \operatorname{stable} Z \operatorname{in} G \Rightarrow \operatorname{stable} \operatorname{wp}.s.Z \operatorname{in} G \rangle$
= {definition of **stable**; omitting range of s}
$\langle \forall s, Z :: \operatorname{stable} Z \operatorname{in} G \Rightarrow \langle \forall t : t \in G : [\operatorname{wp}.s.Z \Rightarrow \operatorname{wp}.t.(\operatorname{wp}.s.Z)] \rangle \rangle$

Now we rewrite the consequent as two conjuncts and deal with each conjunct individually. For each statement s of program F and $\operatorname{stable} Z \operatorname{in} G$, we observe

$\langle \forall t : t \in G : [\operatorname{wp}.s.Z \Rightarrow \operatorname{wp}.t.(\operatorname{wp}.s.Z)] \rangle$
= {omitting the range of t; definition of $\operatorname{wp}.s.Z$}
$\langle \forall t :: [(grd.s \wedge \operatorname{wp}.S.Z) \vee (\neg grd.s \wedge Z) \Rightarrow \operatorname{wp}.t.(\operatorname{wp}.s.Z)] \rangle$
= {predicate calculus}
$\langle \forall t :: [(grd.s \wedge \operatorname{wp}.S.Z) \Rightarrow \operatorname{wp}.t.(\operatorname{wp}.s.Z)] \rangle \wedge$
$\langle \forall t :: [(\neg grd.s \wedge Z) \Rightarrow \operatorname{wp}.t.(\operatorname{wp}.s.Z)] \rangle$

The first conjunct follows from Misra commutativity as shown by this derivation.

$\langle \forall t :: [(grd.s \wedge \operatorname{wp}.S.Z) \Rightarrow \operatorname{wp}.t.(\operatorname{wp}.s.Z)] \rangle$
= {definition of $\operatorname{wp}.t$ and predicate calculus}
$\langle \forall t :: [(grd.s \wedge \operatorname{wp}.S.Z \wedge grd.t) \Rightarrow \operatorname{wp}.T.(\operatorname{wp}.s.Z)] \rangle$
$\Leftarrow$ {from hypothesis $\operatorname{stable} Z \operatorname{in} G: \langle \forall t :: [Z \Rightarrow \operatorname{wp}.t.Z] \rangle$}; $\operatorname{wp}.S$ monotonic}
$\langle \forall t :: [(grd.s \wedge grd.t \wedge \operatorname{wp}.S.(\operatorname{wp}.t.Z)) \Rightarrow \operatorname{wp}.T.(\operatorname{wp}.s.Z)] \rangle$
$\Leftarrow$ {definition of $\operatorname{wp}.t.Z$ and $\operatorname{wp}.s.Z$}
$\langle \forall t :: [(grd.s \wedge grd.t \wedge \operatorname{wp}.S.((grd.t \wedge \operatorname{wp}.T.Z) \vee (\neg grd.t \wedge Z))) \Rightarrow$
$\operatorname{wp}.T.(grd.s \wedge \operatorname{wp}.S.Z)] \rangle$
= {deterministic S; predicate calculus}
$\langle \forall t :: [(grd.s \wedge grd.t \wedge \operatorname{wp}.S.(grd.t \wedge \operatorname{wp}.T.Z)) \Rightarrow$
$\operatorname{wp}.T.(grd.s \wedge \operatorname{wp}.S.Z)] \rangle \wedge$
$\langle \forall t :: [(grd.s \wedge grd.t \wedge \operatorname{wp}.S.(\neg grd.t \wedge Z)) \Rightarrow \operatorname{wp}.T.(grd.s \wedge \operatorname{wp}.S.Z)] \rangle$
= {$\operatorname{wp}.S$ is universally conjunctive; predicate calculus}
$\langle \forall t :: [(grd.s \wedge grd.t \wedge \operatorname{wp}.S.(grd.t) \wedge \operatorname{wp}.(S;T).Z) \Rightarrow$
$\operatorname{wp}.T.(grd.s) \wedge \operatorname{wp}.(T;S).Z] \rangle \wedge$
$\langle \forall t :: [grd.s \wedge grd.t \Rightarrow \neg \operatorname{wp}.S.(\neg grd.t \wedge Z) \vee \operatorname{wp}.T.(grd.s \wedge \operatorname{wp}.S.Z)] \rangle$
= {property S0 and S1 of wp}
$\langle \forall t :: [(grd.s \wedge grd.t \wedge \operatorname{wp}.S.(grd.t) \wedge \operatorname{wp}.(S;T).Z) \Rightarrow$
$\operatorname{wp}.T.(grd.s) \wedge \operatorname{wp}.(T;S).Z] \rangle \wedge$
$\langle \forall t :: [grd.s \wedge grd.t \Rightarrow \operatorname{wp}.S.(grd.t \vee \neg Z)) \vee \operatorname{wp}.T.(grd.s \wedge \operatorname{wp}.S.Z)] \rangle$
$\Leftarrow$ {predicate calculus}
$\langle \forall t :: [(grd.s \wedge grd.t \wedge \operatorname{wp}.S.(grd.t) \wedge \operatorname{wp}.(S;T).Z) \Rightarrow$
$\operatorname{wp}.T.(grd.s) \wedge \operatorname{wp}.(T;S).Z] \rangle \wedge$
$\langle \forall t :: [grd.s \wedge grd.t \Rightarrow \operatorname{wp}.S.(grd.t)] \rangle$
$\Leftarrow$ {rearranging terms}

$$\langle \forall t :: [(grd.s \wedge grd.t \wedge \textbf{wp} .(S; T).Z) \Rightarrow \textbf{wp} .(T; S).Z]\rangle \wedge$$
$$\langle \forall t :: [grd.s \wedge grd.t \Rightarrow \textbf{wp} .S.(grd.t) \wedge \textbf{wp} .T.(grd.t)]\rangle$$
$\Leftarrow$ {definition of Misra commutativity}
$s \, \textbf{co}_m \, G$

The second conjunct follows from Lipton left commutativity as shown by this derivation.

$$\langle \forall t :: [(\neg grd.s \wedge Z) \Rightarrow \textbf{wp} .t.(\textbf{wp} .s.Z)]\rangle$$
$=$ {definition of $\textbf{wp} .t$ and predicate calculus}
$$\langle \forall t :: [(\neg grd.s \wedge Z \wedge grd.t) \Rightarrow \textbf{wp} .T.(\textbf{wp} .s.Z)]\rangle$$
$=$ {definition of $\textbf{wp} .s$ and predicate calculus}
$$\langle \forall t :: [(\neg grd.s \wedge Z \wedge grd.t) \Rightarrow \textbf{wp} .T.((grd.s \wedge \textbf{wp} .S.Z) \vee (\neg grd.s \wedge Z))]\rangle$$
$\Leftarrow$ {predicate calculus}
$$\langle \forall t :: [(\neg grd.s \wedge Z \wedge grd.t) \Rightarrow \textbf{wp} .T.(\neg grd.s \wedge Z)]\rangle$$
$=$ {universal conjunctivity of $\textbf{wp} .T$}
$$\langle \forall t :: [(\neg grd.s \wedge Z \wedge grd.t) \Rightarrow \textbf{wp} .T.(\neg grd.s) \wedge \textbf{wp} .T.Z]\rangle$$
$\Leftarrow$ {hypothesis $\textbf{stable} \, Z \, \textbf{in} \, G$; $[grd.t \wedge Z \Rightarrow \textbf{wp} .T.Z]$}
$$\langle \forall t :: [(\neg grd.s \wedge Z \wedge grd.t) \Rightarrow \textbf{wp} .T.(\neg grd.s)]\rangle$$
$\Leftarrow$ {predicate calculus}
$$\langle \forall t :: [(\neg grd.s \wedge grd.t) \Rightarrow \textbf{wp} .T.(\neg grd.s)]\rangle$$
$\Leftarrow$ {rearranging}
$$\langle \forall t :: [(grd.t \wedge \textbf{wp} .T.(grd.s)) \Rightarrow grd.s]\rangle$$
$\Leftarrow$ {definition of Lipton left commutativity}
$s \, \textbf{lco}_l \, G$

$\square$

Theorem 4.5.2. *Given programs F and G,*

$$(F \, \textbf{co}_m \, (F \, [\!] \, G)) \Rightarrow (F \, \textbf{wdec}_{safe} \, G)$$

Proof. The proof of this theorem follows from the proof of Theorem 4.5.1 upto and including the point where we show $f \, \textbf{co}_m \, G$ implies the first conjunct, with program $F \, [\!] \, G$ instead of G. The following derivation shows that the second conjunct holds trivially rendering any assumption of Lipton commutativity unnecessary. For all statements s in F and $\textbf{stable} \, Z \, \textbf{in} \, F \, [\!] \, G$, we observe

$$\langle \forall u : u \in F \, [\!] \, G : [(\neg grd.s \wedge Z) \Rightarrow \textbf{wp} .u.(\textbf{wp} .s.Z)]\rangle$$
$\Leftarrow$ {From $\textbf{stable} \, Z \, \textbf{in} \, F \, [\!] \, G$, $[Z \Rightarrow \textbf{wp} .s.Z]$; monotonicity of $\textbf{wp} .u$}
$$\langle \forall u : u \in F \, [\!] \, G : [(\neg grd.s \wedge Z) \Rightarrow \textbf{wp} .u.Z]\rangle$$
$\Leftarrow$ {predicate calculus}
$$\langle \forall u : u \in F \, [\!] \, G : [Z \Rightarrow \textbf{wp} .u.Z]\rangle$$
$\Leftarrow$ {From $\textbf{stable} \, Z \, \textbf{in} \, F \, [\!] \, G$, $[Z \Rightarrow \textbf{wp} .u.Z]$}
$true$

$\square$

4.6 Implications for Research in Programming Languages

In this chapter, we have suggested restrictions on parallel programs which when imposed would guarantee that the progress properties of the component programs are preserved in the composition. While the goal of preserving progress properties is a lofty one, the restrictions (such as dec_{safe} and $wdec_{safe}$) are difficult to check for every pair of programs. Conditions such as Lipton and Misra commutativity are slightly more tractable, as they require checking the commutativity of every pair of statements of every pair of programs. However, doing this in practice, goes against the spirit of modularity, as one can no longer treat a program as a black box.

The hope for this research lies in enforcing the proposed restrictions at a *syntactic* level. If the features of a parallel programming language are designed such that they satisfy our restrictions, then we are automatically guaranteed that *all* programs written in that programming language will satisfy those restrictions.

One such example is the feature of *logic variables* (Chandy and Taylor [1990]). A logic variable is a variable shared between components (of a parallel program) that is written at most once. Initially, the value of a logic variable is undefined. During the course of program execution, it may be assigned a value by some component and this value remains fixed for the remaining part of program execution. A *read* action on a logic variable is defined if and only if the variable has a defined value. A *write* action on a logic variable is defined if and only if the variable is undefined. Thus, a read action and a write action of a logic variable Misra–commute with respect to one another. Further, two read actions Misra–commute with one another. However, a write action does not Misra–commute with another write action. This suggests that the variables shared by the components of a parallel program be logic variables, with only one component being able to write to it. Under such circumstances, our theorems show that the components would be weakly decoupled. That is, the progress properties of each component will be preserved in the composition. And on this happy note, we end this chapter.

5. On the Design of Proof Rules for Fair Parallel Programs

Consider the following **do–od** program:

$$
\begin{array}{ll}
\textbf{declare} & a, b : boolean \\
\textbf{do} & true \longrightarrow a := \neg a \\
\text{\textbracketdbl} & true \longrightarrow b := \neg b \\
\text{\textbracketdbl} & b \longrightarrow a := true \\
\textbf{od} &
\end{array}
$$

The program uses two boolean variables a and b and consists of three guarded statements. Each statement consists of a boolean *guard* and a *body*. A statement is said to be *enabled* (*disabled*) in a state if its guard is *true* (*false*) in that state. Operationally speaking, the execution of the program can start in *any* state and proceeds by repeatedly selecting any one of the three statements and executing it. Since at each step, one can select any of the three statements for execution, one can visualize the execution of the program to be structured like a tree: such a tree is called a *computation tree*. The nodes of the tree correspond to the states of the program and the edges of the tree are labelled with the statement selected for execution. For statement t, there is an edge labelled t from node v to w if and only if execution of t transforms the state of node v to the state of node w. It is possible to select a statement for execution even if it is disabled: in this case, the execution of the statement leaves the state unchanged. A path in the tree will be called an *execution sequence* of the program.

It is possible to place constraints on the way statements are selected for execution and regard as legal, only those execution sequences in the computation tree that satisfy these constraints. Such constraints are called *fairness* constraints. For instance, the do–od program is very much like a UNITY program and it is assumed that in an infinite execution of a UNITY program, each statement is executed infinitely often. Such a fairness constraint is termed *unconditional* fairness. An assumption of unconditional fairness is a qualitative guarantee about the rate at which the different processes of a parallel program execute. In terms of the UNITY computational model, it is an assumption about the scheduler that selects statements of the program for execution. There are two points to be noted about such an assumption. First, it provides a useful separation of concerns: the program satisfies its specification provided the scheduler meets its obligation to be unconditionally fair. Second, a fairness constraint provides a basis for building an axiomatization of the progress properties of programs.

For example, in the UNITY proof system for progress, unconditional fairness is instrumental in proving the soundness of the definition of **ensures**. Note that safety properties (such as **unless**) are independent of assumptions of fairness and thus hold of *all* execution sequences.

UNITY's choice of fairness – unconditional fairness – is not sacrosanct. It is merely a useful abstraction that can be easily met in practice: for instance, a scheduler that selects statements in a round–robin fashion is unconditionally fair. Indeed, a number of different fairness assumptions have been used to model the execution of parallel programs. We mention three such constraints below.

– *Minimal Progress*: At each step of the execution, if some statement is enabled, some (possibly different) enabled statement is selected for execution.
– *Weak Fairness*: An execution sequence is *weakly–fair* if and only if each statement that is eventually continuously enabled is infinitely often selected for execution.
– *Strong Fairness*: An execution sequence is *strongly–fair* if and only if each statement that is infinitely often enabled is infinitely often selected for execution.

Each of these constraints gives rise to a different set of legal execution sequences for the program. This means that the properties of the program (that is, the properties of its legal execution sequences) will depend on the fairness constraint assumed for program execution.

In this chapter, our focus will be on proving *progress* properties of programs. We use the *leads-to* operator (Lamport [1977]) to express progress properties. For state predicates X and Y, a program satisfies the progress property X *leads-to* Y, if along *all* fair execution sequences, if the program is in a state in which X is true, it is or will be in a state satisfying Y. For instance, under suitable fairness assumptions,

$$true \ leads-to \ (a \lor b), \text{ and}$$
$$b \ leads-to \ a$$

are possible progress properties for the above program.

In general the progress properties that we can prove for a program will depend on the fairness constraint that is assumed in executing it.

– *Minimal Progress*: With this fairness assumption, we can show that

$$true \ leads-to \ (a \lor b)$$

holds for the **do–od** program given above. Suppose, the program is in a state in which $\neg(a \lor b)$ holds, then only the first two statements of the program are enabled. Minimal progress requires that one of the two be selected for execution. Doing so, results in a state in which $(a \lor b)$ holds. If the program is in a state in which $(a \lor b)$ holds then the property holds trivially.
– *Weak Fairness*: With this fairness assumption, we can show that

$$true \ leads-to \ a$$

holds for the program. Suppose the program is in a state in which $\neg a$ holds. The guard of the first statement is *true* and hence the statement is continuously enabled. Weak fairness requires that it be eventually selected for execution and this results in a state in which a holds. If the program is already in a state in which a holds, the property holds trivially.

Notice that this property does not hold if only minimal progress is assumed. In particular, consider the execution sequence which begins in a state in which $\neg (a \vee b)$ holds. The execution proceeds by repeatedly executing the second statement. Such an execution satisfies the constraint of minimal progress but does not satisfy the property *true leads–to a*.

- *Strong Fairness*: With this fairness assumption, we can show that an even stronger property, namely,

$$true \ leads{-}to \ (a \wedge b)$$

holds for the program. The first two statements are always enabled and are thus infinitely often enabled. Thus, each statement will be selected and executed infinitely often. In particular, each execution of the second statement will negate the value of variable b. Thus, the variable b will be true infinitely often: this means that the guard of the third statement will be true infinitely often and strong fairness will require that it be selected infinitely often for execution. When this happens, variable a will be set to true and the program will reach a state in which $(a \wedge b)$ holds.

The property

$$true \ leads{-}to \ (a \wedge b)$$

does not hold under the constraints of minimal progress and weak fairness. We leave it to the reader to convince himself of this.

These fairness assumptions have formed the basis of several proof rules for proving progress properties of programs that have appeared in the literature. While the notions and notations used for these proof rules vary, there is a strong undercurrent of commonality that runs through them. Our goal is to develop a framework that integrates existing work and brings out this commonality. The preceding example raises the following issues about proving the proofs of progress properties:

- *Proof Rule*: The proofs of the progress properties sketched above are informal. We were fortunate in that the program was simple and the proofs were short. In general, this need not be the case. What we need is a proof rule to show that a program satisfies a progress property rigorously and concisely. Given that the execution of a program satisfies some fairness constraint, what is a proof rule for proving progress properties of the program?
- *Methodology for Proof Rule Design*: The above example illustrated three flavors of fairness. Many more have been reported in the literature. Given an arbitrary fairness constraint, is there a systematic way of *deriving* a proof rule

for it? One would expect a methodology for proof–rule design to have the following characteristics.

- *Applicability*: One should be able to design proof rules for a wide range of fairness notions.
- *Meta–theory*: The soundness and completeness of the proof rules should be easy to guarantee. In particular, one should not redo such meta–theoretic proofs for each notion of fairness.
- *Compositionality*: Is the proof rule *compositional?* That is, given that a property has been proved for a program F, is there a simple way to infer that the same property holds when program F is composed with another program G without having to *reprove* the property for F?
- *Methodology for Program Design*: A careful choice of operators and proof rules for progress can form the basis of a theory that can greatly aid and simplify the process of program design. Such an approach has been taken in UNITY. Can it also be used when using fairness notions other than the unconditional fairness of UNITY?

Experience with the UNITY programming methodology suggests that a simple notion of a program (as a set of statements) and an inductive style of defining progress (in terms of a base relation **ensures** and its transitive, disjunctive closure $\mapsto$) have their advantages. First, one can study the properties of programs without being distracted by language issues such as control structure. Second, while general progress properties (such as the $\mapsto$) do not compose when programs are arbitrarily composed (and they cannot as shown in Chapter 4), basic progress properties (such as **ensures**) do. So, one can reason compositionally about progress properties to some extent. Finally, the choice of an inductive style leads naturally to two operators: **ensures** and $\mapsto$. UNITY has developed a rich set of theorems revolving around these two operators and the operator for safety (**unless**). These theorems have proven to be very useful for program design.

Given these advantages of the UNITY methodology, we take the decision to adopt UNITY's notion of program as the basis of our studies and pose the following question. If one were to replace UNITY's assumption of unconditional fairness by a different notion of fairness, what would the appropriate UNITY–style proof rule look like? It is important to note that once an **ensures** relation is defined, the $\mapsto$ relation (which is the infinite disjunctive, transitive closure of **ensures**) is fixed as well. So our goal of defining a UNITY–style proof rule for a range of fairness assumptions boils down to defining an **ensures** relation for each fairness assumption.

To do so, we introduce two new predicate transformers. The first predicate transformer formalizes the notion of the **g***eneralized* **w***eakest* **p***recondition* of statement s with respect to predicate X and is denoted as **gwp**$.s.X$. The second predicate transformer, defined in terms of **gwp**$.s.X$, captures the notion of the **w***eakest* predicate that **l***eads–t**o* predicate X and is denoted as **wlt**$.X$.

Our framework, phrased in terms of these predicate transformers, advocates the following approach to proof–rule design. First, formulate an intuitively understandable definition of progress under the given fairness assumption, as a formula in the branching time temporal logic, CTL^*. Next, express the CTL^* formula as a logically equivalent formula of the μ-calculus, to obtain fixpoint characterizations of **gwp**$.s$ and **wlt**. Use these fixpoint characterizations as a basis, to extract definitions of **ensures** and $\mapsto$ thus giving rise to a simple UNITY-style proof system for proving progress under the given fairness assumption. We demonstrate the applicability of our framework by designing proof rules for pure nondeterminism, minimal progress, unconditional fairness, weak fairness and strong fairness. Thus we show a *systematic* way of designing proof rules for programs executing under fairness assumptions.

While these proof rules are simpler than those currently known in the literature, they are (as would be expected) logically equivalent to the proof rules suggested in Manna and Pnueli [1984]. Further, they have the additional methodological advantage that their UNITY-like formulation enables one to use the UNITY theory of the *leads-to* in the design and derivation of programs based on different notions of fairness.

A key feature of our work is a simple framework to conduct meta-theoretic arguments about the proof rules. Specifically, we show that if the relations **ensures** and $\mapsto$ and the predicate transformers **gwp**$.s$ and **wlt** meet a simple and easily-checked set of conditions, then the soundness and completeness of the proof rules are easily guaranteed. Further, our proofs of soundness and completeness are conducted in a disciplined and calculational manner without resorting to any complicated machinery (including transfinite ordinals).

It is well-known that the ordinal constants *cannot* be eliminated in proofs of progress properties of programs assuming unbounded nondeterminism. However, it was not known whether ordinals were necessary in a meta-theoretic argument about such proof rules. In particular, all arguments about the soundness and completeness of proof rules for fairness that we have seen have explicitly used ordinals. We believe that we are the first to eliminate them.

We give *two* arguments for the soundness and completeness of our proof rules. A non-constructive argument (in Section 5.4.5) uses fixpoint operators but *no* ordinals and a constructive argument (in Section 5.7) that uses both fixpoint operators and ordinals (as one would expect).

In many treatments of meta-theoretic arguments about fairness, assumptions about the complexity of the assertion language, expressibility of weakest preconditions and relative completeness are tacitly made and not explicated. By drawing comparisons to Hoare triples we show that a notion of completeness of a proof rule for *leads-to* must necessarily be restricted and subject to the same constraint of *relative completeness in the sense of Cook*. We then construct a proof of completeness of *leads-to* under unconditional fairness paying special attention to the roles played by the issues mentioned above.

A restricted version of Section 5.4 (using ordinals and more conditions) appeared in Jutla et al. [1989]. Since then Charanjit Jutla and I have greatly simplified and generalized our framework to deal with more general notions of fairness and have obtained results on compositionality (Jutla and Rao [1992]).

5.1 Logics of Programs

Our goal is to reason about the properties of programs. A number of ways of reasoning about programs have been explored in the literature. One method, as illustrated by branching time temporal logic, is to stay within the semantic domain and reason about the infinite computation trees. Another method, as illustrated by UNITY, is more syntactic in that proof rules are used to deduce properties of the programs.

In this section, we introduce the model of infinite computation trees and briefly review two logics for reasoning about them: namely branching time temporal logic and μ-calculus.

5.1.1 Model of Program Execution

A *state* of a program is an assignment of values to the program variables. It is assumed that the program variables have been declared in the **declare** section of the program and that the values assigned to the program variables are consistent with the types associated with them in the **declare** section.

An *execution* of a program can begin in any state: there are no specific initial conditions. Intuitively speaking, program execution begins in any state and proceeds by repeatedly selecting a (guarded) statement from the **assign** section and executing it with the selection being subject to a *fairness* constraint. For example, a simple fairness constraint may require the eventual execution of each statement whose guard is continuously enabled. Another example is UNITY's fairness constraint which requires that in an infinite execution each statement be selected infinitely often. Since we wish to investigate different notions of fairness, we do not commit ourselves to a particular notion of fairness. Thus, in our model of computation, parallelism is captured by a fair, interleaved execution of the statements of the program with each statement being executed atomically.

More formally, the intended model of a program is a forest of infinite computation trees with the nodes of the trees labelled with program states and the edges with program statements. The root node of the tree is labelled with the state in which program execution is initiated. For each statement t of our program, there is an edge labelled t from node v to node w if and only if execution of t transforms the state of the node v to the state of node w. If predicate X holds in the state of node w, then the state of node v satisfies the **wp**$.t.X$. Apart from the usual predicates, we also have auxiliary propositions $\bar{t}$, for each statement t. The proposition $\bar{t}$ holds at a node if and only if the edge directed into that node is labelled t.

An *execution sequence* of the program is any path in a tree that originates at the root node: an execution sequence is said to be *fair* if it satisfies the fairness constraint being studied.

5.1.2 Temporal Logic

There are many versions of temporal logic and the one most suited to our purposes is the branching time temporal logic named $CTL^\star$. In this logic, the underlying structure of time is assumed to have a branching tree–like nature where each moment in time can have many possible successors. Due to the natural correspondence between this and the tree-like semantics of program execution (outlined in the previous section), the logic can be used to express program properties in a precise and concise manner.

Syntax. The propositional branching time temporal logic, CTL^*, uses the following new operators.

– *Path quantifiers*: A universal quantifier over all executions, **A** (read, *for all paths*) and an existential quantifier over all executions, **E** (read, *exists a path*).
– *Temporal operators*: These are **X** (*next time*), **U** (*until*), **F** (*some time*), **G** (*always*) and **W** (*weak–until*).

These new operators are used to inductively define two classes of formulae: *state formulae* and *path formulae*. We denote the set of state formulae by **StatForm** and the set of path formulae by **PathForm**. Let X be an element of **Pred** (see Section 2.1).

– *State Formulae*: Let p, q and r be elements of **StatForm** and s be an element of **PathForm**. The rules for constructing state formulae are

$$p ::= X \mid (q \wedge r) \mid \neg q \mid \mathbf{E}\,s \mid \mathbf{A}\,s.$$

– *Path Formulae*: Let p, q and r be elements of **PathForm** and s be an element of **StatForm**. The rules for constructing path formulae are

$$p ::= s \mid (q \wedge r) \mid \neg q \mid \mathbf{X}\,q \mid (q\,\mathbf{U}\,r).$$

The set of state formulae generated by the above rules form the language CTL^*. It should be noted that we have effectively treated the set of predicates, **Pred**, as a given set of atomic propositions. This is possible as we don't allow infinitary quantifications over temporal operators. A formula, such as

$$\langle \forall i : i \geq 0 : [x = i \Rightarrow \mathbf{A}(true\,\mathbf{U}(x = i + 1))]\rangle$$

is not allowed by the production rules for state formulae, whereas, a formula, such as,

$$[(x \geq 0) \Rightarrow \mathbf{A}((true\,\mathbf{U}(x > 0)) \wedge \mathbf{X}(x = 0))]$$

is permitted. In the sequel, all quantifications over temporal properties will be finitary: that is, they can be rewritten using the corresponding boolean connectives. This enables us to stay within the realm of propositional branching time temporal logic.

Semantics. The semantics of formulae of CTL^* are defined with respect to the model of infinite computation trees. Such a model can be described by a *temporal structure* $M = (S, R, I)$ where S is the set of states, R is a binary transition relation on S induced by our model of infinite computation trees and I is the interpretation associated with the language of predicates. Specifically, I : **Pred** $\rightarrow 2^S$.

A *fullpath* in the temporal structure, M, $(s_0, s_1, \ldots)$ is a maximal sequence of states beginning in state s_0, such that for all i, $(s_i, s_{i+1}) \in R$. We use the convention that $x = (s_0, s_1, s_2 \ldots)$ denotes a fullpath and that x^i denotes the suffix path $(s_i, s_{i+1}, s_{i+2}, \ldots)$. We write $M, s \models p$ (respectively, $M, x \models p$) to mean that the state formula p (respectively, path formula p) is true in structure M at state s (respectively, path x). We define $\models$ inductively as follows.

For a state s:

- $M, s \models X$ iff $s \in I \ll X \gg$.
- $M, s \models q \wedge r$ iff $M, s \models q$ and $M, s \models r$.
- $M, s \models \neg q$ iff not $(M, s \models q)$.
- $M, s \models \mathbf{E} p$ iff there exists a fullpath x starting at s, $M, x \models p$ for a path formula p.
- $M, s \models \mathbf{A} p$ iff for all fullpaths x starting at s, $M, x \models p$ for a path formula p.

For a path $x = (s_0, s_1, \ldots)$:

- $M, x \models p$ iff $M, s_0 \models p$, for a state formula p.
- $M, x \models q \wedge r$ iff $M, x \models q$ and $M, x \models r$.
- $M, x \models \neg q$ iff not $(M, x \models q)$,
- $M, x \models \mathbf{X} q$ iff $M, x^1 \models q$,
- $M, x \models (q \mathbf{U} r)$ iff there exists $i \geq 0$, $M, x^i \models q$ and for all j, $0 \leq j < i$, $M, x^j \models r$.

For instance, $M, s \models \mathbf{E} \mathbf{X}(p \wedge \bar{t})$, where t is a program statement[1] iff there exists a fullpath $x = (s, s_1, \ldots)$ beginning at s, such that p holds in state s_1 and the transition from state s to s_1 is made by executing statement t.

The remaining temporal operators can be defined as follows.

- *Eventually:* $\mathbf{F} p = true \; \mathbf{U} p$.
- *Always:* $\mathbf{G} p = \neg \mathbf{F} \neg p$
- *Weak Until:* $(p \mathbf{W} q) = (p \mathbf{U} q) \vee \mathbf{G} q$.

Thus, the state formula, $\mathbf{A} \mathbf{F} \mathbf{G} q$, holds at state s iff along all paths starting at s, eventually always q holds. $\mathbf{A} \mathbf{F} \mathbf{G} q$ is also a path formula, and it holds for a path $x = (s_0, s_1, \ldots)$ iff it holds for s_0 as a state formula.

We say that state formula p is *valid*, and write $\models p$, if for every structure M and every state s in M, $M, s \models p$. We define validity for path formulae in a similiar manner.

---

[1] Recall the interpretation of predicate $\bar{t}$ in Section 5.1.1. The predicate $\bar{t}$ holds in a state labelling a node w of the computation tree if and only if the edge directed into node w is labelled t.

In this paper, we will appeal to the following identities between temporal logic and weakest precondition operations, given that the models for temporal logic and our programs are the same.

- *Rule TL-WP0*

$$[\mathbf{E}\,\mathbf{X}(\bar{t} \wedge Z) \equiv \mathbf{wp}\,.t.Z].$$

- *Rule TL-WP1*

$$[\mathbf{A}\,\mathbf{X}\,Z \;\equiv\; \langle \forall t :: \mathbf{wp}\,.t.Z \rangle].$$

- *Rule TL-WP2*

$$[\mathbf{A}\,\mathbf{X}(\bar{t} \Rightarrow Z) \;\equiv\; \mathbf{wp}\,.t.Z].$$

5.1.3 The μ-Calculus

A *fixpoint* construct can be used to increase the power of many modal logics. In this paper, we consider the addition of the fixpoint operator to a simple subset of the $CTL^\star$ consisting of predicates, boolean connectives and the temporal modalities $\mathbf{A}\,\mathbf{X}$ and $\mathbf{E}\,\mathbf{X}$.

Consider a set of equations E, in the unknown dummy x (we write $x : E$ to explicate the dependence on the unknown x). Given an ordering $\subseteq$ on the solutions of E, y is the *least fixpoint* (or the *strongest solution*) of E if and only if

- y solves E.
- $\langle \forall z : z \; solves \; E : y \subseteq z \rangle$.

The least fixpoint is denoted by $\langle \mu x :: E \rangle$. Its dual, the *greatest fixpoint* (or the *weakest solution*), can be defined in a similiar manner and is denoted by $\langle \nu x :: E \rangle$. Many correctness properties of parallel programs can be characterized in terms of the μ-calculus.

Syntax. The syntax of μ-calculus is obtained by extending the language of predicates in three ways:

- *Fixpoint operators:* μ (read, *least fixpoint*) and ν (read, *greatest fixpoint*).
- *Propositional variables:* We denote this set by **PropVar** and denote a representative element by Z.
- *Temporal modalities:* $\mathbf{A}\,\mathbf{X}$ (read, *for all paths, in the next state*) and $\mathbf{E}\,\mathbf{X}$ (read, *exists a path, in the next state*).

The fixpoint operators, propositional variables and the temporal modalities are used to inductively define the formulae of the propositional μ-calculus. This set will be denoted by **MuForm**.

Let p, q and r be elements of **MuForm** and let P be an element of **Pred**. Let $f.Z$ be an element of **MuForm** that is syntactically monotone in the propositional variable Z. That is, all occurrences of Z in the formula f fall under an even number of negations. Given this, the rules for constructing μ-calculus formulae are

$$p ::= P \mid Z \mid (q \wedge r) \mid \neg q \mid \mathbf{A}\,\mathbf{X}\,q \mid \mathbf{E}\,\mathbf{X}\,q \mid \langle \mu Z :: f.Z \rangle \mid \langle \nu Z :: f.Z \rangle.$$

Semantics. A *sentence* is a μ–calculus formula containing no free propositional variables, i.e. no variables unbound by a μ or a ν operator. Sentences are interpreted with respect to a structure $(M = (S, R, I))$, where S is the set of states, R is a binary transition relation induced by our model of infinite computation trees and I is the interpretation associated with the language of predicates. We write $M, s \models p$ to mean that in model M, at state s, formula p holds.

A formula p with free variables $(Z_1, \ldots, Z_n)$ is interpreted as a mapping from $(\mathcal{P}(S))^n$ to $\mathcal{P}(S)$, i.e., it is interpreted as a predicate transformer. We write $p(Z_1, \ldots, Z_n)$ to denote that all free propositional variables of p are among $(Z_1, \ldots, Z_n)$. Let $V_1, \ldots, V_n$ be subsets of S. A valuation $\Lambda = (V_1, \ldots, V_n)$ is an assignment of $(V_1, \ldots, V_n)$, to the free variables $(Z_1, \ldots, Z_n)$ respectively. We write $\Lambda(Z \leftarrow T)$ to denote the valuation identical to Λ except that Z is assigned T. To define $\models$ inductively, we extend $\models$ to formulae with free variables (along with their valuations) as follows:

- $M, s \models P(\Lambda)$ iff $s \in I \ll P \gg$
- $M, s \models Z(\Lambda)$ iff $s \in \Lambda(Z)$
- $M, s \models (q \wedge r)(\Lambda)$ iff $M, s \models q(\Lambda)$ and $M, s \models r(\Lambda)$
- $M, s \models (\neg q)(\Lambda)$ iff not $M, s \models p(\Lambda)$
- $M, s \models (\mathbf{E\,X}\,q)(\Lambda)$ iff there exists $(s, s_1) \in R$ such that $M, s_1 \models q(\Lambda)$
- $M, s \models (\mathbf{A\,X}\,q)(\Lambda)$ iff for all s_1, such that $(s, s_1) \in R$, $M, s_1 \models q(\Lambda)$
- $M, s \models \langle \mu Z :: f.Z \rangle(\Lambda)$ iff $s \in \bigcap \{T \subseteq S | T = \{t | M, t \models f.Z(\Lambda(Z \leftarrow T))\}\}$
- $M, s \models \langle \nu Z :: f.Z \rangle(\Lambda)$ iff $s \in \bigcup \{T \subseteq S | T = \{t | M, t \models f.Z(\Lambda(Z \leftarrow T))\}\}$

The power set of S, $\mathcal{P}(S)$, may be viewed as the complete lattice $(\mathcal{P}(S), S, \phi, \subseteq, \cup, \cap)$. Intuitively, we identify a predicate with the set of states which make it true. Thus, *false* which corresponds to the empty set is the bottom element, *true* which corresponds to S is the top element and implication $(\Rightarrow)$ which corresponds to simple set-theoretic containment provides the partial ordering on the lattice.

Recall the concept of a predicate transformer introduced in section 2.3. A predicate transformer, g, is said to be *monotonic* if and only if

$$[Y \Rightarrow Z] \Rightarrow [g.Y \Rightarrow g.Z].$$

Our interest in the complete lattice of predicates and monotonic predicate transformers stems from the theorem of Knaster–Tarski (Theorem 2.4.1) that guarantees that a monotonic predicate transformer g always has both a least fixpoint, $\langle \mu Z :: g.Z \rangle$, and a greatest fixpoint, $\langle \nu Z :: g.Z \rangle$.

5.2 Methodology for the Design of Proof Rules

We propose the following methodology for the design of proof rules for progress using fairness assumptions.

1. For each fairness assumption, propose a branching time temporal logic formula that expresses progress under the prescribed fairness notion. We choose the branching time logic CTL^* to express our formulae as it is powerful enough to express a wide range of fairness constraints.
2. Find a μ–calculus formula that is logically equivalent to this CTL^* formula. Note that, converting a CTL^* formula to a μ–calculus formula is a well-known procedure (Emerson and Lei [1985], Niwinski [1988]).
3. Using the μ–calculus formula as a guide, extract a sound and relatively complete proof rule for proving progress under the fairness notion assumed.

5.3 From Temporal Logic to μ-Calculus

In this section, we illustrate the first and second steps of our methodology. We use the branching time temporal logic to express different notions of fairness and show equivalent μ–calculus characterizations for the temporal logic formulae. In particular, we consider three different kinds of fairness that have been studied in the literature: minimal progress, weak fairness and strong fairness.

5.3.1 Minimal Progress

The constraint of minimal progress is defined as follows : *in an execution sequence, if some statement is enabled then some (possibly different) enabled statement is executed.*

We define an execution sequence to be *maximal* if it satisfies the minimal progress condition. A program executed under the assumption of *minimal progress* reaches a state satisfying Y if and only if along all *maximal* execution sequences a state satisfying Y is reached. This notion of fairness is captured by the CTL^* formula

$$\mathbf{A}(\mathbf{G}(\langle \exists s :: grd.s \rangle \Rightarrow \langle \exists t :: grd.t \wedge \mathbf{X}\,\overline{t}\rangle) \Rightarrow \mathbf{F}\,Y).$$

We prove the following lemma.

Lemma 5.3.1.

$$\mathbf{A}(\mathbf{G}(\langle \exists s :: grd.s \rangle \Rightarrow \langle \exists t :: grd.t \wedge \mathbf{X}\,\overline{t}\rangle) \Rightarrow \mathbf{F}\,Y) \equiv$$

$$\langle \mu Z :: (\langle \exists s :: grd.s \wedge \langle \forall t : grd.t : \mathbf{E}\,\mathbf{X}(\overline{t} \wedge Z)\rangle\rangle) \vee Y \rangle$$

Proof. We prove the contrapositive; specifically, we show that,

$$\neg\,\mathbf{A}(\mathbf{G}(\langle \exists s :: grd.s \rangle \Rightarrow \langle \exists t :: grd.t \wedge \mathbf{X}\,\overline{t}\rangle) \Rightarrow \mathbf{F}\,Y)$$
$$= \quad \{[\neg\,\mathbf{A}\,X \equiv \mathbf{E}\,\neg X],\ (\neg\,\mathbf{G}\,Y \equiv \mathbf{F}\,\neg Y),\ \text{predicate calculus}\}$$
$$\mathbf{E}(\mathbf{G}(\langle \exists s :: grd.s \rangle \Rightarrow \langle \exists t :: grd.t \wedge \mathbf{X}\,\overline{t}\rangle) \wedge \mathbf{G}\,\neg Y))$$

$=$ $\{(\mathbf{G}\,X \wedge \mathbf{G}\,Y \equiv \mathbf{G}(X \wedge Y))\}$
   $\mathbf{E}\,\mathbf{G}(((\exists s :: grd.s) \Rightarrow (\exists t :: grd.t \wedge \mathbf{X}\,\bar{t})) \wedge \neg Y)$
$=$ $\{\text{predicate calculus}\}$
   $\mathbf{E}\,\mathbf{G}(((\forall s :: \neg grd.s) \vee (\exists t :: grd.t \wedge \mathbf{X}\,\bar{t})) \wedge \neg Y)$
$=$ $\{\text{Proof Obligation, see below}\}$
   $\langle \nu X :: ((\forall s :: \neg grd.s) \vee (\exists t : grd.t : \mathbf{E}\,\mathbf{X}(\bar{t} \wedge Z))) \wedge \neg Y\rangle$
$=$ $\{\text{predicate calculus}\}$
   $\langle \nu X :: (\forall s :: \neg grd.s \vee (\exists t : grd.t : (\mathbf{E}\,\mathbf{X}(\bar{t} \wedge Z)))) \wedge \neg Y\rangle$
$`=$ $\{[\mathbf{E}\,\mathbf{X}\,p \equiv \neg\,\mathbf{A}\,\mathbf{X}\,\neg p]\}$
   $\langle \nu X :: (\forall s :: \neg grd.s \vee (\exists t : grd.t : \neg\,\mathbf{A}\,\mathbf{X}\,\neg(\bar{t} \wedge X))) \wedge \neg Y\rangle$
$=$ $\{[\neg\langle \mu X :: f.X\rangle \equiv \langle \nu X :: \neg f.(\neg X)\rangle]\}$
   $\neg\langle \mu X :: (\exists s :: grd.s \wedge (\forall t : grd.t : \mathbf{A}\,\mathbf{X}(\bar{t} \Rightarrow X))) \vee Y\rangle$

Abbreviating

$$\mathbf{E}\,\mathbf{G}(((\forall s :: \neg grd.s) \vee (\exists t :: grd.t \wedge \mathbf{X}\,\bar{t})) \wedge \neg Y)$$

by Z, our proof obligation is two-fold. We first have to show that Z is a solution of the equation

$$X : [X \equiv ((\forall s :: \neg grd.s) \vee (\exists t : grd.t : \mathbf{E}\,\mathbf{X}(\bar{t} \wedge X))) \wedge \neg Y]$$

and second, that it is the weakest solution.

Ad 0. To show that Z solves the equation, it is sufficient (by Theorem 2.4.1) to show that

$$[Z \Rightarrow \langle (\forall s :: \neg grd.s) \vee (\exists t : grd.t : \mathbf{E}\,\mathbf{X}(\bar{t} \wedge Z))\rangle \wedge \neg Y\rangle].$$

The following derivation proves this.

   Z
$=$ $\{\text{definition of } Z\}$
   $\mathbf{E}\,\mathbf{G}(((\forall s :: \neg grd.s) \Rightarrow (\exists t :: grd.t \wedge \mathbf{X}\,\bar{t})) \wedge \neg Y)$
$\Rightarrow$ $\{[\mathbf{E}\,\mathbf{G}\,X \Rightarrow \mathbf{E}(X \wedge \mathbf{X}\,\mathbf{E}\,\mathbf{G}\,X)]\}$
   $\mathbf{E}(((\forall s :: \neg grd.s) \vee (\exists t :: grd.t \wedge \mathbf{X}\,\bar{t})) \wedge \neg Y \wedge \mathbf{X}\,Z)$
$\Rightarrow$ $\{\text{temporal logic and predicate calculus}\}$
   $\mathbf{E}(((\forall s :: \neg grd.s) \vee (\exists t :: grd.t \wedge \mathbf{X}\,\bar{t} \wedge \mathbf{X}\,Z)) \wedge \neg Y)$
$=$ $\{\text{temporal logic; } [\mathbf{X}\,\bar{t} \wedge \mathbf{X}\,Z \equiv \mathbf{X}(\bar{t} \wedge Z)]\}$
   $\mathbf{E}(((\forall s :: \neg grd.s) \vee (\exists t :: grd.t \wedge \mathbf{X}(\bar{t} \wedge Z))) \wedge \neg Y)$
$\Rightarrow$ $\{\text{temporal logic}\}$
   $(((\forall s :: \neg grd.s) \vee (\exists t :: grd.t \wedge \mathbf{E}\,\mathbf{X}(\bar{t} \wedge Z))) \wedge \neg Y)$

Ad 1. To show that Z is the weakest solution, we have to show that any solution of equation

$$X : (X \equiv (\forall s :: \neg grd.s) \vee (\exists t : grd.t : \mathbf{E}\,\mathbf{X}(\bar{t} \wedge X))) \wedge \neg Y))$$

implies Z.

Assume that X is a solution of the equation and that X holds at a node u. Since X is a solution of the equation, we can conclude that $\neg Y$ holds at u. Two cases arise.

0. $\langle \forall s :: \neg grd.s \rangle$ holds at u. Since all the statements are disabled, effectively there is only one execution, namely the one in which the state of u is repeated infinitely. Further, since the state along this execution does not change, $\langle \forall s :: \neg grd.s \rangle \wedge \neg Y$ holds at each node of the path beginning at u, that is, Z holds at u.

1. $\langle \exists s :: grd.s \rangle$ holds at u. From the definition of X this means that $\langle \exists t : grd.t : \mathbf{E}\,\mathbf{X}(\bar{t} \wedge X) \rangle$ holds at u. Thus, there exists a child (call it v) of u, such that the state of v is obtained by executing statement t in the state of u. Further, $\bar{t} \wedge X$ is true in v. Since X holds at v, the above argument can be repeated with v in place of u. A simple induction argument establishes the existence of a path from u along which $\mathbf{E}\,\mathbf{G}(((\exists s :: grd.s) \Rightarrow \langle \exists t :: grd.t \wedge \mathbf{X}\,\bar{t} \rangle) \wedge \neg Y)$ holds, that is, Z holds. This concludes our proof.   □

Remark on Pure Nondeterminism: The case of pure nondeterminism (that is, no fairness constraint at all) is a special case of minimal progress where the guard of every statement is true. By uniformly substituting *true* for $grd.s$ in the CTL^* formula and Lemma 5.3.1 we obtain the following.

A program executed with no fairness constraint reaches a state satisfying predicate Y if and only if along *all* execution sequences a state satisfying Y is eventually reached.

– CTL^* formula:
$$\mathbf{AF}Y.$$

– Equivalent μ–calculus formula: Using rules TL–WP0 and TL–WP1 to rewrite $\langle \forall t :: \mathbf{E}\,\mathbf{X}(\bar{t} \wedge Z) \rangle$ as $\mathbf{A}\,\mathbf{X}\,Z$ we obtain:

$$[\mathbf{AF}Y \equiv \langle \mu Z :: Y \vee \mathbf{AX}Z \rangle]$$

(*End of Remark*).

5.3.2 Weak Fairness

Weak fairness is defined as follows : *an execution sequence is weakly-fair if and only if each statement that is eventually enabled continuously is infinitely often executed.*

A program which is executed under the constraint of *weak fairness* reaches a state satisfying Y if and only if along *all weakly-fair* execution sequences a state satisfying Y is reached. This notion is accurately captured by the CTL^* formula

$$\mathbf{A}((\forall s :: \mathbf{F}\,\mathbf{G}\,grd.s \Rightarrow \mathbf{G}\,\mathbf{F}(grd.s \wedge \mathbf{X}\,\bar{s})) \Rightarrow \mathbf{F}\,Y).$$

We prove the following lemmata.

Lemma 5.3.2.

$$[\mathbf{A}(Y \ \mathbf{W} \ Z) \ \equiv \ \langle \nu V :: Z \vee (Y \wedge \mathbf{A} \, \mathbf{X} \, V) \rangle]$$

Proof. We abbreviate $\mathbf{A}(Y \ \mathbf{W} \ Z)$ by X. We prove the lemma in two steps. We first show that X solves the equation

$$V : [V \equiv Z \vee (Y \wedge \mathbf{A} \, \mathbf{X} \, V)]$$

and we then show that it is the weakest solution.

Ad 0. To show that X is a solution, it is enough to show (by Theorem 2.4.1) that

$$[X \Rightarrow Z \vee (Y \wedge \mathbf{A} \, \mathbf{X} \, X)].$$

Suppose X holds at a node u. Then, $\mathbf{A}(Y \ \mathbf{W} \ Z)$ holds at u. This means that along any path beginning at u, either Y holds indefinitely or at every node of the path Y holds till a node at which Z holds is reached. That is, either Z holds at u or Y holds at u and X holds at all the children of u. That is $Z \vee (Y \wedge \mathbf{A} \, \mathbf{X} \, X)$ holds at u.

Ad 1. Suppose V is a solution of the equation

$$V : [V \equiv Z \vee (Y \wedge \mathbf{A} \, \mathbf{X} \, V)].$$

To show that X is the weakest solution, we have to show that $[V \Rightarrow X]$. We demonstrate this by proving the contrapositive.

Suppose $\neg X$ holds at a node u. Then there exists a path originating at u such that, $\neg(Y \ \mathbf{W} \ Z)$ holds. That is, there is a sequence of nodes $u, v, \ldots, w, x$ such that $Y \wedge \neg Z$ holds at all the nodes on the segment $u, v, \ldots, w$ and $\neg Y \wedge \neg Z$ holds at x. Since $[\neg V \equiv \neg Z \wedge (\neg Y \vee \mathbf{E} \, \mathbf{X} \, \neg V)]$, we may assert that $\neg V$ holds at x. From the definition of $\neg V$, this means that $\neg V$ holds at w and by a simple induction $\neg V$ holds at u. That is $[\neg X \Rightarrow \neg V]$.   □

Lemma 5.3.3.

$$[\mathbf{A}(\langle \forall s :: \mathbf{F} \, \mathbf{G} \, grd.s \Rightarrow \mathbf{G} \, \mathbf{F}(grd.s \wedge \mathbf{X} \, \bar{s}) \rangle \ \Rightarrow \ \mathbf{F} Y) \ \equiv$$
$$\langle \mu Z :: Y \vee \langle \exists s :: \mathbf{A}((\mathbf{E} \, \mathbf{X}(\bar{s} \wedge Z) \wedge grd.s) \ \mathbf{W} \ Z) \rangle \rangle]$$

Proof. We prove the contrapositive, i.e,

$\qquad \neg \, \mathbf{A}(\langle \forall s :: \mathbf{F} \, \mathbf{G} \, grd.s \Rightarrow \mathbf{G} \, \mathbf{F}(grd.s \wedge \mathbf{X} \, \bar{s}) \rangle \ \Rightarrow \ \mathbf{F} Y)$

$= \quad$ {temporal logic; $[\neg \, \mathbf{A} \, X \equiv \mathbf{E} \, \neg X]$, $[\neg \, \mathbf{F} Y \equiv \mathbf{G} \, \neg Y]$}

$\qquad \mathbf{E} \langle \forall s :: (\mathbf{G} \, \mathbf{F} \, \neg grd.s \vee \mathbf{G} \, \mathbf{F}(grd.s \wedge \mathbf{X} \, \bar{s})) \wedge \mathbf{G} \, \neg Y \rangle$

$= \quad$ {Proof Obligation, see below}

$\qquad \langle \nu X :: \neg Y \wedge \langle \forall s :: \mathbf{E}(X \, \mathbf{U} \, (X \wedge (grd.s \Rightarrow \mathbf{E} \, \mathbf{X}(\bar{s} \wedge X)))) \rangle \rangle$

$= \quad \{ \neg(X \, \mathbf{W} \, Y) \ \equiv \ \neg Y \, \mathbf{U}(\neg X \wedge \neg Y) \}$

$\qquad \langle \nu X :: \neg Y \wedge \langle \forall s :: \mathbf{E} \, \neg(((\mathbf{A} \, \mathbf{X}(\bar{s} \Rightarrow \neg X) \wedge grd.s) \ \mathbf{W} \ \neg X) \rangle \rangle$

$= \quad \{ [\mathbf{E} \, \mathbf{X}(\bar{s} \wedge X) \equiv \mathbf{A} \, \mathbf{X}(\bar{s} \Rightarrow X)] \}$

$\qquad \langle \nu X :: \neg Y \wedge \langle \forall s :: \mathbf{E} \, \neg((\mathbf{E} \, \mathbf{X}(\bar{s} \wedge \neg X) \wedge grd.s) \ \mathbf{W} \ \neg X) \rangle \rangle$

$= \quad \{ [\neg \langle \mu X :: f.X \rangle \ \equiv \ \langle \nu X :: \neg f.(\neg X) \rangle] \}$

$\qquad \neg \langle \mu Z :: Y \vee \langle \exists s :: \mathbf{A}((\mathbf{E} \, \mathbf{X}(\bar{s} \wedge Z) \wedge grd.s) \ \mathbf{W} \ Z) \rangle \rangle$

Abbreviating the expression

$$\mathbf{E}\langle \forall s :: (\mathbf{G}\,\mathbf{F}\,\neg grd.s \vee \mathbf{G}\,\mathbf{F}(grd.s \wedge \mathbf{X}\,\bar{s})) \wedge \mathbf{G}\,\neg Y\rangle$$

by Z, our proof obligation is to show that Z is the weakest solution of

$$X : [X \equiv \neg Y \wedge \langle \forall s :: \mathbf{E}(X\,\mathbf{U}\,(X \wedge (grd.s \Rightarrow \mathbf{E}\,\mathbf{X}(\bar{s} \wedge X))))\rangle]$$

We first show that Z is a solution and then show that it is the weakest solution.

Ad 0. To show that Z solves the equation, it is sufficient to show (by Theorem 2.4.1) that

$$[Z \Rightarrow \neg Y \wedge \langle \forall s :: \mathbf{E}(Z\,\mathbf{U}\,(Z \wedge (grd.s \Rightarrow (\mathbf{E}\,\mathbf{X}(\bar{s} \wedge Z)))))\rangle].$$

We show the two conjuncts separately.

Z
$=$ {definition of Z}
  $\mathbf{E}\langle \forall s :: (\mathbf{G}\,\mathbf{F}\,\neg grd.s \vee \mathbf{G}\,\mathbf{F}(grd.s \wedge \mathbf{X}\,\bar{s})) \wedge \mathbf{G}\,\neg Y\rangle$
$\Rightarrow$ {temporal logic and predicate calculus}
  $\mathbf{E}\,\mathbf{G}\,\neg Y$
$\Rightarrow$ {temporal logic; $\mathbf{G}\,X \Rightarrow X$}
  $\neg Y$

Z
$=$ {definition of Z}
  $\mathbf{E}\langle \forall t :: (\mathbf{G}\,\mathbf{F}\,\neg grd.t \vee \mathbf{G}\,\mathbf{F}(grd.t \wedge \mathbf{X}\,\bar{t})) \wedge \mathbf{G}\,\neg Y\rangle$
$=$ {temporal logic}
  $\mathbf{E}\langle \forall t :: \mathbf{G}(\mathbf{G}\,\mathbf{F}\,\neg grd.t \vee \mathbf{G}\,\mathbf{F}(grd.t \wedge \mathbf{X}\,\bar{t})) \wedge \mathbf{G}\,\neg Y\rangle$
$=$ {interchange quantification}
  $\mathbf{E}\,\mathbf{G}\langle \forall t :: (\mathbf{G}\,\mathbf{F}\,\neg grd.t \vee \mathbf{G}\,\mathbf{F}(grd.t \wedge \mathbf{X}\,\bar{t})) \wedge \mathbf{G}\,\neg Y\rangle$
$=$ {temporal logic and predicate calculus}
  $\mathbf{E}(\mathbf{G}\langle \forall t :: (\mathbf{G}\,\mathbf{F}\,\neg grd.t \vee \mathbf{G}\,\mathbf{F}(grd.t \wedge \mathbf{X}\,\bar{t})) \wedge \mathbf{G}\,\neg Y\rangle \wedge$
  $\langle \forall s :: \mathbf{G}\,\mathbf{F}\,\neg grd.s \vee \mathbf{G}\,\mathbf{F}(grd.s \wedge \mathbf{X}\,\bar{s})\rangle)$
$\Rightarrow$ {temporal logic}
  $\mathbf{E}(\mathbf{G}\langle \forall t :: (\mathbf{G}\,\mathbf{F}\,\neg grd.t \vee \mathbf{G}\,\mathbf{F}(grd.t \wedge \mathbf{X}\,\bar{t})) \wedge \mathbf{G}\,\neg Y\rangle \wedge$
  $\langle \forall s :: \mathbf{G}\,\mathbf{F}(\neg grd.s \vee (grd.s \wedge \mathbf{X}\,\bar{s}))\rangle)$
$\Rightarrow$ {temporal logic}
  $\mathbf{E}(\mathbf{G}\langle \forall t :: (\mathbf{G}\,\mathbf{F}\,\neg grd.t \vee \mathbf{G}\,\mathbf{F}(grd.t \wedge \mathbf{X}\,\bar{t})) \wedge \mathbf{G}\,\neg Y\rangle \wedge$
  $\langle \forall s :: \mathbf{F}(grd.s \Rightarrow (grd.s \wedge \mathbf{X}\,\bar{s}))\rangle)$
$\Rightarrow$ {predicate calculus}
  $\mathbf{E}(\mathbf{G}\langle \forall t :: (\mathbf{G}\,\mathbf{F}\,\neg grd.t \vee \mathbf{G}\,\mathbf{F}(grd.t \wedge \mathbf{X}\,\bar{t})) \wedge \mathbf{G}\,\neg Y\rangle \wedge$
  $\qquad\qquad\qquad\qquad\qquad\qquad \langle \forall s :: \mathbf{F}(grd.s \Rightarrow \mathbf{X}\,\bar{s})\rangle)$
$=$ { $\wedge$ over $\forall$; non–empty programs}
  $\mathbf{E}\langle \forall s :: \mathbf{G}\langle \forall t :: (\mathbf{G}\,\mathbf{F}\,\neg grd.t \vee \mathbf{G}\,\mathbf{F}(grd.t \wedge \mathbf{X}\,\bar{t})) \wedge \mathbf{G}\,\neg Y\rangle \wedge$
  $\qquad\qquad\qquad\qquad\qquad\qquad \mathbf{F}(grd.s \Rightarrow \mathbf{X}\,\bar{s})\rangle$

$\Rightarrow$ {interchange quantification}
$$\langle\forall s :: \mathbf{E}(\mathbf{G}\langle\forall t :: (\mathbf{G}\,\mathbf{F}\,\neg grd.t \lor \mathbf{G}\,\mathbf{F}(grd.t \land \mathbf{X}\,\bar{t})) \land \mathbf{G}\,\neg Y\rangle \land$$
$$\mathbf{F}(grd.s \Rightarrow \mathbf{X}\,\bar{s})))$$

$\Rightarrow$ {temporal logic}
$$\langle\forall s :: \mathbf{E}(\mathbf{G}\,\mathbf{E}\langle\forall t :: (\mathbf{G}\,\mathbf{F}\,\neg grd.t \lor \mathbf{G}\,\mathbf{F}(grd.t \land \mathbf{X}\,\bar{t})) \land \mathbf{G}\,\neg Y\rangle \land$$
$$\mathbf{F}(grd.s \Rightarrow \mathbf{X}\,\bar{s})))$$

$=$ {definition of Z}
$$\langle\forall s :: \mathbf{E}(\mathbf{G}\,Z \land \mathbf{F}(grd.s \Rightarrow \mathbf{X}(\bar{s} \land Z))))\rangle$$

$\Rightarrow$ {temporal logic}
$$\langle\forall s :: \mathbf{E}(\mathbf{G}\,Z \land \mathbf{F}(grd.s \Rightarrow \mathbf{E}\,\mathbf{X}(\bar{s} \land Z))))\rangle$$

$\Rightarrow$ $\{(\mathbf{G}\,X \land \mathbf{F}\,Y \Rightarrow X\,\mathbf{U}(X \land Y))\}$
$$\langle\forall s :: \mathbf{E}(Z\,\mathbf{U}\,(Z \land (grd.s \Rightarrow (\mathbf{E}\,\mathbf{X}(\bar{s} \land Z)))))\rangle$$

Ad 1. To show that Z is the weakest solution, we have to show that any solution of the equation

$$X : [X \equiv \neg Y \land \langle\forall s :: \mathbf{E}(X\,\mathbf{U}\,(X \land (grd.s \Rightarrow (\mathbf{E}\,\mathbf{X}(\bar{s} \land X)))))\rangle]$$

implies Z.

Assume that X is a solution of the equation and that X holds at a node u. We will show that there exists a path beginning at u such that each statement s whose guard is eventually continuously enabled is executed infinitely often along the path and that at each state along the path $\neg Y$ holds. This would imply that for all statements s, $(\mathbf{F}\,\mathbf{G}\,grd.s \Rightarrow \mathbf{G}\,\mathbf{F}(grd.s \land \mathbf{X}\,\bar{s})) \land \mathbf{G}\,\neg Y$, that is, Z holds at u.

Assume that the statements of the program are ordered. Select the first statement, say t. Assume that X holds at u. Since X is a solution of the equation, $\neg Y \land \langle\forall s :: \mathbf{E}(X\,\mathbf{U}\,(X \land (grd.s \Rightarrow \mathbf{E}\,\mathbf{X}(\bar{s} \land X)))))\rangle$ holds at u. Then $\neg Y$ holds at u and for each statement s, there exists a path from u for which $X\,\mathbf{U}(X \land (grd.s \Rightarrow \mathbf{E}\,\mathbf{X}(\bar{s} \land X)))$ holds. Choose the path corresponding to statement t. From $X\,\mathbf{U}(X \land (grd.t \Rightarrow \mathbf{E}\,\mathbf{X}(\bar{t} \land X)))$, there exist nodes v and w and a prefix of the path $u, \ldots, v, w$ such that, X holds at every node on the $u, \ldots, v$ path and $X \land (grd.t \Rightarrow \mathbf{E}\,\mathbf{X}(\bar{t} \land X))$ is true at w. Since X holds at all the nodes on the $u, \ldots, v, w$ path, $\neg Y$ holds at all the nodes as well. Now there are two cases to consider.

Case 0. $grd.t$ holds at node w. Since $X \land (grd.t \Rightarrow \mathbf{wp}.t.X)$ holds at w, there is a child of node w (call it y), such that the state of node y is reached by executing statement t in the state of of node w. Thus statement t can be selected and executed. Since $\mathbf{E}\,\mathbf{X}(\bar{t} \land X)$ holds at w, X holds at y and the same argument can be repeated to extend the path from y for the next statement in the program. The path can be extended by cycling through the statements of the program in this manner.

Case 1. $grd.t$ does not hold at node w. In this case, $\neg grd.t$ holds at node w on the path. This path can be extended to a new node (say y) such that the state of node y is the same as the state of node w and it can be assumed that the state of node y has been obtained by executing statement t in the state of node w (since $grd.t$ is false in w). So X holds in y and the same argument can be repeated to extend the path from y for the next statement in the program. The path can be extended by cycling through the statements of the program in this manner.

For the path so constructed, one can see that if there is a statement s such that $\mathbf{F\,G}\,grd.s$ holds, then $\mathbf{G\,F}(grd.s \wedge \mathbf{X}\,\bar{s})$ holds. That is to say, we can construct a path from u such that for all statements s, $(\mathbf{F\,G}\,grd.s \Rightarrow \mathbf{G\,F}(grd.s \wedge \mathbf{X}\,\bar{s})) \wedge \mathbf{G}\,\neg Y$ holds for the path. In other words, Z holds at u. □

Remark on Unconditional Fairness: Unconditional fairness is defined as follows : *an execution sequence is unconditionally fair if and only if each statement is executed infinitely often.*

A program which is executed under the constraint of *unconditional fairness* reaches a state satisfying Y if and only if along *all unconditionally fair* execution sequences a state satisfying Y is reached.

The case of unconditional fairness is a special case of weak fairness where the guard of every statement is true. By uniformly substituting *true* for $grd.s$ in the $CTL^{\star}$ formula and Lemma 5.3.3 we obtain the following.

– $CTL^{\star}$ formula:

$$\mathbf{A}(\langle \forall s :: \mathbf{G\,F}\,\bar{s}\rangle \;\Rightarrow\; \mathbf{F}\,Y).$$

– Equivalent μ–calculus formula:

$$[\mathbf{A}(\langle \forall s :: \mathbf{G\,F}\,\bar{s}\rangle \;\Rightarrow\; \mathbf{F}\,Y) \;\equiv\; \langle \mu Z :: Y \vee \langle \exists s :: \mathbf{A}(\mathbf{E\,X}(\bar{s} \wedge Z)\;\mathbf{W}\;Z)\rangle\rangle]$$

(End of Remark).

5.3.3 Strong Fairness

Strong fairness is defined as follows : *an execution sequence is strongly–fair if and only if each statement that is enabled infinitely often is executed infinitely often.*

We have investigated the applicability of our framework to strong fairness. It turns out that the proof obligations for strong fairness are more complicated than all the cases previously considered. To prove a property of a program F, one has to prove properties of programs which are related to F : specifically, one has to consider programs that have one statement less than F. We shall denote this by $F - \{s\}$ where s is the omitted statement. Towards this end, we introduce a new notational convention: properties of programs will be parameterized by the name of the program. Till now, the name of the program was implicit in our properties.

A program which is executed under the constraint of *strong fairness* reaches a state satisfying Y if and only if along *all strongly–fair* execution sequences a state satisfying Y is reached. This notion is accurately captured by the $CTL^{\star}$ formula

$$\mathbf{A}(\langle \forall s :: \mathbf{G\,F}\,grd.s \Rightarrow \mathbf{G\,F}(grd.s \wedge \mathbf{X}\,\bar{s})\rangle \Rightarrow \mathbf{F}\,Y).$$

In the following the program being considered is named F and quantifiers over statements will be assumed to range over the statements of F.

Definition 5.3.1. *For a program F, define Θ_F as follows.*

$$[\Theta_F \equiv \langle \forall s :: \mathbf{G\,F}\,grd.s \Rightarrow \mathbf{G\,F}(grd.s \wedge \mathbf{X}\,\bar{s})\rangle].$$

For all programs F, with the definition of Θ_F as given before, we show

$$\Theta_F \;\equiv\; \mathbf{G}\,\Theta_F$$

and

$$\Theta_F \;\equiv\; \mathbf{F}\,\Theta_F.$$

We demonstrate each of the equivalences by a derivation.

$\mathbf{G}\,\Theta_F$
$=$ {definition of Θ_F}
    $\mathbf{G}\langle \forall s :: \mathbf{G\,F}\,grd.s \Rightarrow \mathbf{G\,F}(grd.s \wedge \mathbf{X}\,\bar{s})\rangle$
$=$ {interchange quantification}
    $\langle \forall s :: \mathbf{G}(\mathbf{G\,F}\,grd.s \Rightarrow \mathbf{G\,F}(grd.s \wedge \mathbf{X}\,\bar{s}))\rangle$
$=$ {predicate calculus}
    $\langle \forall s :: \mathbf{G}(\mathbf{F\,G}\,\neg grd.s \vee \mathbf{G\,F}(grd.s \wedge \mathbf{X}\,\bar{s}))\rangle$
$=$ $\{\,\mathbf{F\,G}\,X \equiv \mathbf{G\,F\,G}\,X\,\}$
    $\langle \forall s :: \mathbf{G}(\mathbf{G\,F\,G}\,\neg grd.s \vee \mathbf{G\,F}(grd.s \wedge \mathbf{X}\,\bar{s}))\rangle$
$=$ $\{\,\mathbf{G\,F}\,X \vee \mathbf{G\,F}\,Y \equiv \mathbf{G\,F}(X \vee Y)\,\}$
    $\langle \forall s :: \mathbf{G\,G\,F}(\mathbf{G}\,\neg grd.s \vee (grd.s \wedge \mathbf{X}\,\bar{s}))\rangle$
$=$ {$\mathbf{G}$ idempotent}
    $\langle \forall s :: \mathbf{G\,F}(\mathbf{G}\,\neg grd.s \vee (grd.s \wedge \mathbf{X}\,\bar{s}))\rangle$
$=$ $\{\,\mathbf{G\,F}\,X \vee \mathbf{G\,F}\,Y \equiv \mathbf{G\,F}(X \vee Y)\,\}$
    $\langle \forall s :: \mathbf{G\,F\,G}\,\neg grd.s \vee \mathbf{G\,F}(grd.s \wedge \mathbf{X}\,\bar{s})\rangle$
$=$ $\{\,\mathbf{F\,G}\,X \equiv \mathbf{G\,F\,G}\,X\,\}$
    $\langle \forall s :: \mathbf{F\,G}\,\neg grd.s \vee \mathbf{G\,F}(grd.s \wedge \mathbf{X}\,\bar{s})\rangle$
$=$ {predicate calculus}
    $\langle \forall s :: \mathbf{G\,F}\,grd.s \Rightarrow \mathbf{G\,F}(grd.s \wedge \mathbf{X}\,\bar{s})\rangle$
$=$ {definition of Θ_F}
    Θ_F

The proof of $(\Theta_F \equiv \mathbf{F}\,\Theta_F)$ is by mutual implication. One direction, $(\Theta_F \Rightarrow \mathbf{F}\,\Theta_F)$ follows trivially from temporal logic $(X \Rightarrow \mathbf{F}\,X)$. The other direction is given by the following.

$\mathbf{F}\,\Theta_F$
$=$ {definition of Θ_F}
    $\mathbf{F}\langle \forall s :: \mathbf{G\,F}\,grd.s \Rightarrow \mathbf{G\,F}(grd.s \wedge \mathbf{X}\,\bar{s})\rangle$
$\Rightarrow$ {interchange quantification}
    $\langle \forall s :: \mathbf{F}(\mathbf{G\,F}\,grd.s \Rightarrow \mathbf{G\,F}(grd.s \wedge \mathbf{X}\,\bar{s}))\rangle$
$=$ {predicate calculus}
    $\langle \forall s :: \mathbf{F}(\mathbf{F\,G}\,\neg grd.s \vee \mathbf{G\,F}(grd.s \wedge \mathbf{X}\,\bar{s}))\rangle$
$=$ $\{\,\mathbf{F\,G}\,X \equiv \mathbf{G\,F\,G}\,X\,\}$

$\langle\forall s :: \mathbf{F}(\mathbf{G}\,\mathbf{F}\,\mathbf{G}\,\neg grd.s \vee \mathbf{G}\,\mathbf{F}(grd.s \wedge \mathbf{X}\,\bar{s}.)))$

$=\quad \{\ \mathbf{G}\,\mathbf{F}\,X \vee \mathbf{G}\,\mathbf{F}\,Y \equiv \mathbf{G}\,\mathbf{F}(X \vee Y)\}$

$\langle\forall s :: \mathbf{F}\,\mathbf{G}\,\mathbf{F}(\mathbf{G}\,\neg grd.s \vee (grd.s \wedge \mathbf{X}\,\bar{s})))$

$=\quad \{\ \mathbf{F}\,\mathbf{G}\,\mathbf{F}\,X \equiv \mathbf{G}\,\mathbf{F}\,X\}$

$\langle\forall s :: \mathbf{G}\,\mathbf{F}(\mathbf{G}\,\neg grd.s \vee (grd.s \wedge \mathbf{X}\,\bar{s})))$

$=\quad \{\ \mathbf{G}\,\mathbf{F}\,X \vee \mathbf{G}\,\mathbf{F}\,Y \equiv \mathbf{G}\,\mathbf{F}(X \vee Y)\}$

$\langle\forall s :: \mathbf{G}\,\mathbf{F}\,\mathbf{G}\,\neg grd.s \vee \mathbf{G}\,\mathbf{F}(grd.s \wedge \mathbf{X}\,\bar{s}))$

$=\quad \{\ \mathbf{F}\,\mathbf{G}\,X \equiv \mathbf{G}\,\mathbf{F}\,\mathbf{G}\,X\}$

$\langle\forall s :: \mathbf{F}\,\mathbf{G}\,\neg grd.s \vee \mathbf{G}\,\mathbf{F}(grd.s \wedge \mathbf{X}\,\bar{s}))$

$=\quad \{\text{predicate calculus}\}$

$\langle\forall s :: \mathbf{G}\,\mathbf{F}\,grd.s \Rightarrow \mathbf{G}\,\mathbf{F}(grd.s \wedge \mathbf{X}\,\bar{s}))$

$=\quad \{\text{definition of }\Theta_F\}$

Θ_F

Corollary 5.3.1.

$$\Theta_F \quad\equiv\quad \mathbf{F}\,\mathbf{G}\,\Theta_F.$$

We prove the following lemma (Emerson and Jutla [1988]).

Lemma 5.3.4. *Abbreviate by $\Phi.s.F.Z$,*

$$[\Phi.s.F.Z \quad\equiv\quad (grd.s \Rightarrow \mathbf{A}\,\mathbf{X}(\neg\bar{s} \vee Z)) \wedge \mathbf{A}(\Theta_{F-\{s\}} \Rightarrow \mathbf{F}(grd.s \vee Z))].$$

Then,

$$[\mathbf{A}(\Theta_F \Rightarrow \mathbf{F}\,Y) \quad\equiv\quad \langle\mu Z :: Y \vee \langle\exists s :: \mathbf{A}(\Phi.s.F.Z \mathbf{\ W\ } Z)\rangle\rangle]$$

Proof. First, we derive an expression for $\neg\Phi.s.F.\neg X$.

$\neg\Phi.s.F.\neg X$

$=\quad \{\text{definition of }\Phi\}$

$\neg((grd.s \Rightarrow \mathbf{A}\,\mathbf{X}(\neg\bar{s} \vee \neg X)) \wedge \mathbf{A}(\Theta_{F-\{s\}} \Rightarrow \mathbf{F}(grd.s \vee \neg X)))$

$=\quad \{\text{predicate calculus and temporal logic}\}$

$(grd.s \wedge \mathbf{E}\,\mathbf{X}(\bar{s} \wedge X)) \vee \mathbf{E}(\Theta_{F-\{s\}} \wedge \mathbf{G}(\neg grd.s \wedge X))$

We discharge our proof obligation by showing the contrapositive, that is,

$\neg\,\mathbf{A}(\Theta_F \Rightarrow \mathbf{F}\,Y)$

$=\quad \{\text{temporal logic}\}$

$\mathbf{E}(\Theta_F \wedge \mathbf{G}\,\neg Y)$

$=\quad \{\text{proof obligation}\}$

$\langle\nu X :: \neg Y \wedge \langle\forall s :: \mathbf{E}(X \mathbf{\ U\ }(X \wedge \neg\Phi.s.F.\neg X))\rangle\rangle$

$=\quad \{(\neg(X \mathbf{\ W\ } Y) \equiv \neg Y \mathbf{\ U\ }(\neg X \wedge \neg Y))\ \}$

$\langle\nu X :: \neg Y \wedge \langle\forall s :: \mathbf{E}\,\neg(\Phi.s.F.\neg X \mathbf{\ W\ } \neg X)\rangle\rangle$

$=\quad \{[\neg\langle\mu X :: f.X\rangle \equiv \langle\nu X :: \neg f.(\neg X)\rangle]\}$

$\neg\langle\mu X :: Y \vee \langle\exists s :: \mathbf{A}(\Phi.s.F.X \mathbf{\ W\ } X)\rangle\rangle$

We abbreviate $\mathbf{E}(\Theta_F \wedge \mathbf{G}\,\neg Y)$ by Z. We discharge our proof obligation in two steps. We first show that Z solves the equation

$$X : [X \equiv \neg Y \wedge \langle \forall s :: \mathbf{E}(X\,\mathbf{U}(X \wedge (\neg\Phi.s.F.\neg X)))\rangle]$$

and we then show that it is the weakest solution.

Ad 0. To show that Z is a solution, it is enough to show (by Theorem 2.4.1) that

$$[Z \Rightarrow \neg Y \wedge \langle \forall s :: \mathbf{E}(Z\,\mathbf{U}(Z \wedge \neg\Phi.s.F.\neg Z)))\rangle].$$

We prove each conjunct separately.

$\qquad Z$
$=\quad$ {definition of Z}
$\qquad \mathbf{E}(\Theta_F \wedge \mathbf{G}\,\neg Y)$
$\Rightarrow\quad$ {temporal logic}
$\qquad \mathbf{E}\,\mathbf{G}\,\neg Y$
$\Rightarrow\quad$ {predicate calculus}
$\qquad \neg Y$

$\qquad Z$
$=\quad$ {definition of Z}
$\qquad \mathbf{E}(\Theta_F \wedge \mathbf{G}\,\neg Y)$
$=\quad$ {predicate calculus}
$\qquad \mathbf{E}(\Theta_F \wedge \Theta_F \wedge \mathbf{G}\,\neg Y)$
$=\quad$ {Lemma 5.3.1}
$\qquad \mathbf{E}(\mathbf{G}\,\Theta_F \wedge \Theta_F \wedge \mathbf{G}\,\neg Y)$
$=\quad$ {temporal logic and predicate calculus}
$\qquad \mathbf{E}(\mathbf{G}(\Theta_F \wedge \mathbf{G}\,\neg Y) \wedge \Theta_F)$
$\Rightarrow\quad$ {temporal logic}
$\qquad \mathbf{E}(\mathbf{G}\,\mathbf{E}(\Theta_F \wedge \mathbf{G}\,\neg Y) \wedge \Theta_F)$
$=\quad$ {definition of Z}
$\qquad \mathbf{E}(\mathbf{G}\,Z \wedge \Theta_F)$
$=\quad$ {definition of Θ_F}
$\qquad \mathbf{E}(\mathbf{G}\,Z \wedge \langle \forall s :: \mathbf{G}\,\mathbf{F}\,grd.s \Rightarrow \mathbf{G}\,\mathbf{F}(grd.s \wedge \mathbf{X}\,\bar{s})\rangle \wedge \Theta_F)$
$=\quad$ {temporal logic; Corollary 5.3.1}
$\qquad \mathbf{E}(\mathbf{G}\,Z \wedge \langle \forall s :: \mathbf{G}\,\mathbf{F}\,grd.s \Rightarrow \mathbf{G}\,\mathbf{F}(grd.s \wedge \mathbf{X}\,\bar{s})\rangle \wedge \mathbf{F}\,\mathbf{G}\,\Theta_F \wedge \mathbf{F}\,\mathbf{G}\,Z \wedge \mathbf{G}\,Z)$
$=\quad$ {$\wedge$ over $\forall$; non-empty programs}
$\qquad \mathbf{E}(\mathbf{G}\,Z \wedge \langle \forall s :: (\mathbf{G}\,\mathbf{F}\,grd.s \Rightarrow \mathbf{G}\,\mathbf{F}(grd.s \wedge \mathbf{X}\,\bar{s})) \wedge \mathbf{F}\,\mathbf{G}\,\Theta_F \wedge$
$\qquad\qquad\qquad\qquad\qquad\qquad\qquad \mathbf{F}\,\mathbf{G}\,Z \wedge \mathbf{G}\,Z\rangle)$
$\Rightarrow\quad$ {predicate calculus}
$\qquad \mathbf{E}(\mathbf{G}\,Z \wedge \langle \forall s :: (\mathbf{F}\,\mathbf{G}\,\neg grd.s \wedge \mathbf{F}\,\mathbf{G}\,Z \wedge \mathbf{F}\,\mathbf{G}\,\Theta_F) \vee$
$\qquad\qquad\qquad\qquad\qquad\qquad\qquad (\mathbf{G}\,\mathbf{F}(grd.s \wedge \mathbf{X}\,\bar{s}) \wedge \mathbf{G}\,Z)\rangle)$
$\Rightarrow\quad$ {definition of Θ}
$\qquad \mathbf{E}(\mathbf{G}\,Z \wedge \langle \forall s :: (\mathbf{F}\,\mathbf{G}\,\neg grd.s \wedge \mathbf{F}\,\mathbf{G}\,Z \wedge \mathbf{F}\,\mathbf{G}\,\Theta_{F-\{s\}}) \vee$
$\qquad\qquad\qquad\qquad\qquad\qquad\qquad (\mathbf{G}\,\mathbf{F}(grd.s \wedge \mathbf{X}\,\bar{s}) \wedge \mathbf{G}\,Z)\rangle)$

$\Rightarrow$ {temporal logic}

$\mathbf{E}(\mathbf{G}\,Z \wedge \langle \forall s :: \mathbf{F}\,\mathbf{G}(\neg grd.s \wedge Z \wedge \Theta_{F-\{s\}}) \vee \mathbf{G}\,\mathbf{F}(grd.s \wedge \mathbf{X}(\bar{s} \wedge Z))\rangle)$

$\Rightarrow$ {temporal logic}

$\mathbf{E}(\mathbf{G}\,Z \wedge \langle \forall s :: \mathbf{F}(\mathbf{G}(\neg grd.s \wedge Z) \wedge \Theta_{F-\{s\}}) \vee \mathbf{F}(grd.s \wedge \mathbf{X}(\bar{s} \wedge Z))\rangle)$

$\Rightarrow$ {temporal logic}

$\mathbf{E}(\mathbf{G}\,Z \wedge \langle \forall s :: \mathbf{F}\,\mathbf{E}(\mathbf{G}(\neg grd.s \wedge Z) \wedge \Theta_{F-\{s\}}) \vee \mathbf{F}\,\mathbf{E}(grd.s \wedge \mathbf{X}(\bar{s} \wedge Z))\rangle)$

$=$ {temporal logic}

$\mathbf{E}(\mathbf{G}\,Z \wedge \langle \forall s :: \mathbf{F}(\mathbf{E}(\mathbf{G}(\neg grd.s \wedge Z) \wedge \Theta_{F-\{s\}}) \vee (grd.s \wedge \mathbf{E}\,\mathbf{X}(\bar{s} \wedge Z)))\rangle)$

$=$ {predicate calculus}

$\mathbf{E}(\langle \forall s :: \mathbf{G}\,Z \wedge \mathbf{F}(\mathbf{E}(\mathbf{G}(\neg grd.s \wedge Z) \wedge \Theta_{F-\{s\}}) \vee (grd.s \wedge \mathbf{E}\,\mathbf{X}(\bar{s} \wedge Z)))\rangle)$

$\Rightarrow$ {predicate calculus}

$\langle \forall s :: \mathbf{E}(\mathbf{G}\,Z \wedge \mathbf{F}(\mathbf{E}(\mathbf{G}(\neg grd.s \wedge Z) \wedge \Theta_{F-\{s\}}) \vee (grd.s \wedge \mathbf{E}\,\mathbf{X}(\bar{s} \wedge Z)))\rangle)$

$\Rightarrow$ $\{\mathbf{G}\,X \wedge \mathbf{F}\,Y \Rightarrow X\,\mathbf{U}(X \wedge Y)\}$

$\langle \forall s :: \mathbf{E}(Z\,\mathbf{U}\,(Z \wedge (\mathbf{E}(\mathbf{G}(\neg grd.s \wedge Z) \wedge \Theta_{F-\{s\}}) \vee$
$(grd.s \wedge \mathbf{E}\,\mathbf{X}(\bar{s} \wedge Z))))\rangle)$

Ad 1. To show that Z is the weakest solution, we have to show that any solution of the equation

$$X : [X \equiv \neg Y \wedge \langle \forall s :: \mathbf{E}(X\,\mathbf{U}(X \wedge \neg \Phi.s.F.\neg X))\rangle]$$

implies Z.

Assume that X is a solution of the equation and that X holds at a node u. From the equation, $\neg Y$ holds at u. Choose t to be any statement of the program. Corresponding to t, there exists a path from u on which $X\,\mathbf{U}(X \wedge \neg \Phi.t.F.\neg X)$ holds. From the definition of $\mathbf{U}$, there is a path $u, \ldots, v$, such that at all the nodes on the path X holds and $X \wedge \neg \Phi.t.F.\neg X$ holds at v. Since X holds at all the nodes of the $u, \ldots, v$ path, $\neg Y$ holds at every node of the path as well. From the definition of $\neg \Phi.t.F.\neg X$, two cases can arise.

0. If the first disjunct is true at v, then there exists a path from v, such that $grd.t$ is true in v and $\bar{t} \wedge X$ is true in the second node (call it x) of the path. Thus t can be executed at node v and since X is true at x, the above argument can be repeated with each of the remaining statements of the program, thereby constructing a path from u on which each statement is infinitely often executed. Further, since each X holds at every node, $\neg Y$ holds at every node. That is Z holds at u.

1. If the second disjunct is true at v, then there exists a path from v along which t is only finitely often enabled and $\Theta_{F-\{t\}}$ holds. That is, the path is strongly–fair with respect to F. Further since $\mathbf{G}\,X$ holds along the path, $\mathbf{G}\,\neg Y$ holds as well. Thus we have demonstrated the existence of a strongly–fair path from u along which $\neg Y$ holds. That is, Z holds at u. This concludes our proof obligation. $\square$

This lemma is to be used in conjunction with Lemma 5.3.2 which gives the fixpoint characterization of an expression of the form $\mathbf{A}(Y\,\mathbf{W}\,Z)$.

5.4 From μ-Calculus to UNITY-Style Proof rules

In the previous section, we presented fixpoint characterizations for different notions of fairness. The various fixpoint characterizations share a common structure: they are all of the form

$$\langle \mu Z :: Y \vee \langle \exists s :: \mathbf{gwp}.s.Z \rangle \rangle$$

where s ranges over the statements of the program and $\mathbf{gwp}$ is a function (of s and Z) and is specific to the fairness assumption being studied. Our goal, as dictated by the final step in our methodology, is to use these fixpoint characterizations to extract UNITY style proof rules for proving progress under different notions of fairness. In this section, we use this abstract structure of a fixpoint characterization, to develop a theory that enables us to extract sound and relatively complete UNITY style proof rules.

5.4.1 A Predicate Transformer Approach

Assume that we are given a unary predicate transformer $\mathbf{gwp}.s.X$ for each statement s of a parallel program. Intuitively, the predicate transformer captures the *generalized weakest precondition that establishes predicate* X, by a single helpful transition of the program, in the presence of other (possibly conflicting) transitions.

Remark: In our presentation, the predicate transformer $\mathbf{gwp}$, was obtained as sub–expression of the different fixpoint characterizations for progress under the various fairness constraints. We now give an interpretation of what it means.

In introducing the notion of the *weakest precondition*, Dijkstra defines $\mathbf{wp}.s.X$ as characterizing all possible states, such that if s is executed from a state satisfying $\mathbf{wp}.s.X$, then the execution of s terminates in a state in which X is true. In this model, it is guaranteed that the given statement, s, will be next statement to be selected for execution.

In our model, a program is a set of statements. For a statement s in the set, the only guarantee that we have of its selection for execution is the fairness constraint assumed. It is possible for a number of statements to be executed before statement s is selected, by the fairness constraint, for execution. Using the predicate transformer, $\mathbf{gwp}$, we would like to capture all possible states, such that if program execution is begun in such a state, eventually statement s is selected and executed and its execution establishes the required postcondition. This set of states will be characterized by $\mathbf{gwp}.s.X$, the hidden argument here being the program F to which s belongs. (*End of Remark*).

Given this interpretation, it is natural to expect the predicate transformer $\mathbf{gwp}.s$ to be monotonic. Suppose that we are given:

(P0) $[X \Rightarrow Y] \Rightarrow [\mathbf{gwp}.s.X \Rightarrow \mathbf{gwp}.s.Y]$

We now define a second predicate transformer, that captures the infinite transitive closure of **gwp** .s. To this end, consider the equation :

$$Z : [\, Z \;\equiv\; Y \vee \langle \exists s : s \in F : \mathbf{gwp}.s.Z \,\rangle]$$

The dummy variable s is assumed to quantify over the statements of program F. In the sequel, the range of s will be understood and will not be explicitly mentioned.

Note that from the monotonicity of **gwp** .s, $\exists$ and $\vee$, the right-hand side of the equivalence is monotonic. Thus, by Theorem 2.2.1, the equation has a least fixpoint. Let this solution be called **wlt** .Y. Since **wlt** .Y is the least fixpoint, it satisfies the following conditions :

$$\text{(W0)} \qquad [\, \mathbf{wlt}.Y \;\equiv\; Y \vee \langle \exists s :: \mathbf{gwp}.s.(\mathbf{wlt}.Y) \rangle]$$
$$\text{(W1)} \qquad [\, Y \vee \langle \exists s :: \mathbf{gwp}.s.Z \rangle \;\Rightarrow\; Z] \;\Rightarrow\; [\, \mathbf{wlt}.Y \;\Rightarrow\; Z]$$

W0 states that **wlt** .Y is a solution of the equation and W1 states that it implies all solutions.

Remark : Note that the the definition of **wlt** only depends on **gwp** .s. That is, giving a definition for **gwp** .s completely determines the relation **wlt**. (*End of Remark*).

We now enumerate some useful properties of **wlt**.

$$\text{(W2)} \qquad\qquad [\, Y \;\Rightarrow\; \mathbf{wlt}.Y]$$
$$\text{(W3)} \qquad\quad [\,\langle \exists s :: \mathbf{gwp}.s.(\mathbf{wlt}.Y) \rangle \;\Rightarrow\; \mathbf{wlt}.Y]$$
$$\text{(W4)} \qquad [\, X \;\Rightarrow\; Y] \;\Rightarrow\; [\, \mathbf{wlt}.X \;\Rightarrow\; \mathbf{wlt}.Y]$$
$$\text{(W5)} \qquad\qquad [\, \mathbf{wlt}.(\mathbf{wlt}.Y) \;\equiv\; \mathbf{wlt}.Y]$$

W2 and W3 follow from W0. Property W2 states that **wlt** is weakening. Since the predicate transformer in the equation defining **wlt** .Y is monotonic, by Theorem 2.4.1, **wlt** is monotonic as well. This is asserted by W4. Property W5 expresses the idempotence of **wlt** which follows from its definition as the fixpoint of an equation. Since **wlt** is weakening, monotonic and idempotent, it is a closure operation on predicates.

Having finished our investigation into the properties of **wlt**, we are now in a position to relate it to **gwp** .s.

Lemma 5.4.1. $\langle \forall X :: [\,\langle \exists s :: \mathbf{gwp}.s.X \rangle \;\Rightarrow\; \mathbf{wlt}.X]\rangle$

Proof. For all X,

$$[\,\langle \exists s :: \mathbf{gwp}.s.X \rangle \Rightarrow \mathbf{wlt}.X]$$
$$\Leftarrow \quad \{\text{property W3}\}$$
$$[\,\langle \exists s :: \mathbf{gwp}.s.X \rangle \Rightarrow \langle \exists s :: \mathbf{gwp}.s.(\mathbf{wlt}.X) \rangle]$$
$$\Leftarrow \quad \{\text{predicate calculus}\}$$

$$\langle \forall s :: [\mathbf{gwp}.s.X \Rightarrow \mathbf{gwp}.s.(\mathbf{wlt}.X)] \rangle$$
$$\Leftarrow \quad \{\text{monotonicity of } \mathbf{gwp}.s\}$$
$$\langle \forall s :: [X \Rightarrow \mathbf{wlt}.X] \rangle$$
$$= \quad \{\text{property W2}\}$$
$$true$$

$\square$

5.4.2 A Relational Approach

Remark on Notation: In this section, we will be defining analogs of the UNITY relations: **ensures** and $\mapsto$ for a variety of fairness constraints. Since we will be encountering new notions of fairness, we would like the reader to forget about the UNITY's notion of fairness. Similiarly, we would like the reader to remove all connotations of the UNITY relations **ensures** and $\mapsto$, from his/her mind. To help the reader with this, we will use the more anonymous symbols, $\mathcal{E}$ and $\leadsto$, to denote basic and general progress properties respectively. (*End of Remark on Notation*).

Let $\mathcal{E}$ be a given binary relation on state predicates. Intuitively, each parallel program will have an $\mathcal{E}$ relation associated with it. This $\mathcal{E}$ relation will describe the progress that can be made by a single transition of the given parallel program. In this sense, the relation $\mathcal{E}$ describes the *basic* progress properties of the parallel program. Given this interpretation, it is natural to assume that $\mathcal{E}$ is monotonic. That is, $\mathcal{E}$ satisfies the following basic requirement.

– *condition E0:*

$$\frac{[X \Rightarrow Y]}{(X \ \mathcal{E} \ Y)}$$

We use the relation $\mathcal{E}$ to define the *general* progress properties of a parallel program. To this end, consider the following set L of rules $L0$–$L2$ that define the relation $\triangleright$:

– *Rule L0:*

$$\frac{(X \ \mathcal{E} \ Y)}{(X \triangleright Y)}$$

– *Rule L1:*

$$\frac{(X \triangleright Y) \wedge (Y \triangleright Z)}{(X \triangleright Z)}$$

– *Rule L2:* For an arbitrary set of predicates, W,

$$\frac{\langle \forall X : X \in W : X \triangleright Y \rangle}{(\langle \exists X : X \in W : X \rangle \triangleright Y)}$$

Rule $L0$ states that the $\mathcal{E}$ relation is a subset of the relation $\triangleright$. Transitivity of $\triangleright$ is expressed by $L1$. Rule $L2$ means that $\triangleright$ is disjunctively closed over W, where W is an arbitrary set of predicates. In other words, a relation $\triangleright$ that satisfies the above equations represents the transitive, disjunctive closure of the base relation $\mathcal{E}$. Notice that there can be many such relations: for example, the universal relation, that relates every pair of state predicates satisfies the above equations. For this reason, we focus our attention on the smallest relation that satisfies these equations.

With "$\Rightarrow$" as a partial order on relations we show that the set L of equations in the unknown relation $\triangleright$ has a strongest solution.

Lemma 5.4.2. *There exists a unique strongest relation that solves L. The unique strongest solution of L will be called* leads-to ($\leadsto$).

Proof. The proof follows by showing that the conjunction of all solutions of L is a solution of L. It is the strongest solution of L, since it implies all solutions. $\square$

Remark : Notice that the definition of $\leadsto$ depends only on the definition of $\mathcal{E}$ and the form of the rules $L0$–$L2$. Our methodology of proof rule design derives a new relation $\mathcal{E}$ for a given fairness assumption. By instantiating the equations L with this definition of $\mathcal{E}$, we obtain a proof system (given by $L0$–$L2$) for $\leadsto$ under the given fairness assumption. (*End of Remark*).

Using $E0$ and $L0$ we now observe:

Lemma 5.4.3. $[X \Rightarrow Y] \;\Rightarrow\; X \leadsto Y$

As a Corollary of Lemma 5.4.3 we get the reflexivity of $\leadsto$.

Corollary 5.4.1. $X \leadsto X$

5.4.3 Constraints on *leads-to* and wlt

In section 5.4.1, we defined a predicate transformer **wlt** in terms of a given relation **gwp**$.s$. In section 5.4.2, we defined a relation $\leadsto$ in terms of a given relation $\mathcal{E}$. Our goal is to relate the relation $\leadsto$ to the predicate transformer **wlt**. To attain this end, we require that $\leadsto$ and **wlt** respect certain consistency constraints. With **gwp**$.s$ and **wlt** as defined in Section 5.4.1, $\mathcal{E}$ and $\leadsto$ as defined in Section 5.4.2, these constraints can be stated as

(C0) $(X \; \mathcal{E} \; Y) \;\Rightarrow\; [X \;\Rightarrow\; \mathbf{wlt}.Y]$
(C1) $\langle \forall s :: \mathbf{gwp}.s.X \; \mathcal{E} \; X \rangle$

Remark: Recall that giving a definition of **gwp**$.s$ (for each statement s of the program) fixes the definition of **wlt**. Thus C0 and C1 are really constraints on $\mathcal{E}$ and **gwp**$.s$. In our approach we are given a definition of **gwp**$.s$: we will use constraints C0 and C1 as upper and lower bounds respectively on a possible definition of $\mathcal{E}$. (*End of Remark*).

5.4.4 The predicate transformer led

In order to illustrate the connection between the relation $\leadsto$ and the predicate transformer **wlt** we need one more concept from Knapp [1988]. We introduce this using the following lemma.

Lemma 5.4.4. *The equation* $X: X \leadsto Y$ *has a weakest solution. The weakest solution of* $X: X \leadsto Y$ *is called the* **led.Y** *(read, led-from Y).*

Proof. Abbreviate $X: X \leadsto Y$ by C. We show that the disjunction of all solutions of C solves C. Clearly this is the weakest solution, as it is implied by all the solutions of C.

$$\langle \exists X : X \text{ solves } C : X \rangle \leadsto Y$$
$$\Leftarrow \quad \{L2\}$$
$$\langle \forall X : X \text{ solves } C : X \leadsto Y \rangle$$
$$= \quad \{\text{definition } C \text{ and predicate calculus}\}$$
$$true$$

$\square$

The predicate transformer **led** enjoys the following properties.

$$
\begin{array}{ll}
(\text{LF0}) & \text{led.}Y \leadsto Y \\
(\text{LF1}) & (X \leadsto Y) \Rightarrow [X \Rightarrow \text{led.}Y]
\end{array}
$$

Property LF0 asserts that **led** solves C. Property LF1 asserts that it is the *weakest* solution of C.

5.4.5 Relating *leads-to* and **wlt**

We now present the main Theorem of this section, which shows the close relationship between the relation $\leadsto$ and the predicate transformer **wlt**.

Theorem 5.4.1. $[X \Rightarrow \text{wlt}.Y]$ *iff* $(X \leadsto Y)$

Proof. The proof of the theorem is by mutual implication.

$(\Leftarrow)$

Since *leads-to* $(\leadsto)$ is the strongest solution of the equations $L0$, $L1$ and $L2$, it is sufficient to show that the relation **R** defined as $(X \ \mathbf{R} \ Y) \equiv [X \Rightarrow \text{wlt}.Y]$ solves the same equations. The result follows.

Equation L0 :

$$(X \ \mathcal{E} \ Y)$$
$$\Rightarrow \quad \{C0\}$$
$$[X \Rightarrow \text{wlt}.Y]$$
$$= \quad \{\text{definition of } \mathbf{R}\}$$
$$(X \ \mathbf{R} \ Y)$$

Equation L1 (transitivity):

$$(X \; \mathbf{R} \; Y) \wedge (Y \; \mathbf{R} \; Z)$$
$=$ {definition of $\mathbf{R}$}
$$[X \; \Rightarrow \; \mathbf{wlt}.Y] \wedge [Y \; \Rightarrow \; \mathbf{wlt}.Z]$$
$\Rightarrow$ {monotonicity of $\mathbf{wlt}$}
$$[X \; \Rightarrow \; \mathbf{wlt}.Y] \wedge [\mathbf{wlt}.Y \; \Rightarrow \; \mathbf{wlt}.(\mathbf{wlt}.Z)]$$
$\Rightarrow$ {transitivity of $\Rightarrow$}
$$[X \; \Rightarrow \; \mathbf{wlt}.(\mathbf{wlt}.Z)]$$
$\Rightarrow$ {W5 with $Y := Z$}
$$[X \; \Rightarrow \; \mathbf{wlt}.Z]$$
$=$ {definition of $\mathbf{R}$}
$$(X \; \mathbf{R} \; Z)$$

Equation L2 (disjunction):

$$\langle \forall X :: X \; \mathbf{R} \; Y \rangle$$
$=$ {definition of $\mathbf{R}$}
$$\langle \forall X :: [X \; \Rightarrow \; \mathbf{wlt}.Y] \rangle$$
$=$ {interchange quantifications}
$$[\langle \forall X :: X \; \Rightarrow \; \mathbf{wlt}.Y \rangle]$$
$=$ {predicate calculus}
$$[\langle \exists X :: X \rangle \; \Rightarrow \; \mathbf{wlt}.Y]$$
     {definition of $\mathbf{R}$}
$$\langle \exists X :: X \rangle \; \mathbf{R} \; Y$$

$(\Rightarrow)$

0. $\langle \forall s :: \mathbf{gwp}.s.(\mathbf{led}.Y) \; \mathcal{E} \; \mathbf{led}.Y \rangle$
       ,Constraint C1 with $X := \mathbf{led}.Y$
1. $\langle \forall s :: \mathbf{gwp}.s.(\mathbf{led}.Y) \; \leadsto \; \mathbf{led}.Y \rangle$
       ,0 and Rule $L0$
2. $\langle \exists s :: \mathbf{gwp}.s.(\mathbf{led}.Y) \rangle \; \leadsto \; \mathbf{led}.Y$
       ,1 and Rule $L2$
3. $\mathbf{led}.Y \; \leadsto \; Y$
       ,Property LF0 of the led
4. $\langle \exists s :: \mathbf{gwp}.s.(\mathbf{led}.Y) \rangle \; \leadsto \; Y$
       ,From 2, 3 and the transitivity of $\leadsto$
5. $Y \; \leadsto \; Y$
       ,Corollary 5.4.1
6. $(\langle \exists s :: \mathbf{gwp}.s.(\mathbf{led}.Y) \rangle \vee Y) \; \leadsto \; Y$
       ,From 4, 5 and the disjunctivity of $\leadsto$
7. $[\langle \exists s :: \mathbf{gwp}.s.(\mathbf{led}.Y) \rangle \vee Y \; \Rightarrow \; \mathbf{led}.Y]$
       ,From 6 and Property LF1 of led
8. $[\mathbf{wlt}.Y \; \Rightarrow \; \mathbf{led}.Y]$
       ,From 7 and Property W1 with $Z := \mathbf{led}.Y$

9. wlt.$Y \rightsquigarrow$ led.Y
      ,8 and Lemma 5.4.3
10. $X \rightsquigarrow$ wlt.Y
      ,From hypothesis $[X \Rightarrow$ wlt.$Y]$ and Lemma 5.4.3
11. $X \rightsquigarrow Y$
      ,From 10, 9, 3 and transitivity of $\rightsquigarrow$

$\square$

5.4.6 Summary

We recapitulate our main result and summarize the results of this section. We are given a unary predicate transformer **gwp**.s that satisfies P0 i.e.,

$$[X \Rightarrow Y] \Rightarrow [\text{gwp}.s.X \Rightarrow \text{gwp}.s.Y].$$

This fixes the interpretation of **wlt**. We are also given a binary relation $\mathcal{E}$ on predicates that satisfies $E0$ i.e.,

$$[X \Rightarrow Y] \Rightarrow (X \, \mathcal{E} \, Y).$$

This fixes the interpretation of $\rightsquigarrow$. If the definitions of $\mathcal{E}$ and **gwp**.s satisfy the consistency conditions C0 and C1 i.e.,

$$(X \, \mathcal{E} \, Y) \Rightarrow [X \Rightarrow \text{wlt}.Y].$$

$$\langle \forall s :: \text{gwp}.s.Y \, \mathcal{E} \, Y \rangle$$

then our theorem states that,

$$[X \Rightarrow \text{wlt}.Y] \text{ iff } (X \rightsquigarrow Y).$$

5.5 Proof Rules

5.5.1 Defining $\mathcal{E}$ from gwp.s

The first three steps of the proposed methodology gave us to a definition of the predicate transformer, **gwp**.s, for the various fairness constraints. We now present two lemmas that permit us to extract a definition of $\mathcal{E}$, given a definition of **gwp**.s. We will use these two lemmas in the subsequent sections to define $\mathcal{E}$ relations for different notions of fairness.

Lemma 5.5.1. *Given a definition of a monotonic predicate transformer* **gwp**.s *that is devoid of fixpoint operators, we define $\mathcal{E}$ by*

$$X \, \mathcal{E} \, Y \equiv \langle \exists s :: [X \Rightarrow Y \vee \text{gwp}.s.Y] \rangle$$

These definitions of $\mathcal{E}$ and **gwp**.s *satisfy E0 and consistency conditions C0 and C1.*

Proof. It is easy to see that $E0$ holds. The following two derivations show that C0 and C1 hold.

$$X \; \mathcal{E} \; Y$$
$=$ {definition of $\mathcal{E}$}
$$\langle \exists s :: [X \Rightarrow Y \vee \mathbf{gwp}.s.Y] \rangle$$
$\Rightarrow$ {predicate calculus}
$$[X \Rightarrow Y \vee \langle \exists s :: \mathbf{gwp}.s.Y \rangle]$$
$\Rightarrow$ {property W2 and Lemma 5.4.1}
$$[X \Rightarrow \mathbf{wlt}.Y]$$

$$\langle \forall s :: \mathbf{gwp}.s.Y \; \mathcal{E} \; Y \rangle$$
$=$ {definition of $\mathcal{E}$}
$$\langle \forall s :: [\mathbf{gwp}.s.Y \Rightarrow Y \vee \langle \exists s :: \mathbf{gwp}.s.Y \rangle] \rangle$$
$=$ {predicate calculus}
$$true$$

$\square$

Lemma 5.5.2. *Given a definition of a monotonic predicate transformer* $\mathbf{gwp}.s$ *that is of the form*

$$\mathbf{gwp}.s.Y \;\equiv\; \langle \nu Z :: Y \vee h.s.Y.Z \rangle$$

we define $\mathcal{E}$ *by*

$$X \; \mathcal{E} \; Y \;\equiv\; \langle \exists s :: [X \Rightarrow Y \vee h.s.Y.(X \vee Y)] \rangle$$

These definitions of $\mathcal{E}$ *and* $\mathbf{gwp}.s$ *satisfy* $E0$ *and consistency conditions C0 and C1.*

Proof. It is easy to see that $E0$ holds. The following two derivations show that C0 and C1 hold.

$$X \; \mathcal{E} \; Y$$
$=$ {definition of $\mathcal{E}$}
$$\langle \exists s :: [X \Rightarrow Y \vee h.s.Y.(X \vee Y)] \rangle$$
$\Rightarrow$ {predicate calculus}
$$\langle \exists s :: [X \vee Y \Rightarrow Y \vee h.s.Y.(X \vee Y)] \rangle$$
$\Rightarrow$ {property of greatest fixpoints}
$$\langle \exists s :: [X \vee Y \Rightarrow \langle \nu Z :: Y \vee h.s.Y.Z \rangle] \rangle$$
$\Rightarrow$ {definition of $\mathbf{gwp}.s$}
$$\langle \exists s :: [X \vee Y \Rightarrow \mathbf{gwp}.s.Y] \rangle$$
$\Rightarrow$ {predicate calculus}
$$\langle \exists s :: [X \Rightarrow \mathbf{gwp}.s.Y] \rangle$$
$\Rightarrow$ {predicate calculus}
$$[X \Rightarrow \langle \exists s :: \mathbf{gwp}.s.Y \rangle]$$
$\Rightarrow$ {Lemma 5.4.1}
$$[X \Rightarrow \mathbf{wlt}.Y]$$

$\langle \forall s :: \mathbf{gwp}.s.Y \; \mathcal{E} \; Y \rangle$

$=$ {definition of $\mathcal{E}$}

$\langle \forall s :: \langle \exists t :: [\mathbf{gwp}.s.Y \;\Rightarrow\; Y \vee h.t.Y.(\mathbf{gwp}.s.Y \vee Y)] \rangle \rangle$

$\Leftarrow$ {predicate calculus}

$\langle \forall s :: \langle \exists t :: [\mathbf{gwp}.s.Y \vee Y \;\Rightarrow\; Y \vee h.t.Y.(\mathbf{gwp}.s.Y \vee Y)] \rangle \rangle$

$\Leftarrow$ {definition of $\mathbf{gwp}.s$ as a fixpoint}

$\langle \forall s :: \langle \exists t :: [Y \vee h.s.Y.(\mathbf{gwp}.s.Y \vee Y) \vee Y \;\Rightarrow\; Y \vee h.t.Y.(\mathbf{gwp}.s.Y \vee Y)] \rangle \rangle$

$\Leftarrow$ {predicate calculus}

true

□

5.5.2 Minimal Progress

By examining the fixpoint characterization for minimal progress we obtain the following definition for $\mathbf{gwp}.s$.

$$[\mathbf{gwp}.s.Z \;\equiv\; grd.s \wedge \langle \forall t : grd.t : \mathbf{e}\,\mathbf{X}(\bar{t} \wedge Z) \rangle]$$

Using Rule TL-WP0, we rewrite $\mathbf{gwp}.s$ as follows.

$$[\mathbf{gwp}.s.Z \;\equiv\; grd.s \wedge \langle \forall t : grd.t : \mathbf{wp}.t.Z \rangle]$$

To be able to define a proof system for minimal progress we need to define the relation $\mathcal{E}$. Using Lemma 5.5.1, we propose the following definition for $\mathcal{E}$:

$$(X \; \mathcal{E} \; Y) \;\equiv\; \langle \forall t :: [X \wedge \neg Y \wedge grd.t \;\Rightarrow\; \mathbf{wp}.t.Y] \rangle$$

$$\wedge \; \langle \exists s :: [X \wedge \neg Y \;\Rightarrow\; grd.s] \rangle$$

This definition of $\mathcal{E}$ along with the rules L (see Section 5.4.2) constitutes a sound and complete proof rule for proving progress properties under minimal progress.

Remark on Pure Nondeterminism: The case of pure nondeterminism (that is, no fairness constraint at all) is a special case of minimal progress where the guard of every statement is true. By uniformly substituting *true* for $grd.s$ in the definition of $\mathbf{gwp}.s$ and definition of $\mathcal{E}$ we obtain the following.

– Definition of $\mathbf{gwp}.s$:

$$[\mathbf{gwp}.s.Z \;\equiv\; \langle \forall t :: \mathbf{E}\,\mathbf{X}(\bar{t} \wedge Z) \rangle]$$

Using Rule TL-WP0, we rewrite this as,

$$[\mathbf{gwp}.s.Z \;\equiv\; \langle \forall t :: \mathbf{wp}.t.Z \rangle]$$

– Definition of $\mathcal{E}$:

$$(X \; \mathcal{E} \; Y) \;\equiv\; \langle \forall s :: [X \wedge \neg Y \;\Rightarrow\; \mathbf{wp}.s.Y] \rangle$$

(*End of Remark*).

5.5.3 Weak Fairness

By examining the fixpoint characterization for weak fairness we obtain the following definition of **gwp** .*s*.

$$[\mathbf{gwp} \,.s.Z \;\equiv\; \langle \nu Y :: Z \vee (\mathbf{A\,X}\,Y \wedge \mathbf{E\,X}(\bar{s} \wedge Z) \wedge grd.s)\rangle]$$

Using Rules TL-WP1 and TL-WP0, we rewrite **gwp** .*s* as

$$[\mathbf{gwp} \,.s.Z \;\equiv\; \langle \nu Y :: Z \vee (\langle \forall t :: \mathbf{wp} \,.t.Y\rangle \wedge \mathbf{wp} \,.s.Z \wedge grd.s)\rangle]$$

To be able to define a proof system for weak fairness, we need to define the predicate transformer $\mathcal{E}$. Using Lemma 5.5.2, we propose the following definition for $\mathcal{E}$:

$$(X \,\mathcal{E}\, Y) \;\equiv\; \begin{aligned}&\langle \forall s :: [X \wedge \neg Y \;\Rightarrow\; \mathbf{wp} \,.s.(X \vee Y)]\rangle \\ &\wedge \langle \exists s :: [X \wedge \neg Y \;\Rightarrow\; \mathbf{wp} \,.s.Y \wedge grd.s]\rangle\end{aligned}$$

This definition of $\mathcal{E}$ along with the rules L (see Section 5.4.2) constitutes a sound and complete proof rule for proving progress properties under weak fairness.

Remark on Unconditional Fairness: The case of unconditional fairness is a special case of weak fairness where the guard of every statement is true. By uniformly substituting *true* for *grd.s* in the definition of **gwp** .*s* and definition of $\mathcal{E}$ we obtain the following.

– Definition of **gwp** .*s*:

$$[\mathbf{gwp} \,.s.Z \;\equiv\; \langle \nu Y :: Z \vee (\mathbf{A\,X}\,Y \wedge \mathbf{E\,X}(\bar{s} \wedge Z))\rangle]$$

Using rules TL-WP0 and TL-WP1 this can be rewritten as

$$[\mathbf{gwp} \,.s.Z \;\equiv\; \langle \nu Y :: Z \vee (\langle \forall t :: \mathbf{wp} \,.t.Y\rangle \wedge \mathbf{wp} \,.s.Z)\rangle]$$

– Definition of $\mathcal{E}$:

$$(X \,\mathcal{E}\, Y) \;\equiv\; \begin{aligned}&\langle \forall s :: [X \wedge \neg Y \;\Rightarrow\; \mathbf{wp} \,.s.(X \vee Y)]\rangle \\ &\wedge \langle \exists s :: [X \wedge \neg Y \;\Rightarrow\; \mathbf{wp} \,.s.Y]\rangle\end{aligned}$$

(End of Remark).

5.5.4 Strong Fairness

By examining the fixpoint characterization for strong fairness we obtain the following definition of **gwp** .*s.Z*.

$$\langle \nu Y :: Z \vee (\mathbf{A\,X}\,Y \wedge (grd.s \Rightarrow \mathbf{A\,X}(\bar{s} \Rightarrow Z)) \wedge \mathbf{wlt} \,.(F - \{s\}).(grd.s \vee Z))\rangle.$$

Using rules TL-WP1 and TL-WP2, we can rewrite **gwp** .*s* as

$$\langle \nu Y :: (\langle \forall t :: \mathbf{wp} \,.t.Y\rangle \wedge (grd.s \Rightarrow \mathbf{wp} \,.s.Z) \wedge \mathbf{wlt} \,.(F - \{s\}).(grd.s \vee Z)) \vee Z\rangle.$$

To be able to define a proof system strong fairness, we need to define the predicate transformer $\mathcal{E}$. Using Lemma 5.5.2, we have

$$
\begin{aligned}
(X \; \mathcal{E} \; Y \; \text{in} \; F) \quad \equiv \quad & \langle \forall s :: \; [X \wedge \neg Y \Rightarrow \mathbf{wp}\,.s.(X \vee Y)] \rangle \wedge \\
& \langle \exists s :: \; [X \wedge \neg Y \Rightarrow \mathbf{wlt}\,.\{F - \{s\}\}.(grd.s \vee Y)] \wedge \\
& \quad [X \wedge \neg Y \wedge grd.s \Rightarrow \mathbf{wp}\,.s.Y] \rangle
\end{aligned}
$$

The second line in the above definition can be replaced by $X \wedge \neg Y \rightsquigarrow grd.s \vee Y$ in $F - \{s\}$, by induction on the number of statements in the program. The base case is the empty program: the $\rightsquigarrow$ properties of empty program are those that hold due to logical implication.

This definition of $\mathcal{E}$ along with the rules L (see Section 5.4.2) constitutes a sound and complete proof rule for proving progress properties under strong progress. The rule above is similiar to the one presented in Lehmann et al. [1981], the difference being that our rule has been systematically derived.

5.6 Examples

In this section, we will use the proof rules obtained towards the end of Section 5.5 to prove progress properties of some example programs. One of the advantages of having the same format for the proof rules is that one can prove and use theorems of the progress operator, $\rightsquigarrow$, that hold regardless of the notion of fairness that they are based upon. For instance, the second example presented here uses induction over $\rightsquigarrow$.

Example 5.6.1. Consider the example presented in the introduction. We now apply the apply the proof rules that we have developed to formally derive the progress properties that were informally proved in the introduction.

$$
\begin{array}{ll}
\mathbf{declare} & a, b : boolean \\
\mathbf{assign} & true \longrightarrow a := \neg a \\
[\![& true \longrightarrow b := \neg b \\
[\![& b \longrightarrow a := true \\
\mathbf{end} &
\end{array}
$$

For minimal progress, we show that the property $true \rightsquigarrow (a \vee b)$ holds.

$$
\begin{array}{ll}
& true \rightsquigarrow (a \vee b) \\
\Leftarrow & \{\text{Rule } L0\} \\
& true \; \mathcal{E} \; (a \vee b) \\
= & \{\text{definition of } \mathcal{E}\} \\
& \langle \forall s :: [\neg a \wedge \neg b \wedge grd.s \Rightarrow \mathbf{wp}\,.s.(a \vee b)] \rangle \; \wedge \; \langle \exists s :: [\neg a \wedge \neg b \Rightarrow grd.s] \rangle \\
= & \{\text{instantiating}\} \\
& [\neg a \wedge \neg b \Rightarrow \neg a \vee b] \; \wedge \; [\neg a \wedge \neg b \Rightarrow a \vee \neg b] \; \wedge \\
& [\neg a \wedge \neg b \wedge b \Rightarrow true \vee b] \; \wedge \; \langle \exists s :: [\neg a \wedge \neg b \Rightarrow grd.s] \rangle \\
= & \{\text{predicate calculus; the first statement for the last conjunct}\} \\
& true
\end{array}
$$

For weak fairness, we show that the property $true \leadsto a$ holds.

$\quad true \leadsto a$

$\Leftarrow \quad$ {Rule $L0$}

$\quad true \; \mathcal{E} \; a$

$= \quad$ {definition of $\mathcal{E}$}

$\quad \langle \forall s :: [\neg a \Rightarrow \mathbf{wp}.s.(true \vee a)] \rangle \;\wedge\; \langle \exists s :: [\neg a \Rightarrow \mathbf{wp}.s.a] \rangle$

$= \quad$ {$[\mathbf{wp}.s.true \equiv true]$}

$\quad \langle \exists s :: [\neg a \Rightarrow \mathbf{wp}.s.a] \rangle$

$= \quad$ {the first statement of the program}

$\quad true$

For strong fairness, we show that the property $true \leadsto (a \wedge b)$ holds.

$\quad true \leadsto (a \wedge b)$

$\Leftarrow \quad$ {Rule $L0$}

$\quad true \; \mathcal{E} \; (a \wedge b)$

$= \quad$ {definition of $\mathcal{E}$}

$\quad \langle \forall s :: [\neg a \vee \neg b \Rightarrow \mathbf{wp}.s.(true \vee (a \wedge b))] \rangle \;\wedge$

$\quad \langle \exists s :: \neg a \vee \neg b \leadsto grd.s \vee (a \wedge b) \text{ in } F - \{s\} \;\wedge$

$\quad [(\neg a \vee \neg b) \wedge grd.s \Rightarrow \mathbf{wp}.s.(a \wedge b)] \rangle$

$= \quad$ {$[\mathbf{wp}.s.true \equiv true]$}

$\quad \langle \exists s :: \neg a \vee \neg b \leadsto grd.s \vee (a \wedge b) \text{ in } F - \{s\} \;\wedge$

$\quad [(\neg a \vee \neg b) \wedge grd.s \Rightarrow \mathbf{wp}.s.(a \wedge b)] \rangle$

$\Leftarrow \quad$ {instantiating using the third statement}

$\quad (\neg a \vee \neg b \leadsto b \vee (a \wedge b) \text{ in } F - \{b \rightarrow a := true\}) \;\wedge\; [(\neg a \vee \neg b) \wedge b \Rightarrow b]$

$= \quad$ {predicate calculus}

$\quad (\neg a \vee \neg b \leadsto b \text{ in } F - \{b \rightarrow a := true\})$

$\Leftarrow \quad$ {Rule $L0$}

$\quad (\neg a \vee \neg b \; \mathcal{E} \; b \text{ in } F - \{b \rightarrow a := true\})$

$= \quad$ {definition of $\mathcal{E}$}

$\quad \langle \forall s :: [(\neg a \vee \neg b) \wedge \neg b \Rightarrow \mathbf{wp}.s.((\neg a \vee \neg b) \vee b)] \rangle \;\wedge$

$\quad \langle \exists s :: [(\neg a \vee \neg b) \wedge \neg b \leadsto grd.s \vee b \text{ in } F - \{s, b \rightarrow a := true\}] \;\wedge$

$\quad [(\neg a \vee \neg b) \wedge \neg b \wedge grd.s \Rightarrow \mathbf{wp}.s.b] \rangle$

$= \quad$ {$[\mathbf{wp}.s.true \equiv true]$}

$\quad \langle \exists s :: [(\neg a \vee \neg b) \wedge \neg b \leadsto grd.s \vee b \text{ in } F - \{s, b \rightarrow a := true\}] \;\wedge$

$\quad [(\neg a \vee \neg b) \wedge \neg b \wedge grd.s \Rightarrow \mathbf{wp}.s.b] \rangle$

$\Leftarrow \quad$ {instantiating using the second statement}

$\quad (\neg b \leadsto true \vee b \text{ in } F - \{true \rightarrow b := \neg b, b \rightarrow a := true\}) \wedge$

$\quad [\neg b \wedge true \Rightarrow \neg b] \rangle$

$= \quad$ {predicate calculus}

$\quad true$

Example 5.6.2. As mentioned in the introduction, one of the advantages of having a uniform style for the proof rules for progress is that one can build a useful theory for proving progress properties of programs. One such theorem is an induction principle for proving progress. It is stated as follows.

Let W be a well-founded set under the relation $<$. Let M be a function (also called a *metric*) from program states to W. Then the induction theorem is

$$\frac{\langle \forall m : m \in W : (X \wedge M = m) \rightsquigarrow (X \wedge M < m) \vee Y \rangle}{X \rightsquigarrow Y}$$

The hypothesis of the induction rule states that a program state in which X holds is eventually followed by a state in which Y holds or a state in which X holds and the value of the metric M is lower. Since the well-foundedness of the set W means that the value of M cannot decrease indefinitely, eventually a state is reached in which Y holds.

We will use this principle of induction in the following example.

$$\begin{array}{ll}
\textbf{declare} & i, j : integer \\
\textbf{assign} & i > j \longrightarrow i := i - 1 \\
\parallel & i \leq j \longrightarrow i := i + 1 \\
\parallel & i > j \longrightarrow j := j + 1 \\
\textbf{end}
\end{array}$$

With the assumption of weak fairness, we formally show that $true \rightsquigarrow (i = j)$. That is, beginning in any state, the program will eventually reach a state in which the two variables have the same value.

We first present an informal proof of the progress property. Assume that the variables i and j have initial values I and J. There will be three cases to consider, namely, when I is less than, equal to and greater that J. Consider the case where I is less than J. In this case, only the second statement of the program is enabled and remains enabled till, by the constraint of weak fairness, it is eventually executed. This has the effect of increasing the value of i by 1. If i is still less than j, this reasoning can be repeated. Eventually, the program reaches a state in which i and j have the same values. One can reason about the other two cases (i equal to j and i greater than j) in a similiar way.

A formal derivation of the same property is presented below.

$$\begin{array}{ll}
& true \rightsquigarrow (i = j) \\
= & \{\text{arithmetic}\} \\
& true \rightsquigarrow (\mid i - j \mid = 0) \\
\Leftarrow & \{\text{induction with } W \text{ the set of natural numbers under the } < \text{ ordering}\} \\
& \{\text{and the metric } M \text{ as } \mid i - j \mid\} \\
& \langle \forall m : m \geq 0 : (true \wedge \mid i - j \mid = m) \rightsquigarrow (true \wedge \mid i - j \mid < m) \vee (\mid i - j \mid = 0) \rangle \\
= & \{\text{predicate calculus}\} \\
& \langle \forall m : m \geq 0 : (\mid i - j \mid = m) \rightsquigarrow (\mid i - j \mid < m) \vee (\mid i - j \mid = 0) \rangle \\
\Leftarrow & \{\text{disjunctivity with } (\mid i - j \mid = 0) \rightsquigarrow (\mid i - j \mid = 0)\} \\
& \langle \forall m : m > 0 : (\mid i - j \mid = m) \rightsquigarrow (\mid i - j \mid < m) \vee (\mid i - j \mid = 0) \rangle \\
\Leftarrow & \{\text{consequence weakening}\} \\
& \langle \forall m : m > 0 : (\mid i - j \mid = m) \rightsquigarrow (\mid i - j \mid = (m - 1)) \rangle \\
\Leftarrow & \{\text{definition of absolute value}\} \\
& \langle \forall m : m > 0 : (i - j) = m \rightsquigarrow (i - j) = (m - 1) \rangle \wedge \\
& \langle \forall m : m < 0 : (i - j) = m \rightsquigarrow (i - j) = (m + 1) \rangle
\end{array}$$

$\Leftarrow$ {Rule L0}
$$\langle \forall m : m > 0 : (i-j) = m \; \mathcal{E} \; (i-j) = (m-1)\rangle \; \wedge$$
$$\langle \forall m : m < 0 : (i-j) = m \; \mathcal{E} \; (i-j) = (m+1)\rangle$$
$\Leftarrow$ {definition of $\mathcal{E}$ for weak fairness}
     $true$

With the assumption of strong fairness, we can show a much stronger property, namely, that the value of the variable j can increase without bound. This can be formally expressed as $(j \geq K) \rightsquigarrow (j > K)$.

We first present an informal proof of the progress property. The preceding proof shows that $true \rightsquigarrow (i = j)$ holds for the program if the program is executed under the assumption of weak fairness. We show below that any progress property that holds for a program under the assumption of weak fairness continues to hold when it is executed under the assumption of strong fairness as. Therefore $true \rightsquigarrow (i = j)$ holds under the assumption of strong fairness as well. Suppose the program is in a state in which variables i and j have the value K. In such a state, only the second statement is enabled continuously (and hence infinitely often). When it is eventually executed, the value of i is $K+1$ is the new program state. In the new state, the guards of the first and third statements are enabled. If the first statement is executed (and the third statement is ignored), the value of i decreases to K. Once again i and j have the same value and the guards of the first and third statements are disabled. If this pattern of program execution is repeated, the guard of the third statement is infinitely often true. By the constraint of strong fairness, it is eventually selected for execution and doing so will increment the value of j. So eventually the value of j increases unboundedly.

The following derivation shows that any progress property proved under the assumption of weak fairness continues to hold if strong fairness is assumed.

$(X \rightsquigarrow Y) \; (under \; weak \; fairness)$
$=$ {Theorem 5.4.1}
     $[X \; \Rightarrow \; \mathbf{A}(\langle \forall s :: \mathbf{F} \, \mathbf{G} \, grd.s \Rightarrow \mathbf{G} \, \mathbf{F}(grd.s \wedge \mathbf{X} \, \bar{s})\rangle \; \Rightarrow \; \mathbf{F} \, Y)]$
$\Rightarrow$ {temporal logic $[\mathbf{F} \, \mathbf{G} \, grd.s \Rightarrow \mathbf{G} \, \mathbf{F} \, grd.s]$}
     $[X \; \Rightarrow \; \mathbf{A}(\langle \forall s :: \mathbf{G} \, \mathbf{F} \, grd.s \Rightarrow \mathbf{G} \, \mathbf{F}(grd.s \wedge \mathbf{X} \, \bar{s})\rangle \; \Rightarrow \; \mathbf{F} \, Y)]$
$=$ {Theorem 5.4.1}
     $(X \rightsquigarrow Y) \; (under \; strong \; fairness)$

We have already proved that that $true \rightsquigarrow (i = j)$ holds when the above program is executed under the assumption of weak fairness. By consequence weakening, this means that $true \rightsquigarrow (i \geq j)$ holds. Notice that $(j \geq K)$ **unless** $false$ holds for the program. Using the following theorem (also called, the PSP Theorem)

$$X \rightsquigarrow Y$$
$$\frac{U \; \textbf{unless} \; V}{(X \wedge U) \rightsquigarrow (U \wedge Y) \vee V}$$

we conclude $(j \geq K) \rightsquigarrow (i \geq j) \land (j \geq K)$. While this progress property was proved assuming weak fairness, it continues to hold when the program is executed with strong fairness.

The following derivation shows that $(i \geq j) \land (j \geq K) \rightsquigarrow (j > K)$

$\quad (i \geq j) \land (j \geq K) \rightsquigarrow (j > K)$
$\Leftarrow \quad \{\text{Rule L0}\}$
$\quad (i \geq j) \land (j \geq K) \, \mathcal{E} \, (j > K)$
$\Leftarrow \quad \{\text{Definition of } \mathcal{E}\}$
$\quad \langle \forall s :: [(i \geq j) \land (j = K) \Rightarrow \mathbf{wp}\,.s.(((i \geq j) \land (j \geq K)) \lor (j > K))]\rangle \, \land$
$\quad \langle \exists s :: (i \geq j) \land (j = K) \rightsquigarrow grd.s \lor (j > K)$
$\qquad\quad \textbf{in } F - \{s\} \, \land$
$\quad [(i \geq j) \land (j = K) \land grd.s \Rightarrow \mathbf{wp}\,.s.(j > K)]\rangle$
$\Leftarrow \quad \{\text{instantiating using the third statement}\}$
$\quad \langle \forall s :: [(i \geq j) \land (j = K) \Rightarrow \mathbf{wp}\,.s.(((i \geq j) \land (j \geq K)) \lor (j > K))]\rangle \, \land$
$\quad \langle \exists s :: (i \geq j) \land (j = K) \rightsquigarrow (i > j) \lor (j > K)$
$\qquad\quad \textbf{in } F - \{(i > j) \longrightarrow j := j + 1\} \, \land$
$\quad [(i \geq j) \land (j = K) \land (i > j) \Rightarrow (j + 1 > K)]\rangle$
$\Leftarrow \quad \{\text{predicate calculus and definitions of } \mathbf{wp}\}$
$\quad true$

By transitivity (Rule L1) on the two progress properties, $(j \geq K) \rightsquigarrow (i \geq j) \land (j \geq K)$ and $(i \geq j) \land (j \geq K) \rightsquigarrow (j > K)$, we conclude $(j \geq K) \rightsquigarrow (j > K)$. Since $[(j = K) \Rightarrow (j \geq K)]$, we get

$$(j = K) \rightsquigarrow (j > K)$$

That is, the value of j increases without bound.

5.7 On a Notion of Completeness of *leads–to*

For many of the rules for proving progress under assumptions of fairness, the expressiveness of the assertion language and the nature of the completeness proven is not very clear. The assertion language is usually assumed to be a first–order language augmented with fixpoint operators, a sort denoting the ordinals, constants for all the recursive ordinals and an ordering relation on the ordinals. With respect to completeness, most authors (Gerth and Pnueli [1988], Sanders [1990], Knapp [1990]) prove completeness *relative* to the completeness of some existing temporal logic: often the temporal logic chosen is too powerful and as a consequence, the assumptions underlying the completeness result are not clear.

In this section, we briefly review the notion of completeness for Hoare triples and show that many of the same considerations apply to the completeness of the $\rightsquigarrow$. The best result that one can hope for is *completeness in the sense of Cook*. We then illustrate, how our completeness result for unconditional fairness can be used to *construct* a proof of the progress property that holds in the model. Our careful treatment clearly illustrates the roles played by the complexity of the assertion language, relative completeness, expressibility of weakest preconditions and the nature of the sets used in the disjunction axiom L2.

5.7.1 Reviewing Completeness

As the first step of our investigation, we trace the problems that were encountered in defining the notion of completeness for Hoare triples (Apt [1981]) and draw parallels to the $\rightsquigarrow$ relation.

Let AL denote a suitable language for assertions and PL denote a language for programming constructs. Let H denote a proof system for Hoare logic, T denote a proof system for assertions of AL and L denote a proof system for the $\rightsquigarrow$ relation.

- The systems H and L, by themselves, cannot guarantee completeness for Hoare triples and the $\rightsquigarrow$ relation. Specifically, $\{true\}\, x := t\, \{true\}$ and $true \rightsquigarrow true$ are true of all models but are unprovable in H and L respectively. One needs an axiomatic theory for the language of assertions to prove $true \Rightarrow true$. The solution lies in augmenting H and L with a proof system for assertions, namely T.

- While adding an axiomatic system for AL allows one to prove some additional assertions, it does not solve the problem of incompleteness. If AL can express statements of arithmetic, then by Gödel's incompleteness theorem the set of validities of AL is not recursively enumerable. That is there exist true assertions of the AL that are unprovable. Such an assertion, say P, can be expressed by the Hoare triple $\{true\}\, skip\, \{P\}$ or as the property $true \rightsquigarrow P$ for the program containing only the skip statement. Clearly, the Hoare triple and the progress property hold in the model but *cannot* be proved in H and L, even when the latter are augmented with T. This source of incompleteness stems from the complexity of the assertion language AL. One possible solution is to restrict it, so that Gödel assertions cannot be expressed.

- Consider a very simple assertion language consisting of the two assertions *true* and *false*. The set of programs for which the Hoare triple $\{true\}\, S\, \{false\}$ holds are precisely those programs that diverge on all possible inputs. It is known that this set is not recursively enumerable (Hopcroft and Ullman [1979]). This is a valid Hoare triple that cannot be derived in H. One can construct a similiar example for the $\rightsquigarrow$ operator as well. In (Pachl [1990]), Jan Pachl has shown that a non-recursively enumerable set, namely, the set of instances of the Post's Correspondence Problem that don't have a solution can be encoded as a set of $\rightsquigarrow$ properties of a program.

This example shows that curtailing the expressive power of the assertion language alone is not a solution to the incompleteness of Hoare logic. To factor out the incompleteness that is due to the assertion language, one introduces the notion of *relative completeness*. This can be informally stated as follows: For all models M and Hoare triples Φ, if $\models_M \Phi$ then $Tr_M \vdash_H \Phi$ where Tr_M are all the assertions that are true in the model M and we are permitted to use these assertions in the proof of Φ.

- Introducing relative completeness does not eliminate the problem of incompleteness. An additional source of incompleteness is the inability to express (or name) sets of states which occur during program execution by predicates. One such example is given by Wand (Wand [1978]). Wand exhibits a simple while program and a partial correctness Hoare triple corresponding to it. While the Hoare triple is valid in the model described, it cannot be derived in a proof system for Hoare triples even by assuming relative completeness. This is because it is impossible to express the invariant of the while program using the assertion language described.

  While Wand's example was a Hoare triple for a while program, the exact same argument can be readily extended to a $\leadsto$ property of the same while program recast as a program admissible in our formalism. This shows that relative completeness alone is not enough to remedy the incompleteness of the $\leadsto$ operator of UNITY.

- As a means of incorporating expressibility of assertions that occur during program execution, Cook (Cook [1978]) introduced the notion of expressibility of the *weakest precondition*[2]. This was used to define a new notion of completeness – *completeness in the sense of Cook*. A proof system H for PL is *complete in the sense of Cook*, if for every model M in which the weakest precondition is expressible and for every Hoare triple Φ, if $\models_M \Phi$, then $Tr_M \vdash_G \Phi$. Notice that this notion of completeness uses relative completeness as well.

  To overcome the problems associated with the completeness of $\leadsto$ it is necessary to define a notion of completeness akin to that of Cook. In the following derivation, for the case of unconditional fairness, we show exactly where it is necessary to appeal to expressibility of weakest preconditions.

5.7.2 Constructing a Proof of Progress

In this section we give a *constructive* proof of completeness of the proof system for unconditional fairness. Since the proof is constructive, we have to use ordinals unlike the proof of Theorem 5.4.1.

Assume that a property $X \leadsto Y$ holds in the intended model of execution for a program F executed on the assumption of unconditional fairness. On the basis of our framework, we may assert that

$$[\mathbf{A}(\langle \forall s :: \mathbf{G}\,\mathbf{F}\,\bar{s}\rangle \Rightarrow \mathbf{F}\,Y) \ \equiv \ \text{wlt}.Y]$$

where wlt.Y is given by,

$$[\text{wlt}.Y \ \equiv \ \langle \mu Z :: Y \vee \langle \exists s :: \text{gwp}.s.Z\rangle\rangle]$$

and gwp.$s.Z$ is given by,

$$[\text{gwp}.s.Z \ \equiv \ \langle \nu V :: ((\langle \forall t :: \text{wp}.t.V\rangle \wedge \text{wp}.s.Z) \vee Z\rangle].$$

---

[2] Actually Cook introduced expressibility of the strongest postcondition but showed that the concepts were equivalent.

Further, if $X \rightsquigarrow Y$ holds in the intended model of computation trees, then using the above, we may assert that $[X \Rightarrow \mathbf{wlt}.Y]$. We now show how to construct a derivation of $X \rightsquigarrow Y$ explicating all our assumptions as we go along.

1. To express the predicate transformer $\mathbf{gwp}.s.Y$, the assertion language should contain fixpoint operators and propositional variables which can be bound by these fixpoint operators. Furthermore, it requires the expressibility of the weakest preconditions ($\mathbf{wp}.s$) of all the statements. This is where completeness in the sense of Cook comes in.

2. The first step of our derivation shows that

$$\mathbf{gwp}.s.Y \ \mathcal{E} \ Y.$$

While this proof has been omitted in the interest of brevity, it can be found in Jutla et al. [1989].

3. From 2, using L0, we can infer that

$$\mathbf{gwp}.s.Y \rightsquigarrow Y.$$

4. From 3, using the disjunction axiom of $\rightsquigarrow$ L2, over a *finite* set of program statements, we can infer that,

$$\langle \exists s :: \mathbf{gwp}.s.Y \rangle \rightsquigarrow Y.$$

5. Since $\mathbf{wlt}.Y$ is expressed as the strongest solution of a monotonic predicate transformer, we know by the Theorem of Knaster–Tarski, that it can be expressed as

$$\mathbf{wlt}.Y \ \equiv \ \langle \exists \alpha :: f^{\alpha}.Y \rangle$$

where the predicate transformer f is defined as,

$$[f^0.Y \ \equiv \ false]$$
$$[f^{i+1}.Y \ \equiv \ (Y \vee \langle \exists s :: \mathbf{gwp}.s.(f^i.Y) \rangle)]$$
$$[f^{\alpha}.Y \ \equiv \ \langle \exists \beta : \beta < \alpha : f^{\beta}.Y \rangle]$$

The expression of each of the iterates of f upto the closure ordinal, requires the assertion language to contain a sort corresponding to the ordinals and an ordering relation $<$ on the ordinals. Using these we can show that each of the $f^{\alpha}.Y$ is expressible in the assertion language. Using this definition of $\mathbf{wlt}$ and 4 we show that,

$$\langle \forall \alpha :: f^{\alpha}.Y \rightsquigarrow Y \rangle.$$

The proof of this fact requires us to use the disjunction axiom L2 over a set of ordinals less than a fixed ordinal α. Application of the disjunction axiom once again over the set of ordinals less than the closure ordinal yields,

$$\mathbf{wlt}.Y \rightsquigarrow Y.$$

Notice that all applications of the disjunction axiom were confined to well-ordered sets.

6. We have not yet made use of the fact that in the model $[X \Rightarrow \textbf{wlt}.Y]$ holds. Since $\textbf{wlt}.Y$ is expressible in the assertion language (see 5) $[X \Rightarrow \textbf{wlt}.Y]$ is a truth of the assertion language in the model of computation trees. It is at this point that *relative* completeness enters the picture. If we could assume the existence of a derivation for such an assertion, then by Lemma 5.4.3, we have $X \rightsquigarrow \textbf{wlt}.Y$. This along with the conclusion of 5, permits us to deduce,

$$X \rightsquigarrow Y$$

6. Reasoning About Probabilistic Parallel Programs

In the last chapter, we presented a framework for the design of proof rules for proving progress properties under a variety of fairness assumptions. The use of the framework was exemplified by fairness assumptions such as minimal progress, weak fairness and strong fairness: these assumptions have proved to be useful for reasoning about progress properties of parallel programs.

A fairness assumption that has become important in the past few years is the one associated with a "coin toss". A coin is fair, in the sense that if it is tossed repeatedly then eventually it is guaranteed to come up heads (or tails, as the case may be). One of the first papers to use coin–tossing as a transition of an algorithm was Michael Rabin's seminal paper Rabin [1976] on Probabilistic Algorithms. Ever since then it has been widely recognized that using probabilistic transitions in the design and analysis of algorithms has several advantages. Often these algorithms are simpler and more efficient, in terms of time, space, and communication complexity, than their deterministic[1] counterparts (Rabin [1976], Rabin [1982a], Rabin [1982b], Herman [1990], see Gupta et al. [1994] for a survey). With the advent of multiprocessing and distributed computing, it has been realized that for certain problems it is possible to construct a probabilistic algorithm where no deterministic one exists. This is true especially for problems involving the resolution of symmetry. In the last decade, several such algorithms for synchronization, communication, and coordination of parallel programs have appeared in the literature (Francez and Rodeh [1980], Itai and Rodeh [1981], Lehmann and Rabin [1981], Cohen et al. [1984], Herman [1990]).

This gain in simplicity, efficiency, and solvability is not without a price. An integral part of algorithm design is a proof of correctness, and for probabilistic algorithms, one has to sacrifice the traditional notion of correctness for a quantitative notion: correctness with a probability between 0 and 1.

In this chapter we address this problem of correctness for probabilistic parallel programs. Since the term *probabilistic* has been used with various connotations, we begin with an informal definition of the class of algorithms of interest. We are interested in those algorithms that in addition to the usual deterministic transitions, permit *coin-tossing* as a legal transition. Informally, we allow transitions of the form

$$x := \text{outcome of the toss of a } \textit{fair} \text{ coin.}$$

---

[1] We use the term *deterministic* to mean *nonprobabilistic*.

This simple addition enables us to express many known probabilistic algorithms concisely.

We distinguish between two notions of correctness: *deterministic* and *probabilistic*. The former is defined to capture the traditional notion of absolute correctness of our algorithms. For the latter, rather than specify a quantitative measure, we reason about the more qualitative notion: correctness *with probability 1*. To understand the difference between the two notions intuitively, consider tossing a coin repeatedly: while there is no certainty that it will come up heads, it is guaranteed to come up heads eventually, with probability 1. In the sequel, properties of interest will be classified as *deterministic* or *holding with probability 1* depending on the notion of correctness used. It is important to note that even probabilistic programs can have deterministic properties.

Following the usual practice in program verification, we will investigate two classes of properties for probabilistic programs, namely, *safety* and *progress* properties. For reasons having to do with the way Alpern and Schneider [1985] define safety, it does not make sense to define the notion of a safety property that holds with probability 1. Thus, we require *safety* properties to hold deterministically. For *progress*, we are interested in proving a restricted class of properties, namely, those that are attained with probability 1. Furthermore, we are interested in those progress properties that are independent of the actual probability values attached to the individual alternatives of a probabilistic transition: the only assumption we allow ourselves is that these values are nonzero and that the sum of the values over a given transition is 1.

How realistic are these restrictions? In our experience, there are many probabilistic algorithms in the literature that satisfy these restrictions. These include algorithms for the dining philosophers problem (Lehmann and Rabin [1981]), mutual exclusion (Rabin [1982b], Cohen et al. [1984], Hart et al. [1983]), self-stabilization (Herman [1990], Israeli and Jalfon [1990]), asynchronous consensus (Ben-Or [1983]) and leader election (Itai and Rodeh [1981]). The work in this paper is applicable to these algorithms. At the same time, there is a large class of interesting applications in cryptography and security that use randomization, but that do not satisfy these restrictions. Some of these are correct with probability $1 - \epsilon$ (and not with probability 1 as we require), where ϵ can be made as small as required by suitably iterating the algorithm. A typical example of such a problem is that of primality testing, where one can increase one's confidence in the primality of a number by checking for more divisors. Yet other algorithms rely on the actual probability values attached to the outcomes of the probabilistic transition: for instance, applications based on the Gambler's ruin paradigm require the probabilistic transition to be perfectly fair. The results of this paper do not apply to such algorithms. This, at present, is a limitation of our work, and we hope to remove it in the future.

It should be noted that, even with the imposed restrictions, the proofs of such a constrained class of properties can be quite tenuous and tricky: [2] a suggestion

---

[2] For a compelling example of how unintuitive probabilistic reasoning can be, consider the following example: two coins are independently tossed ad infinitum. Is it the case

for a proof principle for such properties first appeared in Hart et al. [1983]. The proof principle was shown to be sound and complete for a class of finite state programs, that is, programs with a fixed number of processes and variables ranging over finite domains. The proof principle provided the basis for a decision procedure for mechanically determining whether a program satisfied a progress property with probability 1.

This proof principle has been the essence of several proof systems proposed since then. In Lehman and Shelah [1982], the authors generalized the temporal propositional logic of linear time to handle random events as well. In Hart and Sharir [1984], two propositional probabilistic temporal logics based on temporal logics of branching time are presented. However, these papers do not address the methodological question of designing probabilistic programs.

In Pnueli [1983], Amir Pnueli introduced the concept of *extreme fairness*. One of the results of the paper shows that a property that holds for all extremely fair computations holds with probability 1. Thus, extreme fairness is a sufficient condition to be satisfied by a scheduler in executing probabilistic programs. A proof rule based on extreme fairness and linear–time temporal logic was presented. This proof rule has been used to prove some difficult algorithms in Pnueli [1983], Pnueli and Zuck [1984] and Pnueli and Zuck [1986]. Though this method was the first to tackle sizably complex probabilistic programs, it has been shown to be incomplete. That is, there exist properties expressible in linear–time temporal logic that hold with probability 1, but that do not hold on some extremely fair computation. Second, the complexity of the proof rule makes it difficult to understand and apply. Part of the complexity stems from the interplay of randomization and parallelism, but the lack of an accompanying proof methodology does little to alleviate the difficulty. In Zuck [1986], Lenore Zuck introduced α-fairness and showed that temporal logic properties that hold with probability 1 for a finite–state program are precisely those that hold over all α-fair computations of the program.

In Hart and Sharir [1985], the proof principle of Hart et al. [1983] is generalized to develop conditions for the qualitative analysis of *infinite–state* probabilistic programs. To the author's knowledge, no proof system incorporating these conditions has yet been proposed.

Researchers have also investigated the question of probabilistic model checking. That is, given a finite–state probabilistic program and its temporal logic specification, do the computations of the program satisfy the specification with probability 1? This question was first raised in Vardi [1985] and was solved by automata theoretic methods extended to incorporate probabilistic transitions. The time complexity of the algorithm suggested to answer this question is double exponential in the size of the specification. Pnueli and Zuck (private communication regarding probabilistic verification by tableaux, 1989) develop a tableaux-based method to model checking and present an algorithm whose time complexity is single exponential in the size of the specification. This line

---

that with probability 1 the system reaches a state in which both coins show heads? For details, see Example 6.13.1 in Section 6.13.

of research diverges from ours: these methods are essentially *a posteriori*, they assume that a program is given, whereas we wish to derive the program from the specification.

Probabilistic transitions have also been studied in the context of process algebras. Giacalone et al. [1989] present PCCS, a calculus for reasoning about communicating probabilistic processes. PCCS, which is based on Milner's synchronous calculus (Milner [1983]), provides a setting to study various kinds of equivalences for probabilistic processes, and to construct sound and complete axiomatizations for them (Jou and Smolka [1990]). In other important related work, citejp90 present a probabilistic powerdomain of evaluations that is used to give the semantics of a language with a probabilistic parallel construct.

In this chapter, we try to show that probabilistic parallel algorithms can be specified, refined, and derived with the same rigor and elegance that applies to parallel algorithms. By synthesizing ideas from Hart et al. [1983] and Pnueli [1983], the theory of predicate transformers (Dijkstra and Scholten [1990]), and UNITY (Chandy and Misra [1988]), we construct a theory to reason about probability and parallelism.

We use the idea of extreme fairness and a generalization of the UNITY model of computation to develop a methodology to reason about probabilistic parallel programs. We generalize the UNITY model in two ways. First, we reintroduce the **initially** section that had been dropped in the last two chapters. Second, a program will be a set of probabilistic multiple assignment statements: such a statement is a generalization of the multiple assignments that we had introduced earlier. An execution of a program begins in a state satisfying the initial condition and proceeds by repeatedly picking a statement from the set and executing it, with the caveat of *unconditional fairness* — that is, in an infinite execution sequence every statement is executed infinitely often. While *unconditional fairness* is required in the selection of a statement to be executed, we require a different notion of fairness called, *extreme fairness*, in the selection of an alternative of a probabilistic statement. Extreme fairness is a useful abstraction that allows us to axiomatize and reason about properties that hold with probability 1.

By defining the *weakest precondition* (wp-semantics) for a probabilistic statement appropriately, we show that the UNITY relation **unless** and its associated theory can be used to reason about the safety properties of probabilistic programs as well. This is in keeping with our decision to treat all safety properties deterministically. In a like manner, we show how the theory of the UNITY relations **ensures** and ↦ (read, *leads-to*) can be extended to reason about progress properties that hold *deterministically*.

The wp-semantics are not adequate to specify and verify progress properties that *hold with probability 1*.[3] It is necessary to define a new predicate transformer **wpp** (read, *weakest probabilistic precondition*) to capture the inherent nondeterminacy of the probabilistic construct. The **wpp** is the dual of **wp** and this is reflected in its properties. It turns out that the predicate transformer

---

[3] To see the necessity of a new operator, see Section 6.5 and Example 6.13.2 in Section 6.13.

wpp along with the notion of *extreme fairness* provides the right generalization of **wp** (or Hoare triples, for that matter). The predicate **wpp**.$s.X$ characterizes all states such that, if statement s is executed infinitely often from such a state, then infinitely often the execution of s terminates in a state satisfying predicate X. Further, it provides the basis for generalizing the relations **unless, ensures** and $\mapsto$ to new relations **upto, entails** and $\models\!\!\Rightarrow$ (read, *probabilistically leads-to*), respectively. Using this small set of operators, we construct a powerful theory in which specifications can be clearly stated and refined using a set of inference rules: further, the choice of operators is such that they provide heuristic guidance in extracting the program text from the final specification. We have investigated the properties of these operators in detail.

As with other proof theories, our proof theory is not compositional with respect to general progress properties. However, we have results on deriving basic progress properties of a composite probabilistic program from those of its components. Specifically, **unless, upto, ensures** and **entails** properties compose in our model.

One of the important features of our theory is that our operators are not powerful enough to reason about the individual state transitions of a program. As a consequence, we are able to avoid the incompleteness of Pnueli [1983]. We show that our proof system is sound and complete for proving properties of *finite-state* probabilistic programs.

Our proof system is novel in that it shows that probabilistic programs are amenable to the same process of specification, refinement, and verification as sequential and parallel programs. We illustrate our proof system by examples from random walk and (two-process) mutual exclusion problems. Furthermore, our proof system allows both probabilistic and deterministic properties to be manipulated within a unified framework. This, along with the compositional features of the operators that we introduce, allows one to reuse proofs of existing programs (both probabilistic and deterministic) and to reason in a compositional manner. The most complicated example that we have proved in our system is the paradigm of *eventual determinism* (Rao [1990]).

6.1 The Programming Model

Our programming model is a generalization of UNITY. Recall that a UNITY program consists of four parts: a collection of variable declarations, a set of abbreviations, a set of initial conditions, and a *finite* set of statements. These sections are called **declare, always, initially,** and **assign** respectively. The statements in the **assign** section are restricted to be deterministic conditional multiple assignment statements. The syntax of a probabilistic parallel program will be the same as that of a UNITY program with one change: we generalize UNITY's multiple assignment statement to a *probabilistic multiple assignment*. This will be basic transition in our model.

We now describe the format of a multiple assignment statement as used in UNITY and a probabilistic assignment statement as used in our computational model.

6.1.1 Deterministic Statements

Recall that the only statement allowed in a UNITY program is the *multiple assignment (MA)*. This can be informally presented as

$$MA :: x := e.$$

In general, x is a list of variables, and e is a list of expressions. We restrict an expression to be a well–defined function of the state. Notice that this allows expressions to be defined by cases, provided that there is a unique, well–defined value for the expression in each state. This is required to guarantee that every assignment statement is *deterministic*. The assignment succeeds only if the number and types of variables match the number and types of the corresponding expressions.

6.1.2 Probabilistic Statements

The only statement that we allow in our computational model is the *probabilistic assignment statement (PA)*. This can be informally presented as

$$PA :: \quad x := e.0 \mid e.1 \mid \cdots \mid e.(k-1).$$

As in a multiple assignment statement, x is a list of variables and each $e.i$ $(0 \leq i \wedge i < k)$ is a list of expressions. Again, the only restriction we impose is that the expression be a well–defined function of the state.

A probabilistic assignment is executed as follows: a *k–sided coin* is tossed. The outcome of the coin toss determines which list of expressions, $e.i$, is to be assigned to the list of variables x. Thus, a PA can give rise to one of k different assignments. Each of these possible assignments will be called a *mode* of the PA.

It is important to note the following points about a probabilistic assignment statement. First, we did not specify the notion of fairness that will be assumed in the execution of such a statement. Specifically, we do not attach a probability value to a mode: we only require that each mode have a nonzero probability of occurrence and that the sum of probabilities over all of the modes equal 1. It is unnecessary to make these probabilities explicit because we are only interested in those properties of the program that hold for arbitrary probability distributions. Second, in the case of only one mode ($k = 1$), a probabilistic statement specializes to a deterministic statement as in UNITY.

6.1.3 Executing a UNITY Program

We recapitulate the notion of executing a UNITY program. A *state* of a UNITY program is an assignment of values to the variables of the program. It is assumed that these variables have been declared in the **declare** section of the program and that the values assigned to the variables are consistent with the type associated with the variables in the **declare** section.

An *execution* of a UNITY program begins in a state that satisfies the initial conditions. It proceeds by repeatedly selecting a statement from the **assign** section and executing it with the selection being subject to a *fairness* constraint: in an infinite execution, each statement is selected infinitely often. Such a fairness constraint is termed *unconditional fairness*. In other words, an execution of a UNITY program is a sequence of states, beginning in a state that satisfies the initial conditions, with the transitions between the states being effected by a fair selection of the statements of the UNITY program. Thus, in the UNITY model of computation, parallelism is captured by a fair, interleaved execution of the statements of the program with each statement being executed atomically. In this sense, a UNITY program may be looked upon as a set of unconditionally fair execution sequences.

6.1.4 Executing a Probabilistic Parallel Program

Our model of program execution is a generalization of UNITY's. Just as in UNITY, an execution of a probabilistic program begins in a state that satisfies the initial condition, and proceeds by repeatedly selecting a statement from the **assign** section and executing it with the selection being subject to *unconditional* fairness. Recall that a statement of a probabilistic parallel program is a probabilistic multiple assignment, which is a generalization of UNITY's multiple assignment statement. Executing a probabilistic multiple assignment, such as PA, can give rise to k possible outcomes, where each outcome is associated with executing one mode of PA, whereas executing UNITY's deterministic multiple assignment gave rise to exactly one possible outcome. This means that UNITY's concept of a *linear* execution needs to be generalized to a *treelike* structure for probabilistic programs, with the nodes of the tree corresponding to the states of the probabilistic program and the edges corresponding to the transitions. Such a treelike structure is called a *schedule*, and every path in the schedule is called an *execution sequence* of the probabilistic program. An execution sequence is *unconditionally fair* if each statement of the probabilistic program is infinitely often selected for execution. For the purposes of this paper, a schedule is *unconditionally fair* if all of its execution sequences are unconditionally fair.[4] Thus, in our model, a program can be looked upon as a set of unconditionally fair schedules. For such a model, a program satisfies a property with probability 1 if, for *all* unconditionally fair schedules, the measure of the set of execution sequences of the schedule that satisfy the property is 1.

We now formalize the notion of fairness required in selecting the mode to be executed (or, equivalently, the fairness required in tossing the coin). Let X

---

[4] As pointed out by Hart et al. [1983], for a schedule to be unconditionally fair, it is enough to require that the measure of the set of unconditionally fair execution sequences of the schedule be 1.

be a predicate over program variables. An execution sequence, σ, is *extremely fair with respect to X* if for all probabilistic statements PA, if PA is executed infinitely often from states of σ satisfying X, then every mode of the PA is executed infinitely often from states of σ satisfying X.

An execution is *extremely fair* if it is extremely fair with respect to all first-order expressible predicates X.

In Pnueli [1983], Amir Pnueli established that, to prove that a property holds with probability 1, it is sufficient to show that it holds over all extremely fair executions. Thus, by assuming that the execution of the probabilistic statements is extremely fair in our computational model, we are assured by Pnueli's result that all properties hold with probability 1.

Remark. The following is an alternative to extreme fairness. Assume that the probability distribution of the modes of a probabilistic statement is independent of the state in which it is executed. With such an assumption, we can show the following theorem.

Theorem 6.1.1. *Given a probabilistic program with one probabilistic multiple assignment statement, PA, and an unconditionally fair schedule, assume that the probability distribution associated with PA's modes is independent of the state in which it is executed. Then, with probability 1, each of its modes is executed infinitely often.*

Proof. Let A_n be the set of all execution sequences such that the ith mode of the probabilistic statement is executed in the nth state of the execution. Then,

$$lim\ sup_{n \to \infty}\ A_n = \bigcap_{n=1}^{\infty} \bigcup_{k=n}^{\infty} A_k$$

is the set of all execution sequences in which the ith mode is chosen infinitely often. Since the probability distribution of the modes is independent of the states, one can apply the second Borel–Cantelli theorem to infer that

$$P(lim\ sup_{n \to \infty}\ A_n) = 1.$$

$\square$

From this it follows that any property that holds for all sequences in $lim\ sup\ A_n$ (i.e., of all extremely fair sequences) holds with probability 1. This analysis was done assuming that there was only one probabilistic statement that was being executed. If more than one probabilistic statement is being scheduled, then the validity of this result would depend on assumptions about the scheduling of the probabilistic statements with respect to one another. (*End of Remark*).

In summary, our computational model requires two notions of fairness: *unconditional fairness* in the selection of statements to be executed, and *extreme fairness* in the execution of a statement.

6.2 The weakest Precondition

In this chapter we will make extensive use of a unary predicate transformer, namely, the *weakest precondition* (wp) predicate transformer, introduced in Dijkstra [1975]. Recall that for a statement t and a predicate X, the *weakest precondition* of t with respect to X is denoted by $\mathbf{wp}.t.X$. It characterizes precisely those states beginning in which each execution of statement t is guaranteed to terminate in a state in which predicate X holds.

We now describe *weakest precondition* semantics of a multiple assignment statement as used in UNITY and a probabilistic assignment statement as used in our computational model.

6.2.1 Deterministic Statements

Recall the syntax of a multiple assignment statement, MA:

$$MA \;::\; x := e.$$

Formally, the *weakest precondition* semantics of a conditional multiple assignment is defined as follows.

$$[\mathbf{wp}.MA.X \equiv \{x := e\}X].$$

Theorem 6.2.1. *The predicate transformer $\mathbf{wp}.MA$ is universally conjunctive.*

Proof. The universal conjunctivity of $\mathbf{wp}.MA$ follows from the universal conjunctivity of the operation of substitution. The interested reader is referred to Dijkstra and Scholten [1990] (see p. 117, chap. 6). □

To prove the disjunctivity of $\mathbf{wp}.MA$ requires some more groundwork. We have to make use of the fact that the statement is *deterministic*. Using this, we can show the following,

Theorem 6.2.2. *The predicate transformer $\mathbf{wp}.MA$ is universally disjunctive.*

Proof. The universal disjunctivity of $\mathbf{wp}.MA$ follows from the univeral disjunctivity of the operation of substitution and the determinacy of the statement MA (see p. 117, chap 6 in Dijkstra and Scholten [1990]). □

6.2.2 Probabilistic Statements

Recall the syntax of a probabilistic statement, PA.

$$PA \;::\; x := e.0 \mid e.1 \mid \cdots \mid e.(k-1).$$

Formally, the *weakest precondition* semantics of a probabilistic assignment statement is defined as follows:

$$[\mathbf{wp}.PA.X \equiv \langle \forall i : 0 \le i \wedge i < k : \{x := e.i\}X \rangle].$$

We now investigate the junctivity properties of this predicate transformer.

Theorem 6.2.3. *The predicate transformer* **wp**.*PA is universally conjunctive.*

Proof. The universal conjunctivity of **wp**.*PA* follows from the universal conjunctivity of the universal quantification and the operation of substitution (see p. 117, chap. 6 in Dijkstra and Scholten [1990]).   □

Theorem 6.2.4. *The predicate transformer* **wp**.*PA is or–continuous.*

Proof. The or–continuity of **wp**.*PA* follows from the universal disjunctivity of substitution and from the assumption that a probabilistic statement has a finite number of modes (see p. 141, chap. 7 in Dijkstra and Scholten [1990]).   □

Theorem 6.2.5. *The predicate transformer* **wp**.*PA is not finitely disjunctive.*

Proof. Consider the statement

$$S \,::\, x := heads \mid tails$$

and the assertions

$$[X \equiv (x = heads)] \wedge [Y \equiv (x = tails)].$$

Then

$$
\begin{aligned}
& \mathbf{wp}.S.(X \vee Y) \\
= \ & \{\text{Definition of } \mathbf{wp}.PA\} \\
& \{x := heads\}(X \vee Y) \wedge \{x := tails\}(X \vee Y) \\
= \ & \{\text{Axiom of assignment}\} \\
& (heads = heads \vee heads = tails) \wedge (tails = heads \vee tails = tails) \\
= \ & \{\text{predicate calculus}\} \\
& true
\end{aligned}
$$

whereas

$$
\begin{aligned}
& \mathbf{wp}.S.X \vee \mathbf{wp}.S.Y \\
= \ & \{\text{Definition of } \mathbf{wp}.S\} \\
& (\{x := heads\}X \wedge \{x := tails\}X) \vee (\{x := heads\}Y \wedge \{x := tails\}Y) \\
= \ & \{\text{Axiom of assignment}\} \\
& (heads = heads \wedge tails = heads) \vee (heads = tails \wedge tails = tails) \\
= \ & \{\text{predicate calculus}\} \\
& false
\end{aligned}
$$

□

Corollary 6.2.1. *The predicate transformer* **wp**.*PA is truth-preserving.*

$$[\mathbf{wp}.PA.true \equiv true].$$

Proof. Follows from the universal conjunctivity of **wp**.*PA* and from the fact that universal quantification over an empty set is true.   □

Corollary 6.2.2. *(Law of the Excluded Miracle)*

$$[\textbf{wp}.PA.false \equiv false].$$

Proof. Since universal quantification and the operation of substitution obey the Law of the Excluded Miracle, we can conclude that **wp**.*PA* also obeys the same law.   □

6.3 Reasoning About Safety

In this section our aim is to define and develop a theory to reason about the safety properties of a probabilistic program. Recall that in UNITY, safety properties are expresses using the **unless** relation. The **unless** is a binary relation on state predicates and is formally defined as follows:

$$\frac{\langle \forall s : s \, in \, F : [X \wedge \neg Y \Rightarrow \textbf{wp}.s.(X \vee Y)] \rangle}{(X \textbf{ unless } Y)}$$

where the dummy s quantifies over the statements of a UNITY program F and where X and Y are state predicates.

Intuitively, X **unless** Y means that in all executions, if X holds in some state of the execution, X continues to hold in succeeding states as long as Y does not hold: if Y never holds, then X holds forever.

One of the contributions of UNITY is a rich theory to combine **unless** properties: these can be used both to deduce new **unless** properties and to refine safety specifications. All of the rules in the theory are based on the following four postulates.

1. Reflexivity and anti-reflexivity:

$$X \textbf{ unless } X$$

$$X \textbf{ unless } \neg X.$$

2. Consequence weakening:

$$\frac{X \textbf{ unless } Y, [Y \Rightarrow Z]}{X \textbf{ unless } Z}$$

3. General conjunction and disjunction: For i ranging over an arbitrary set I,

$$\frac{\langle \forall i :: X.i \text{ unless } Y.i \rangle}{\langle \forall i :: X.i \rangle \text{ unless } \langle \forall i :: X.i \vee Y.i \rangle \wedge \langle \exists i :: Y.i \rangle \quad \text{(General conjunction)}}$$
$$\langle \exists i :: X.i \rangle \text{ unless } \langle \forall i :: \neg X.i \vee Y.i \rangle \wedge \langle \exists i :: Y.i \rangle \quad \text{(General disjunction)}$$

Using the rule of consequence weakening, the following are special cases of general conjunction and disjunction:

Simple conjunction and simple disjunction:

$$\frac{X \text{ unless } Y}{U \text{ unless } V}$$
$$(X \wedge U) \text{ unless } (Y \vee V) \quad \text{(simple conjunction)}$$
$$(X \vee U) \text{ unless } (Y \vee V) \quad \text{(simple disjunction)}$$

4. Cancellation:

$$\frac{X \text{ unless } Y, \ \ Y \text{ unless } Z}{(X \vee Y) \text{ unless } Z}$$

As mentioned in the introduction to this chapter, we are interested in defining a relation for proving deterministic safety properties of probabilistic parallel programs. Since a UNITY program is a special case of a probabilistic program, we would like the relation to be a generalization of UNITY relation for safety, namely, the **unless**. By doing so, we hope to draw on the extensive repertoire of theorems of **unless** that have already been discovered.

If the definition of **unless** (as given in UNITY and reproduced above) is to satisfy the four postulates given above and, hence, the rich calculus of **unless** as developed in UNITY, it is sufficient for the predicate transformer **wp**.s (where s is a statement of the UNITY program) to satisfy the condition of *universal conjunctivity*. That is,

$$[\langle \forall X : X \in W : \textbf{wp}.s.X \rangle \equiv \textbf{wp}.s.\langle \forall X : X \in W : X \rangle],$$

where W is an arbitrary set of predicates.

Recall that, in our computational model, we had generalized the multiple assignment statement of UNITY to a probabilistic assignment statement (PA). But, by Theorem 6.2.3, the predicate transformer **wp**.PA is also universally conjunctive, and this means that we can use the **unless** relation and its theory, as developed in UNITY, to reason about the safety properties of probabilistic programs as well.

6.4 UNITY and Progress: ensures and $\mapsto$

Probabilistic programs could have progress properties that hold deterministically. In this section we extend the machinery of UNITY to prove deterministic progress properties of probabilistic programs.

Recall that the basis of the definition of progress in UNITY is the **ensures** operator. The **ensures** operator is a binary relation on state predicates and is formally defined as

$$\frac{X \text{ unless } Y, \; \langle \exists s : s \, in \, F : [X \wedge \neg Y \Rightarrow \mathbf{wp}.s.Y] \rangle}{X \text{ ensures } Y}$$

where s ranges over the statements of the UNITY program F and where X and Y are state predicates.

Intuitively, an **ensures** property strengthens an **unless** property by ruling out the possibility that a program remains in a state satisfying X forever. It does so by postulating the existence of a statement s, which when executed in a state satisfying $X \wedge \neg Y$ is guaranteed to terminate in a state satisfying Y. So, if the program is in a state satisfying X, the **unless** part of the proof obligation guarantees that the only way that a program leaves such a state (if ever) is by transiting to a state satisfying Y. The existence of statement s and the requirement of unconditional fairness guarantee that eventually statement s is executed and the program transits to a state satisfying Y.

In UNITY, general progress properties are expressed using the *leads–to* operator (denoted, $\mapsto$). The $\mapsto$ operator is a binary relation on state predicates and is formally defined as the strongest relation that satisfies the following three conditions:

1. *Base case:*
$$\frac{X \text{ ensures } Y}{X \mapsto Y}$$

2. *Transitivity:*
$$\frac{X \mapsto Y, \; Y \mapsto Z}{X \mapsto Z}$$

3. *Disjunctivity:* For an arbitrary set of predicates, W:
$$\frac{\langle \forall X : X \in W : X \mapsto Y \rangle}{\langle \exists X : X \in W : X \rangle \mapsto Y}$$

That is, the relation $\mapsto$ is the transitive, disjunctive closure of the **ensures** relation. Intuitively, the property $X \mapsto Y$ means that if X holds in a state of an unconditionally fair execution sequence, then Y holds either in that state or in a later state.

Just as in the case of the **unless** relation, one of the important contributions of UNITY is a powerful theory to manipulate progress properties. The basic postulates underlying the theory of **ensures** are the following.

1. Reflexivity:
$$X \text{ ensures } X$$

2. Consequence weakening:
$$\frac{X \text{ ensures } Y, \; [Y \Rightarrow Z]}{X \text{ ensures } Z}$$

3. Impossibility:

$$\frac{X \text{ ensures } false}{[\neg X]}$$

4. Conjunction:

$$\frac{\begin{array}{c} U \text{ ensures } V, \\ X \text{ unless } Y \end{array}}{(U \wedge X) \text{ ensures } (U \wedge Y) \vee (X \wedge V) \vee (V \wedge Y)}$$

5. Disjunction:

$$\frac{X \text{ ensures } Y}{(X \vee Z) \text{ ensures } (Y \vee Z)}$$

6. E–continuity: For a weakening sequence of predicates $X.i$,

$$\frac{\langle \forall i :: X.i \text{ ensures } Y \rangle}{\langle \exists i :: X.i \rangle \text{ ensures } Y}$$

Just as in the case of the **unless** relation, we would like to use the UNITY relations **ensures** and $\mapsto$ to reason about the deterministic progress properties of probabilistic parallel programs as well. If the definition of **ensures** (as given in UNITY and reproduced above) is to satisfy the above postulates and the theory of **ensures** as developed in UNITY, it is sufficient for the predicate transformer **wp** $.s$ to meet the following conditions.

1. Law of the Excluded Miracle:

$$[\mathbf{wp}.s.false \equiv false]$$

2. Finite conjunctivity:

$$[\mathbf{wp}.s.X \wedge \mathbf{wp}.s.Y \equiv \mathbf{wp}.s.(X \wedge Y)]$$

Fortunately, by Corollary 6.2.2, the predicate transformer **wp** $.PA$ satisfies the Law of the Excluded Miracle. By Theorem 6.2.3, it is universally conjunctive, and hence, by Theorem 2.2.1, it is finitely conjunctive as well. Thus, we can use the **ensures** relation and its theory as developed in UNITY to reason about **ensures** properties of probabilistic parallel programs.

The important postulates about the $\mapsto$ are the following:

1. Implication:

$$\frac{[X \Rightarrow Y]}{X \mapsto Y}$$

2. Impossibility:

$$\frac{X \mapsto false}{[\neg X]}$$

3. Disjunction: For i ranging over an arbitrary set I,

$$\frac{\langle \forall i :: X.i \mapsto Y.i \rangle}{\langle \exists i :: X.i \rangle \mapsto \langle \exists i :: Y.i \rangle}$$

4. Cancellation:
$$\frac{W \mapsto (X \vee Y), \; Y \mapsto Z}{W \mapsto (X \vee Z)}$$

5. Progress–Safety–Progress (PSP):

$$\frac{X \mapsto Y, \; U \text{ unless } V}{(X \wedge U) \mapsto (Y \wedge U) \vee V}$$

6. Completion: For i ranging over any finite set I,

$$\frac{\langle \forall i :: X.i \mapsto Y.i \rangle, \quad \langle \forall i :: X.i \text{ unless } Z \rangle}{\langle \forall i :: X.i \rangle \mapsto \langle \forall i :: Y.i \rangle \vee Z}$$

7. Induction principle: Let $(W, \prec)$ be a well–founded set. Let M be a metric mapping program states to W. Then

$$\frac{\langle \forall m : m \in W : (X \wedge M = m) \mapsto (X \wedge M \prec m) \vee Y \rangle}{X \mapsto Y}$$

Now, the theorems about $\mapsto$ in UNITY depend on the properties of **unless** and **ensures**, and the definition of $\mapsto$. We have shown that the properties of **unless** and **ensures** continue to hold even with the more general probabilistic statements of our computational model. Thus retaining the UNITY definition of $\mapsto$, we can use the theory developed in UNITY to reason about the *deterministic* progress properties in our computational model.

6.5 Deterministic Versus Probabilistic Correctness

The theory of the UNITY relations **unless**, **ensures**, and $\mapsto$ is sufficient to reason about the deterministic safety and progress properties of probabilistic programs. However, the notions of **ensures** and $\mapsto$ are inadequate to reason about progress properties that hold with probability 1.

Consider the program of example 6.13.2 in Section 6.13 (Pnueli [1983]) reproduced here for convenience:

```
declare      b : integer
initially    b = 0
assign       b := b + 1  if  (b mod 3) ≤ 1
          ∥  b := b + 2  if  (b mod 3) ≤ 1
end
```

For this program, it is not the case that

$$true \mapsto (b \bmod 3 = 2)$$

Consider the execution sequence in which the two statements are alternately executed, leading to the following sequence of values for b:

$$0, 1, 3, 4, 6, 7, \ldots.$$

This execution sequence is *unconditionally fair* with respect to the two statements but no state of the execution satisfies $(b \bmod 3 = 2)$. Thus, the program does not satisfy the progress property *deterministically*.

Now consider the probabilistic program.

> **declare** $b : integer$
> **initially** $b = 0$
> **assign** $b := b + 1 \mid b + 2$ **if** $(b \bmod 3) \le 1$
> **end**

Suppose that the first alternative is taken with a nonzero probability p and that the second alternative is taken with a nonzero probability q. This program has only one schedule, namely, the one shown in figure 6.1. For this schedule, we can

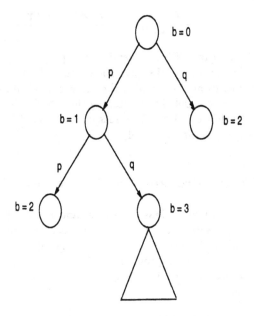

Fig. 6.1. Schedule for the probabilistic program of Section 7

compute the probability that a state satisfying $(b \bmod 3 = 2)$ is reached:

$$
\begin{aligned}
P(b \bmod 3 = 2) \;&=\; q + p^2 + p * q * P(b \bmod 3 = 2) \\
\Rightarrow \quad \{\text{arithmetic, } q = 1 - p\} \\
P(b \bmod 3 = 2) \;&=\; 1
\end{aligned}
$$

That is, the measure of the set of execution sequences on which this property is attained is 1. There is only one execution sequence that does not have this property, namely, the one that strictly alternates the execution of the two modes, and its measure is 0. We say that *true probabilistically leads-to* $(b \bmod 3 = 2)$ and write this as

$$true \Longmapsto (b \bmod 3 = 2).$$

We were fortunate in that there is only one schedule for the program given above. In general, a probabilistic program would have more than one statement and, thus, an infinite set of schedules. To verify that a given progress property holds with probability 1 would require doing an analytical exercise (similiar to the one above) for all the *unconditionally* fair schedules, and that would be an impossible task. Clearly, we need a simpler way.

In the next three sections, we show how each of the **unless, ensures** and $\mapsto$ can be generalized to reason effectively about properties that hold with probability 1.

6.6 The weakest Probabilistic Precondition

The predicate transformer **wp** allows us to define safety properties of probabilistic programs. For defining probabilistic progress properties, it turns out that **wp**.s is too restrictive. Intuitively, **wp**.PA requires *all* modes of the probabilistic statement PA to behave in the same manner, whereas for progress, it is enough if there *exists* a single helpful mode that establishes a desired property. This weaker notion is nicely captured by the predicate transformer **w**eakest **p**robabilistic **p**recondition (denoted, **wpp**).

The predicate transformer **wpp** is defined as follows:

$$[\textbf{wpp}.PA.X \equiv \langle \exists i : 0 \leq i \wedge i < k : \{x := e.i\}X \rangle].$$

Note that for a deterministic statement s (i.e., a statement with a single mode), the **wpp**.s is the same as **wp**.s. The only difference between **wp**.PA and **wpp**.PA is the presence of an existential quantifier in place of a universal one. In this sense, **wpp**.PA is the dual of **wp**.PA, and this is reflected in its properties.

Remark. In introducing the notion of the *weakest precondition*, Dijkstra defines **wp**.s.X as characterizing all possible states such that, if s is executed from a state satisfying **wp**.s.X, then the execution of s terminates in a state in which X is true.

The predicate transformer **wpp**.s.X considered along with the notion of extreme fairness generalizes this idea. It characterizes all possible states such that, if s is executed *infinitely often* from a state satisfying **wpp**.s.X, then *infinitely often* the execution of s terminates in a state in which X is true. (*End of Remark*).

Theorem 6.6.1. *The predicate transformer* **wpp** *.PA is and–continuous.*

Proof. The and–continuity of the predicate transformer **wpp** *.PA* follows from the universal conjunctivity of the operation of substitution and the finite range of i (see p. 99, chap. 6 in Dijkstra and Scholten [1990]).   □

Theorem 6.6.2. *The predicate transformer* **wpp** *.PA is* not *finitely conjunctive.*

Proof. We use the same example as for Theorem 6.2.5, which serves for **wpp** *.CPA* as well. Consider the statement

$$S :: x := heads \mid tails$$

and the assertions

$$[X \equiv (x = heads)] \wedge [Y \equiv (x = tails)].$$

Then

$$\begin{aligned}
& \mathbf{wpp}.S.(X \wedge Y) \\
= \ & \{\text{predicate calculus}\} \\
& \mathbf{wpp}.S.false \\
= \ & \{\text{definition of } \mathbf{wpp}.S\} \\
& false
\end{aligned}$$

whereas

$$\begin{aligned}
& \mathbf{wpp}.S.X \vee \mathbf{wpp}.S.Y \\
= \ & \{\text{definition of } \mathbf{wpp}.S\} \\
& (\{x := heads\}X \vee \{x := tails\}X) \wedge (\{x := heads\}Y \vee \{x := tails\}Y) \\
= \ & \{\text{axiom of assignment}\} \\
& (heads = heads \vee tails = heads) \wedge (heads = tails \vee tails = tails) \\
= \ & \{\text{predicate calculus}\} \\
& true
\end{aligned}$$

□

Theorem 6.6.3. *The predicate transformer* **wpp** *.PA is universally disjunctive.*

Proof. The universal disjunctivity of **wpp** *.PA* follows from the universal disjunctivity of existential quantification and the operation of substitution (see p. 117, chap. 6 in Dijkstra and Scholten [1990]).   □

Corollary 6.6.1. *The predicate transformer* **wpp** *.PA is truth preserving:*

$$[\mathbf{wpp}.s.true \equiv true].$$

Proof. Since the operation of substitution is universally disjunctive (see p. 117, chap. 6 in Dijkstra and Scholten [1990]), it is truth preserving, and **wpp** $.PA$ is truth preserving. □

Corollary 6.6.2. *The predicate transformer* **wpp** $.PA$ *is strict:*

$$[\textbf{wpp}.s.false \equiv false].$$

Proof. Follows from the universal disjunctivity of **wpp** $.PA$ and the fact that existential quantification over an empty set is false. □

6.7 Relating wp and wpp

In this section we present theorems relating the predicate transformers **wp** and **wpp**.

Theorem 6.7.1. *For all statements s,*

$$[\textbf{wp}.s.X \Rightarrow \textbf{wpp}.s.X].$$

Proof. For a probabilistic statement PA, we have the following derivation:

$$
\begin{array}{ll}
& \textbf{wp}.PA.X \\
= & \{\text{definition of } \textbf{wp}.PA\} \\
& \langle \forall i :: \{x := e.i\}X \rangle \\
\Rightarrow & \{\text{predicate calculus, range nonempty}\} \\
& \langle \exists i :: \{x := e.i\}X \rangle \\
= & \{\text{definition of } \textbf{wpp}.PA\} \\
& \textbf{wpp}.PA.X
\end{array}
$$

□

Theorem 6.7.2. *For all statements s,*

$$[\textbf{wp}.s.X \wedge \textbf{wpp}.s.Y \Rightarrow \textbf{wpp}.s.(X \wedge Y)].$$

Proof. For a probabilistic statement PA, we have the following derivation:

$$
\begin{array}{ll}
& \textbf{wp}.PA.X \wedge \textbf{wpp}.PA.Y \\
= & \{\text{definition of } \textbf{wp}.PA \text{ and } \textbf{wpp}.PA\} \\
& \langle \forall i :: \{x := e.i\}X \rangle \wedge \langle \exists i :: \{x := e.i\}Y \rangle \\
& \{\wedge \text{ over } \exists\} \\
& \langle \exists i :: \langle \forall i :: \{x := e.i\}X \rangle \wedge \{x := e.i\}Y \rangle \\
\Rightarrow & \{\text{instantiation}\} \\
& \langle \exists i :: \{x := e.i\}X \wedge \{x := e.i\}Y \rangle \\
= & \{\text{universal conjunctivity of multiple assignment}\} \\
& \langle \exists i :: \{x := e.i\}(X \wedge Y) \rangle
\end{array}
$$

$=$ {definition of **wpp**.PA}
    wpp.PA.$(X \wedge Y)$

$\square$

Theorem 6.7.3. *For all statements s,*

$$[\mathbf{wp}.s.(X \vee Y) \Rightarrow \mathbf{wp}.s.X \vee \mathbf{wpp}.s.Y].$$

Proof. For a probabilistic statement PA, we have the following derivation:

    wp.PA.$(X \vee Y)$
$=$ {definition of **wp**.PA}
    $\langle \forall i :: \{x := e.i\}(X \vee Y)\rangle$
    {universal disjunctivity of multiple assignment}
    $\langle \forall i :: \{x := e.i\}X \vee \{x := e.i\}Y\rangle$
$\Rightarrow$ {predicate calculus}
    $\langle \forall i :: \{x := e.i\}X\rangle \vee \langle \exists i :: \{x := e.i\}Y\rangle$
$=$ {definition of **wp**.PA and **wpp**.PA}
    wp.$PA.X \vee$ **wpp**.$PA.Y$

$\square$

6.8 Reasoning about Progress

In this section we develop a relation to reason about progress with probability 1. To do so, we introduce three new relations: **upto**, **entails**, and $\rightsquigarrow$ (read, *prompts*). The predicate transformer, **wpp** allows us to generalize the UNITY relations **unless** to **upto** and **ensures** to **entails**. We then introduce the relation $\rightsquigarrow$ as the reflexive, transitive closure of **entails** and $\mapsto$. These relations provide the basis for defining the relation $\Longmapsto$ (read, *probabilistically leads–to*), the probabilistic analog of the deterministic leads–to $\mapsto$.

6.8.1 TheRelation upto

We begin by generalizing the relation **unless**. Consider the definition of **unless**:

$$\frac{\langle \forall s :: [X \wedge \neg Y \Rightarrow \mathbf{wp}.s.(X \vee Y)]\rangle}{X \text{ unless } Y}$$

We use Theorem 6.7.3 to weaken this definition to obtain the definition of **upto**:

$$\frac{\langle \forall s :: [X \wedge \neg Y \Rightarrow \mathbf{wp}.s.X \vee \mathbf{wpp}.s.Y]\rangle}{X \text{ upto } Y}$$

Intuitively, X **upto** Y captures the following idea: If X holds at any point during the execution of a program, then either

1. Y never holds and X continues to hold forever; or
2. Y holds eventually (it may hold initially when X holds) and X continues to hold until Y holds; or
3. X continues to hold until $\neg X$ holds eventually; the transition from X to $\neg X$ being made by a statement that *could have* taken it to a state satisfying Y.

The interesting (third) case arises when a probabilistic statement PA is executed in a state satisfying $X \wedge \neg Y$. Suppose that not all modes of the PA when executed lead to a state satisfying X and, furthermore that there exists a mode that will take it to a state satisfying Y. Since there are no guarantees on which mode will be executed, execution of PA can lead to a state satisfying $\neg X$, even though there exists a mode that can take it to Y.

One of the consequences of this definition is that, in general, **upto** includes **unless** and if all statements are deterministic (i.e., multiple assignments) the definition of **upto** reduces to **unless**.

Theorem 6.8.1. *The* **upto** *is a generalization of* **unless***:*

$$(X \text{ unless } Y) \Rightarrow (X \text{ upto } Y).$$

Furthermore, for a program consisting of only deterministic statements,

$$(X \text{ unless } Y) \equiv (X \text{ upto } Y).$$

Proof.

$$(X \text{ upto } Y)$$
$\Leftarrow$ {definition of **upto**}
$$\langle \forall s :: [X \wedge \neg Y \Rightarrow \mathbf{wp}.s.X \vee \mathbf{wpp}.s.Y] \rangle$$
$\Leftarrow$ {Theorem 6.7.3}
$$\langle \forall s :: [X \wedge \neg Y \Rightarrow \mathbf{wp}.s.(X \vee Y)] \rangle$$
$=$ {definition of **unless**}
$$(X \text{ unless } Y)$$

For a program consisting only of deterministic statements,

$$(X \text{ upto } Y)$$
$\Leftarrow$ {definition **upto**}
$$\langle \forall s :: [X \wedge \neg Y \Rightarrow \mathbf{wp}.s.X \vee \mathbf{wpp}.s.Y] \rangle$$
$=$ {definition of **wpp** for deterministic statements}
$$\langle \forall s :: [X \wedge \neg Y \Rightarrow \mathbf{wp}.s.X \vee \mathbf{wp}.s.Y] \rangle$$
$=$ {**wp**.MA is universally disjunctive}
$$\langle \forall s :: [X \wedge \neg Y \Rightarrow \mathbf{wp}.s.(X \vee Y)] \rangle$$
$=$ {definition of **unless**}
$$(X \text{ unless } Y)$$

In the last steps of both the derivations given above, we have appealed to the definition of **unless** to replace an expression (in terms of **wp**) by an **unless** property. Given that the **unless** was introduced in Section 6.3 by using an inference rule rather than an equivalence, this requires more justification. Intuitively speaking, there are only two ways of inferring **unless** properties: first, by use of the inference rule; and, second, by the use of the substitution axiom (to be introduced in Section 6.10). To avoid inconsistencies in our logic due to the substitution axiom, the presentation of operators like the **unless** has to be by means of an inference rule and not by means of an equivalence. However, it is shown by Misra (Misra [1990]) that, for purposes of proving theorems about the **unless** (such as the one above), it is sufficient to consider only the case where the **unless** was inferred using the inference rule. A more elaborate discussion of this topic is beyond the purview of this book, and we refer the reader to Misra [1990]. □

The relation **upto** is weaker than **unless** and, accordingly, enjoys a smaller set of properties.

1. Reflexivity and Anti-Reflexivity:

$$X \text{ upto } X$$

$$X \text{ upto } \neg X$$

$(X \text{ upto } X)$
$=$ {definition of **upto**}
$\langle \forall s :: [X \wedge \neg X \Rightarrow \text{wp}.s.X \vee \text{wpp}.s.X] \rangle$
$=$ {predicate calculus}
$\langle \forall s :: [false \Rightarrow \text{wp}.s.X \vee \text{wpp}.s.X] \rangle$
$=$ {predicate calculus}
$true$

$(X \text{ upto } \neg X)$
$=$ {definition of **upto**}
$\langle \forall s :: [X \wedge X \Rightarrow \text{wp}.s.X \vee \text{wpp}.s.(\neg X)] \rangle$
$\Leftarrow$ {predicate calculus and Theorem 6.7.3}
$\langle \forall s :: [X \Rightarrow \text{wp}.s.(X \vee \neg X)] \rangle$
$=$ {by Corollary 6.6.1, **wpp**.s is truth preserving}
$\langle \forall s :: [X \Rightarrow true] \rangle$
$=$ {predicate calculus}
$true$

2. Consequence Weakening:

$$\frac{\begin{array}{c} X \text{ upto } Y \\ [Y \Rightarrow Z] \end{array}}{X \text{ upto } Z}$$

$(X \text{ upto } Y) \wedge [Y \Rightarrow Z]$
$=$ {definition of **upto**}
$\langle \forall s :: [X \wedge \neg Y \Rightarrow \text{wp}.s.X \vee \text{wpp}.s.Y] \rangle \wedge [Y \Rightarrow Z]$
$\Rightarrow$ {by Theorem 6.6.3 and Theorem 2.2.1, **wpp**.s is monotonic}

$$\langle \forall s :: [X \wedge \neg Y \Rightarrow \textbf{wp}.s.X \vee \textbf{wpp}.s.Y] \rangle \wedge [\textbf{wpp}.s.Y \Rightarrow \textbf{wpp}.s.Z] \wedge$$
$$[\neg Z \Rightarrow \neg Y]$$

$\Rightarrow \quad$ {transitivity of $\Rightarrow$}

$\qquad \langle \forall s :: [X \wedge \neg Z \Rightarrow \textbf{wp}.s.X \vee \textbf{wpp}.s.Z] \rangle$

$= \quad$ {definition of upto}

$\qquad X$ **upto** Z

3. **Partial Conjunction:**

$$\frac{\begin{array}{c} X \textbf{ upto } Y \\ X' \textbf{ upto } Y' \end{array}}{(X \wedge X') \textbf{ upto } ((X' \wedge Y) \vee Y')} \quad , \text{conjunction}$$

$\qquad (X \textbf{ upto } Y) \wedge (X' \textbf{ upto } Y')$

$= \quad$ {definition of upto}

$\qquad \langle \forall s :: [X \wedge \neg Y \Rightarrow \textbf{wp}.s.X \vee \textbf{wpp}.s.Y] \rangle \wedge$
$\qquad \langle \forall s :: [X' \wedge \neg Y' \Rightarrow \textbf{wp}.s.X' \vee \textbf{wpp}.s.Y'] \rangle$

$\Rightarrow \quad$ {predicate calculus}

$\qquad \langle \forall s :: [X \wedge X' \wedge \neg(Y \vee Y') \Rightarrow$
$\qquad\qquad\qquad (\textbf{wp}.s.X \wedge \textbf{wp}.s.X') \vee (\textbf{wp}.s.X \wedge \textbf{wpp}.s.Y') \vee$
$\qquad\qquad\qquad (\textbf{wp}.s.X' \wedge \textbf{wpp}.s.Y) \vee (\textbf{wpp}.s.Y \wedge \textbf{wpp}.s.Y')] \rangle$

$\Rightarrow \quad$ {Theorem 6.2.3 and Theorem 6.7.2 and weakening}

$\qquad \langle \forall s :: [X \wedge X' \wedge \neg(Y \vee Y') \Rightarrow$
$\qquad\qquad\qquad \textbf{wp}.s.(X \wedge X') \vee \textbf{wpp}.s.(X' \wedge Y) \vee \textbf{wpp}.s.Y'] \rangle$

$= \quad$ {Theorem 6.6.3}

$\qquad \langle \forall s :: [X \wedge X' \wedge \neg(Y \vee Y') \Rightarrow$
$\qquad\qquad\qquad \textbf{wp}.s.(X \wedge X') \vee \textbf{wpp}.s.((X' \wedge Y) \vee Y')] \rangle$

$= \quad$ {predicate calculus}

$\qquad \langle \forall s :: [X \wedge X' \wedge \neg((X' \wedge Y) \vee Y') \Rightarrow$
$\qquad\qquad\qquad \textbf{wp}.s.(X \wedge X') \vee \textbf{wpp}.s.((X' \wedge Y) \vee Y')] \rangle$

$\qquad$ {definition of upto}

$\qquad (X \wedge X') \textbf{ upto } ((X' \wedge Y) \vee Y')$

4. **Simple Conjunction and Simple Disjunction:**

$$\frac{\begin{array}{c} X \textbf{ upto } Y \\ X' \textbf{ upto } Y' \end{array}}{\begin{array}{cc} (X \wedge X') \textbf{ upto } (Y \vee Y') & , \text{simple conjunction} \\ (X \vee X') \textbf{ upto } (Y \vee Y') & , \text{simple disjunction} \end{array}}$$

$\qquad (X \textbf{ upto } Y) \wedge (X' \textbf{ upto } Y')$

$\Rightarrow \quad$ {Conjunction}

$\qquad (X \wedge X') \textbf{ upto } ((X' \wedge Y) \vee Y')$

$\Rightarrow \quad$ {Consequence Weakening}

$\qquad (X \wedge X') \textbf{ upto } (Y \vee Y')$

$(X \text{ upto } Y) \wedge (X' \text{ upto } Y')$

= {definition of **upto**}

$\langle \forall s :: [X \wedge \neg Y \Rightarrow \mathbf{wp}.s.X \vee \mathbf{wpp}.s.Y] \rangle \wedge$
$\qquad\qquad\qquad \langle \forall s :: [X' \wedge \neg Y' \Rightarrow \mathbf{wp}.s.X' \vee \mathbf{wpp}.s.Y'] \rangle$

$\Rightarrow$ {By Theorem 6.2.3 and Theorem 2.2.1 **wp**.s is monotonic;}
{By Theorem 6.6.3 and Theorem 2.2.1 **wpp**.s is monotonic}

$\langle \forall s :: [(X \wedge \neg Y) \vee (X' \wedge \neg Y') \Rightarrow \mathbf{wp}.s.(X \vee X') \vee \mathbf{wpp}.s.(Y \vee Y')] \rangle$

$\Rightarrow$ {predicate calculus}

$\langle \forall s :: [(X \vee X') \wedge \neg(Y \vee Y') \Rightarrow \mathbf{wp}.s.(X \vee X') \vee \mathbf{wpp}.s.(Y \vee Y')] \rangle$

= {definition of **upto**}

$(X \vee X') \text{ upto } (Y \vee Y')$

5. Conjunction with **unless**:

$$\frac{X \text{ unless } Y}{\qquad X' \text{ upto } Y' \qquad}$$
$$\overline{(X \wedge X') \text{ upto } (X \wedge Y') \vee (X' \wedge Y) \vee (Y \wedge Y')}$$

$(X \text{ unless } Y) \wedge (X' \text{ upto } Y')$

= {definition of **unless** and **upto**}

$\langle \forall s :: [X \wedge \neg Y \Rightarrow \mathbf{wp}.s.(X \vee Y)] \rangle \wedge$
$\qquad\qquad\qquad \langle \forall s :: [X' \wedge \neg Y' \Rightarrow \mathbf{wp}.s.X' \vee \mathbf{wpp}.s.Y'] \rangle$

$\Rightarrow$ {predicate calculus}

$\langle \forall s :: [(X \wedge X' \wedge \neg Y \wedge \neg Y') \Rightarrow$
$\qquad\qquad \mathbf{wp}.s.(X \vee Y) \wedge (\mathbf{wp}.s.X' \vee \mathbf{wpp}.s.Y')] \rangle$

$\Rightarrow$ {predicate calculus and Theorem 6.7.2}

$\langle \forall s :: [(X \wedge X' \wedge \neg Y \wedge \neg Y') \Rightarrow$
$\qquad\qquad \mathbf{wp}.s.(X \wedge X') \vee \mathbf{wpp}.s.((X' \wedge Y) \vee (X \wedge Y') \vee (Y \wedge Y'))] \rangle$

= {predicate calculus and definition of **upto**}

$(X \wedge X') \text{ upto } (X \wedge Y') \vee (X' \wedge Y) \vee (Y \wedge Y')$

Many of the properties of **unless** are not inherited by **upto**. In particular, conjunction, disjunction, general conjunction, and general disjunction do not hold for **upto**. Further, the rule of cancellation

$$\frac{X \text{ upto } Y,}{\qquad Y \text{ upto } Z \qquad}$$
$$\overline{(X \vee Y) \text{ upto } Z}$$

does not hold for **upto**. This is not a problem, as **upto** is almost never used for specifications; its utility lies in defining operators for progress. There will be few manipulations involving **upto**.

The following corollaries hold for **upto**. These are all proved using the basic properties listed above. They do not depend on the definition of **upto**.

1. Implication

$$\frac{[X \Rightarrow Y]}{X \text{ upto } Y}$$

0. X **upto** X
  ,Reflexivity
1. $[X \Rightarrow Y]$
  ,Given
2. X **upto** Y
  ,Consequence Weakening using 0 and 1

2.

$$\frac{[\neg X \Rightarrow Y]}{X \text{ upto } Y}$$

0. X **upto** $\neg X$
  ,Anti-Reflexivity
1. $[\neg X \Rightarrow Y]$
  ,Given
2. X **upto** Y
  ,Consequence Weakening using 0 and 1

3.

$$\frac{X \text{ upto } (Y \vee Z)}{(X \wedge \neg Y) \text{ upto } (Y \vee Z)}$$

0. X **upto** $(Y \vee Z)$
  ,Given
1. $\neg Y$ **upto** Y
  ,Anti-Reflexivity
2. $(X \wedge \neg Y)$ **upto** $(Y \vee Z)$
  ,Simple Conjunction on 0 and 1

4.

$$\frac{(X \wedge \neg Y) \text{ upto } (Y \vee Z)}{X \text{ upto } (Y \vee Z)}$$

0. $(X \wedge Y)$ **upto** Y
  ,Implication Theorem above
1. $(X \wedge \neg Y)$ **upto** $(Y \vee Z)$
  ,Given
2. X **upto** $(Y \vee Z)$
  ,Simple Disjunction on 0 and 1

5.

$$\frac{(X \vee Y) \text{ upto } Z}{X \text{ upto } (Y \vee Z)}$$

0. $(X \lor Y)$ **upto** Z
        ,Given
1. $\neg Y$ **upto** Y
        ,Anti-Reflexivity
2. $(X \land \neg Y)$ **upto** $(Y \lor Z)$
        ,Simple Conjunction on 0 and 1
3. X **upto** $(Y \lor Z)$
        ,Corollary 4 given above

6.

$$X \text{ upto } true$$

0. X **upto** X
        ,Reflexivity
1. $[X \Rightarrow true]$
        ,predicate calculus
2. X **upto** $true$
        ,Consequence weakening using 0 and 1

7.

$$true \text{ upto } X$$

0. X **upto** X
        ,Reflexivity
1. $\neg X$ **upto** X
        ,Anti-Reflexivity
2. $true$ **upto** X
        ,Simple Disjunction on 0 and 1

8.

$$false \text{ upto } X$$

0. X **upto** X
        ,Reflexivity
1. $\neg X$ **upto** X
        ,Anti-Reflexivity
2. $false$ **upto** X
        ,Simple Conjunction on 0 and 1

6.8.2 TheRelation entails

We propose a new relation **entails** to generalize **ensures**. Consider the definition of **ensures**.

$$\frac{(X \text{ unless } Y) \land \langle \exists s :: [X \land \neg Y \Rightarrow \mathbf{wp}.s.Y] \rangle}{X \text{ ensures } Y}$$

We use Theorem 6.7.1 to weaken this definition to obtain the definition of **entails**:

$$\frac{(X \text{ upto } Y) \land \langle \exists s :: [X \land \neg Y \Rightarrow \textbf{wpp}.s.Y] \rangle}{X \text{ entails } Y}$$

The intuitive meaning of (X **entails** Y) is that, if X is infinitely often true in a computation, then Y is infinitely often true. The claim that Y is infinitely often true is justified as follows: let an X–state be a state satisfying predicate X. Suppose $X \land \neg Y$ holds at some point in the execution of the program. By the first conjunct, the only way a program can reach a $\neg X$–state is to execute a statement that *may lead to* a Y–state. Note that the second conjunct assures us of the existence of such a statement s that has a mode whose execution in a $(X \land \neg Y)$–state would lead to a Y–state. By *unconditional fairness*, s must be executed, causing the program to transit to a $\neg X$–state. If X is infinitely often true, then each time the transition from an X–state to a $\neg X$–state is made, it is done by executing a statement whose execution could have resulted in a Y–state. From the finiteness of the set of statements, some statement t whose execution could have lead to a Y–state is executed infinitely often from X–states. By *extreme fairness*, every mode of t is executed infinitely often from X–states. In particular, the mode leading to a Y–state is executed infinitely often. It follows that Y is infinitely often true.

The ideas introduced in our computational model, unconditional fairness and extreme fairness, were all intended to justify this definition of the **entails** relation. The relation **entails** plays an important role in the design of probabilistic programs. Besides being the keystone of the proof theory of progress properties, it has a methodological significance as well. In extracting a program from a specification, each **entails** property can usually be translated to a single probabilistic statement. This will be illustrated by an example in a later section.

Theorem 6.8.2. *The* **entails** *generalizes* **ensures***:*

$$(X \textbf{ ensures } Y) \Rightarrow (X \textbf{ entails } Y)$$

Furthermore, for a program consisting only of deterministic statements,

$$(X \textbf{ ensures } Y) \equiv (X \textbf{ entails } Y).$$

Proof.

    (X **entails** Y)
$\Leftarrow$ {definition of **entails**}
    (X **upto** Y) $\land \langle \exists s :: [X \land \neg Y \Rightarrow \textbf{wpp}.s.Y] \rangle$
$\Leftarrow$ {**upto** include **unless**; Theorem 6.8.1}
    (X **unless** Y) $\land \langle \exists s :: [X \land \neg Y \Rightarrow \textbf{wp}.s.Y] \rangle$
$=$ {definition of **ensures**}
    (X **ensures** Y)

For a program consisting only of deterministic statements,

$(X$ entails $Y)$
$\Leftarrow$ {definition of entails}
$(X$ upto $Y) \wedge \langle \exists s :: [X \wedge \neg Y \Rightarrow \mathbf{wpp}.s.Y] \rangle$
$=$ {definition of upto and wp for deterministic statements}
$(X$ unless $Y) \wedge \langle \exists s :: [X \wedge \neg Y \Rightarrow \mathbf{wp}.s.Y] \rangle$
$=$ {definition of ensures}
$(X$ ensures $Y)$

$\square$

Since **entails** is a generalization of **ensures**, it enjoys a smaller set of properties.

1. Reflexivity:

$$X \text{ entails } X$$

X entails X
$=$ {definition of entails}
$(X$ upto $X) \wedge \langle \exists s :: [X \wedge \neg X \Rightarrow \mathbf{wpp}.s.X] \rangle$
$\Leftarrow$ {Reflexivity of upto and predicate calculus}
$\langle \exists s :: [false \Rightarrow \mathbf{wpp}.s.X] \rangle$
$=$ {predicate calculus}
$true$

2. Consequence Weakening:

$$\frac{X \text{ entails } Y, \; [Y \Rightarrow Z]}{X \text{ entails } Z}$$

$(X$ entails $Y) \wedge [Y \Rightarrow Z]$
$=$ {definition of entails}
$(X$ upto $Y) \wedge \langle \exists s :: [X \wedge \neg Y \Rightarrow \mathbf{wpp}.s.Y] \rangle \wedge [Y \Rightarrow Z]$
$\Rightarrow$ {Consequence Weakening for upto; Monotonicity of wpp.s}
$(X$ upto $Z) \wedge \langle \exists s :: [X \wedge \neg Z \Rightarrow \mathbf{wpp}.s.Y] \rangle \wedge [\mathbf{wpp}.s.Y \Rightarrow \mathbf{wpp}.s.Z]$
$\Rightarrow$ {transitivity of implication}
$(X$ upto $Z) \wedge \langle \exists s :: [X \wedge \neg Z \Rightarrow \mathbf{wpp}.s.Z] \rangle$
$=$ {definition of entails}
$(X$ entails $Z)$

3. Impossibility:

$$\frac{X \text{ entails } false}{[\neg X]}$$

$(X$ entails $false)$
$=$ {definition of entails}
$(X$ upto $false) \wedge \langle \exists s :: [X \wedge \neg false \Rightarrow \mathbf{wpp}.s.false] \rangle$
$\Rightarrow$ {Corollary 6.6.2}
$\langle \exists s :: [X \Rightarrow false] \rangle$
$=$ {predicate calculus}
$[\neg X]$

4. Conjunction with **unless**:

$$\frac{\begin{array}{c} X \text{ entails } Y \\ X' \text{ unless } Y' \end{array}}{(X \wedge X') \text{ entails } (X \wedge Y') \vee (X' \wedge Y) \vee (Y \wedge Y')}$$

$\quad\quad (X \text{ entails } Y) \wedge (X' \text{ unless } Y')$

$= \quad \{\text{definition of } \textbf{entails}\}$

$\quad\quad (X \textbf{ upto } Y) \wedge \langle \exists s :: [X \wedge \neg Y \Rightarrow \textbf{wpp} .s.Y]\rangle \wedge (X' \textbf{ unless } Y')$

$\Rightarrow \quad \{\text{conjunction with } \textbf{unless} \text{ for } \textbf{upto}; \text{ definition of } \textbf{upto}\}$

$\quad\quad ((X \wedge X') \textbf{ upto } (X \wedge Y') \vee (X' \wedge Y) \vee (Y \wedge Y')) \wedge$

$\quad\quad \langle \exists s :: [(X \wedge X' \wedge \neg Y \wedge \neg Y') \Rightarrow (\textbf{wpp} .s.Y \wedge \textbf{wp} .s.(X' \vee Y'))]\rangle$

$\Rightarrow \quad \{\text{Theorem 6.7.2}\}$

$\quad\quad ((X \wedge X') \textbf{ upto } (X \wedge Y') \vee (X' \wedge Y) \vee (Y \wedge Y')) \wedge$

$\quad\quad \langle \exists s :: [(X \wedge X' \wedge \neg Y \wedge \neg Y') \Rightarrow \textbf{wpp} .s.((X' \wedge Y) \vee (Y' \wedge Y))]\rangle$

$\Rightarrow \quad \{\text{Weakening the consequence of the second conjunct}\}$

$\quad\quad ((X \wedge X') \textbf{ upto } (X \wedge Y') \vee (X' \wedge Y) \vee (Y \wedge Y')) \wedge$

$\quad\quad \langle \exists s :: [(X \wedge X' \wedge \neg Y \wedge \neg Y') \Rightarrow$

$\quad\quad\quad\quad\quad\quad \textbf{wpp} .s.((X' \wedge Y) \vee (Y' \wedge Y) \vee (X \wedge Y'))]\rangle$

$= \quad \{\text{definition of } \textbf{entails}\}$

$\quad\quad ((X \wedge X') \text{ entails } (X \wedge Y') \vee (X' \wedge Y) \vee (Y \wedge Y'))$

5. Conjunction with **upto**:

$$\frac{\begin{array}{c} X \text{ entails } Y \\ X' \text{ upto } Y' \end{array}}{(X \wedge X') \text{ entails } (X' \wedge Y) \vee Y'}$$

$\quad\quad (X \text{ entails } Y) \wedge (X' \textbf{ upto } Y')$

$= \quad \{\text{definition of } \textbf{entails} \text{ and } \textbf{upto}\}$

$\quad\quad (X \textbf{ upto } Y) \wedge (X' \textbf{ upto } Y') \wedge \langle \exists s :: [X \wedge \neg Y \Rightarrow \textbf{wpp} .s.Y]\rangle$

$= \quad \{\text{conjunction for } \textbf{upto}; \text{ definition of } \textbf{upto}\}$

$\quad\quad ((X \wedge X') \textbf{ upto } ((X' \wedge Y) \vee Y)) \wedge$

$\quad\quad \langle \exists s :: [X \wedge X' \wedge \neg Y \wedge \neg Y' \Rightarrow (\textbf{wp} .s.X' \vee \textbf{wpp} .s.Y') \wedge \textbf{wpp} .s.Y]\rangle$

$= \quad \{\text{predicate calculus}\}$

$\quad\quad ((X \wedge X') \textbf{ upto } ((X' \wedge Y) \vee Y)) \wedge$

$\quad\quad \langle \exists s :: [X \wedge X' \wedge \neg Y \wedge \neg Y' \Rightarrow$

$\quad\quad\quad\quad\quad\quad (\textbf{wp} .s.X' \wedge \textbf{wpp} .s.Y) \vee (\textbf{wpp} .s.Y' \wedge \textbf{wpp} .s.Y)]\rangle$

$\Rightarrow \quad \{\text{weaken consequence of second conjunct using Theorem 6.7.2}\}$

$\quad\quad ((X \wedge X') \textbf{ upto } ((X' \wedge Y) \vee Y)) \wedge$

$\quad\quad \langle \exists s :: [X \wedge X' \wedge \neg Y \wedge \neg Y' \Rightarrow (\textbf{wpp} .s.(X' \wedge Y) \vee \textbf{wpp} .s.Y')]\rangle$

$= \quad \{\text{universal disjunctivity of } \textbf{wpp} .s\}$

$\quad\quad ((X \wedge X') \textbf{ upto } ((X' \wedge Y) \vee Y)) \wedge$

$\quad\quad \langle \exists s :: [X \wedge X' \wedge \neg Y \wedge \neg Y' \Rightarrow \textbf{wpp} .s.((X' \wedge Y) \vee Y')]\rangle$

$= \quad \{\text{definition of } \textbf{entails}\}$

$\quad\quad ((X \wedge X') \textbf{ upto } ((X' \wedge Y) \vee Y))$

6. Disjunction:

$$\frac{X \text{ entails } Y}{(X \vee Z) \text{ entails } (Y \vee Z)}$$

X entails Y
$=$ {definition of entails}
       $(X \text{ upto } Y) \wedge \langle \exists s :: [X \wedge \neg Y \Rightarrow \text{wpp}.s.Y] \rangle$
$=$ {reflexivity of upto}
       $(X \text{ upto } Y) \wedge (Z \text{ upto } Z) \wedge \langle \exists s :: [X \wedge \neg Y \Rightarrow \text{wpp}.s.Y] \rangle$
$\Rightarrow$ {simple disjunction for upto}
       $(X \vee Z) \text{ upto } (Y \vee Z) \wedge \langle \exists s :: [X \wedge \neg Y \Rightarrow \text{wpp}.s.Y] \rangle$
$\Rightarrow$ {predicate calculus; monotonicity of wpp.s}
       $((X \vee Z) \text{ upto } (Y \vee Z)) \wedge \langle \exists s :: [(X \vee Z) \wedge \neg(Y \vee Z) \Rightarrow$
       $\quad \text{wpp}.s.(Y \vee Z)] \rangle$
$=$ {definition of entails}
       $(X \vee Z) \text{ entails } (Y \vee Z)$

Of all the properties of **ensures**, the conjunction rule does not hold for **entails**. The following corollaries hold for **entails**. They follow from the basic properties listed above. They do not depend on the definition of **entails**.

1. Implication

$$\frac{[X \Rightarrow Y]}{X \text{ entails } Y}$$

0. X entails X
           ,Reflexivity of **entails**
1. $[X \Rightarrow Y]$
           ,Given
2. X entails Y
           ,Consequence Weakening on 0 and 1

2.

$$\frac{X \text{ entails } (Y \vee Z)}{(X \wedge \neg Y) \text{ entails } (Y \vee Z)}$$

0. X entails $(Y \vee Z)$
           ,Given
1. $\neg Y \text{ upto } Y$
           ,Anti-Reflexivity of **upto**
2. $(X \wedge \neg Y) \text{ entails } ((\neg Y \wedge Z) \vee Y)$
           ,Conjunction with **upto** for **entails** using 0 and 1
3. $(X \wedge \neg Y) \text{ entails } (Y \vee Z)$
           ,predicate calculus on 2

3.

$$\frac{(X \vee Y) \text{ entails } Z}{X \text{ entails } (Y \vee Z)}$$

0. $(X \lor Y)$ **entails** Z
        ,Given
1. $\neg Y$ **upto** Y
        ,Anti-Reflexivity of **upto**
2. $(X \land \neg Y)$ **entails** $((\neg Y \land Z) \lor Y)$
        ,Conjunction with **upto** for **entails** using 0 and 1
3. X **entails** $(Y \lor Z)$
        ,Disjunction on 3 using $Z := X \land Y$ and predicate calculus

6.8.3 TheRelation $\rightsquigarrow$

The relation **entails** is tied closely to the program. We abstract from this by defining the relation $\rightsquigarrow$ (read, *prompts*) to be the reflexive, transitive closure of **entails** and $\longmapsto$.

1. Base case:
$$\frac{(X \text{ entails } Y)}{(X \rightsquigarrow Y)}$$

2. Leads–to:
$$\frac{X \longmapsto Y}{X \rightsquigarrow Y}$$

3. Transitivity:
$$\frac{X \rightsquigarrow Y, \ Y \rightsquigarrow Z}{X \rightsquigarrow Z}$$

The definition of $\rightsquigarrow$ satisfies the following properties. The proofs of these properties require induction on the definition of $\rightsquigarrow$ given above.

1. Implication:
$$\frac{[X \Rightarrow Y]}{X \rightsquigarrow Y}$$

0. $[X \Rightarrow Y]$
        ,Given
1. X **entails** Y
        ,Corollary 1 of **entails**
2. $X \rightsquigarrow Y$
        ,definition of $\rightsquigarrow$

2. Impossibility:
$$\frac{X \rightsquigarrow false}{[\neg X]}$$

The proof is by induction on the definition of $\rightsquigarrow$. The base cases are proved by the impossibility properties of **entails** and $\longmapsto$. The induction step is proved by

0. $(X \rightsquigarrow Y) \wedge (Y \rightsquigarrow false)$
    ,Given
1. $(X \rightsquigarrow Y) \wedge [\neg Y]$
    ,Induction hypothesis
2. $(X \rightsquigarrow false)$
    ,From 1
3. $[\neg X]$
    ,Induction hypothesis

3. Disjunction:
$$\frac{(X \rightsquigarrow Y)}{(X \vee Z) \rightsquigarrow (Y \vee Z)}$$

The proof is by induction on $\rightsquigarrow$. The base cases follow from the disjunction properties of **entails** and $\longmapsto$. The induction step is as follows.

0. $(X \rightsquigarrow U) \wedge (U \rightsquigarrow Y)$
    ,Given
1. $(X \vee W \rightsquigarrow U \vee W) \wedge (U \vee W \rightsquigarrow Y \vee W)$
    ,Induction hypothesis, twice
2. $(X \vee W \rightsquigarrow Y \vee W)$
    ,Transitivity of $\rightsquigarrow$

4. Finite Disjunction:
$$\frac{(X \rightsquigarrow Z), (Y \rightsquigarrow Z)}{(X \vee Y) \rightsquigarrow Z}$$

0. $(X \rightsquigarrow Z) \wedge (Y \rightsquigarrow Z)$
    ,Given
1. $(X \vee Y \rightsquigarrow Z \vee Y) \wedge (Y \vee Z \rightsquigarrow Z \vee Z)$
    ,Disjunction, twice
2. $(X \vee Y \rightsquigarrow Z)$
    ,Transitivity of $\rightsquigarrow$

5. Cancellation:
$$\frac{U \rightsquigarrow V \vee W, \ W \rightsquigarrow X}{U \rightsquigarrow V \vee X}$$

0. $(U \rightsquigarrow V \vee W) \wedge (W \rightsquigarrow X)$
    ,Given
1. $(U \rightsquigarrow V \vee W) \wedge (V \vee W \rightsquigarrow V \vee X)$
    ,Disjunction on second property of 0
2. $(U \rightsquigarrow V \vee X)$
    ,Transitivity of $\rightsquigarrow$

6. PSP (Progress-Safety-Progress):

$$\frac{X \rightsquigarrow Y, \ U \ \textbf{unless} \ V}{(X \wedge U) \rightsquigarrow (Y \wedge U) \vee V}$$

The proof is by induction on the definition of $\leadsto$. The base cases follow from the conjunction with **unless** rule of **entails** and $\mapsto$ and consequence weakening. The induction step is as follows.

0. $(X \leadsto Z) \wedge (Z \leadsto Y) \wedge (U \text{ unless } V)$
   ,Given
1. $((X \wedge U) \leadsto (U \wedge Z) \vee V) \wedge$
   $((Z \wedge U) \leadsto (U \wedge Y) \vee V)$
   ,Applying induction hypothesis twice
2. $(X \wedge U) \leadsto (Y \wedge U) \vee V$
   ,Cancellation on 1

7. Completion Theorem (Proof Omitted):
   For any finite set of predicates, $X.i, Y.i, 0 \leq i < N$:

$$\frac{\langle \forall i :: X.i \leadsto Y.i \vee Z \rangle \quad \langle \forall i :: Y.i \text{ unless } Z \rangle}{\langle \wedge i :: X.i \rangle \leadsto \langle \wedge i :: Y.i \rangle \vee Z}$$

6.8.4 Probabilistically Leads–to: $\Longmapsto$

In this chapter, we shall express all probabilistic progress properties using the relation $\Longmapsto$ (read, *probabilistically leads–to*). A program has the property $X \mid \Longmapsto Y$ if, once X becomes true, Y will become true with probability 1. The $\Longmapsto$ is defined to be the strongest relation satisfying the following three axioms:

1. Base case:

$$\frac{X \text{ unless } Y, \ X \leadsto Y}{X \Longmapsto Y}$$

2. Transitivity:

$$\frac{X \Longmapsto Y, \ Y \Longmapsto Z}{X \Longmapsto Z}$$

3. Disjunctivity: For an arbitrary set W,

$$\frac{\langle \forall X : X \in W : X \Longmapsto Z \rangle}{\langle \exists X : X \in W : X \rangle \Longmapsto Z}$$

According to the first axiom, if X is true at any point in the execution of a program, by X **unless** Y it remains true indefinitely or until Y becomes true. In the former case, X is infinitely often true, and by $X \leadsto Y$, Y is infinitely often true. In either case, Y becomes true. The second axiom ensures that $\Longmapsto$ is transitively closed, and the third axiom ensures that $\Longmapsto$ is disjunctively closed.

Probabilistically leads–to is a generalization of the UNITY leads–to. That is:

Theorem 6.8.3. $(X \mapsto Y) \Rightarrow (X \Longmapsto Y)$.

Proof. The proof is by an induction on the definition of $\mapsto$.

1. Base case:

$$(X \text{ ensures } Y)$$
$\Rightarrow$ {definition of **ensures**}
$$(X \text{ unless } Y) \wedge (X \text{ entails } Y)$$
$\Rightarrow$ {definition of $\Longmapsto$}
$$(X \Longmapsto Y)$$

2. Induction step (transitivity):

$$(X \mapsto Y) \wedge (Y \mapsto Z)$$
$\Rightarrow$ {Induction hypothesis, twice}
$$(X \Longmapsto Y) \wedge (Y \Longmapsto Z)$$
$\Rightarrow$ {Transitivity of $\Longmapsto$}
$$(X \Longmapsto Z)$$

3. Induction step (disjunction):

$$\langle \forall X :: X \mapsto Y \rangle$$
$\Rightarrow$ {Induction hypothesis}
$$\langle \forall X :: X \Longmapsto Y \rangle$$
$\Rightarrow$ {Disjunctivity of $\Longmapsto$}
$$(\langle \exists X :: X \rangle \Longmapsto Z)$$

$\square$

The probabilistically leads-to ($\Longmapsto$) enjoys all the properties of $\mapsto$. The proofs of these properties require induction on the definition of $\mapsto$ given above.

1. Implication:

$$\frac{[X \Rightarrow Y]}{X \Longmapsto Y}$$

   0. $[X \Rightarrow Y]$
         ,Given
   1. $X \mapsto Y$
         ,Property of $\mapsto$
   2. $X \Longmapsto Y$
         ,1 and Theorem 6.8.3

2. Impossibility:

$$\frac{X \Longmapsto \text{false}}{[\neg X]}$$

The proof is by induction on the definition of $\Longmapsto$.

Base Case:

0. $(X$ **unless** $false) \wedge (X$ **entails** $false)$
    ,Given
1. $[\neg X]$
    ,Impossibility property of **entails**

Induction Step (transitivity):

0. $(X \Longmapsto Y) \wedge (Y \Longmapsto false)$
    ,Given
1. $(X \Longmapsto Y) \wedge [\neg Y]$
    ,Induction hypothesis
2. $(X \Longmapsto false)$
    ,From 1
3. $[\neg X]$
    ,Induction hypothesis

Induction Step (disjunctivity):

0. $\langle \forall X :: X \Longmapsto false \rangle$
    ,Given
1. $[\langle \forall X :: \neg X \rangle]$
    ,Induction hypothesis
2. $[\neg \langle \exists X :: X \rangle]$
    ,predicate calculus

3. General Disjunction:

$$\frac{\langle \forall m : m \in W : X.m \Longmapsto Y.m \rangle}{\langle \exists m : m \in W : X.m \rangle \Longmapsto \langle \exists m : m \in W : Y.m \rangle}$$

0. $[Y.m \Rightarrow \langle \exists m :: Y.m \rangle]$
    ,predicate calculus
1. $\langle \forall m :: X.m \Longmapsto Y.m \rangle$
    ,Given
2. $\langle \forall m :: X.m \Longmapsto \langle \exists m :: Y.m \rangle \rangle$
    ,0, Implication and transitivity of $\Longmapsto$
3. $\langle \exists m :: X.m \rangle \Longmapsto \langle \exists m :: Y.m \rangle \rangle$
    ,disjunctivity of $\Longmapsto$

4. Cancellation:

$$\frac{U \Longmapsto V \vee W, \ W \Longmapsto X}{U \Longmapsto V \vee X}$$

0. $(U \Longmapsto V \vee W) \wedge (W \Longmapsto X)$
    ,Given
1. $(U \Longmapsto V \vee W) \wedge (V \vee W \Longmapsto V \vee X)$
    ,Disjunction on second conjunct of 0
2. $(U \Longmapsto V \vee X)$
    ,Transitivity of $\Longmapsto$

5. PSP (Progress-Safety-Progress):

$$\frac{X \Longmapsto Y, \; U \textbf{ unless } V}{(X \wedge U) \Longmapsto (Y \wedge U) \vee V}$$

The proof is by induction on the definition of $\Longmapsto$.
Base case:

0. $(X \textbf{ unless } Y) \wedge (X \textbf{ entails } Y) \wedge (U \textbf{ unless } V)$
   ,Given
1. $(X \wedge U \textbf{ unless } (Y \wedge U) \vee V) \wedge ((X \wedge U) \textbf{ entails } (Y \wedge U) \vee V)$
   ,Conjunction of the two **unless** properties;
   ,Conjunction with **unless** for enta:ls
2. $(X \wedge U \Longmapsto (Y \wedge U) \vee V)$
   ,definition of $\Longmapsto$

Induction Step (transitivity):

0. $(X \Longmapsto Y) \wedge (Y \Longmapsto Z) \wedge (U \textbf{ unless } V)$
   ,Given
1. $((X \wedge U) \Longmapsto (Y \wedge U) \vee V) \wedge ((Y \wedge U) \Longmapsto (Z \wedge U) \vee V)$
   ,Induction hypothesis, twice
2. $((X \wedge U) \Longmapsto (Z \wedge U) \vee V)$
   ,Cancellation

Induction Step (disjunctivity):

0. $\langle \forall X :: X \Longmapsto Y \rangle \wedge (U \textbf{ unless } V)$
   ,Given
1. $\langle \forall X :: (X \wedge U) \Longmapsto (Y \wedge U) \vee V \rangle$
   ,Induction hypothesis
2. $\langle \exists X :: X \wedge U \rangle \Longmapsto (Y \wedge U) \vee V$
   ,Disjunctivity of $\Longmapsto$
3. $\langle \exists X :: X \rangle \wedge U \Longmapsto (Y \wedge U) \vee V$
   ,predicate calculus

6. Completion Theorem (Proof Omitted):
   For any finite set of predicates, $X.i, Y.i, 0 \leq i < N$:

$$\frac{\langle \forall i :: X.i \Longmapsto Y.i \vee Z \rangle}{\langle \forall i :: Y.i \textbf{ unless } Z \rangle}{\langle \wedge i :: X.i \rangle \Longmapsto \langle \wedge i :: Y.i \rangle \vee Z}$$

6.9 An Induction Principle for Probabilistic Leads-to

An interesting property of $\Longmapsto$ is its transitivity, and one can use this to formulate a principle of induction over well-founded sets. Let $(W, \prec)$ be a well-founded set, and let M be a metric[5] mapping the states of the program to W. Then the

---

[5] Traditionally, in program verification, the term *metric* has been used to describe functions that are used to prove the termination of programs. Such a function is not a metric in the topologoical sense of the word.

induction principle states the following:

$$\frac{\langle \forall m : m \in W : X \wedge (M = m) \Longmapsto (X \wedge M \prec m) \vee Y \rangle}{X \Longmapsto Y}$$

Intuitively, the hypothesis of the induction principle states that, from any program state in which X holds, execution of the program leads to a state in which either Y is true or the value of the metric is decreased. Since the range of the metric is a well-founded set, the metric cannot decrease indefinitely. It follows that a state satisfying Y is attained. The theorem can be formally proved by appealing to the definition of $\Longmapsto$.

6.10 Substitution Axiom

The substitution axiom has been introduced in UNITY as a generalization of Leibniz's principle of substitution of equals for equals. Informally, the substitution axiom states that if $x = y$ then x can be substituted for y in all program properties. Of particular importance is the case where a program invariant I can be substituted for *true* and vice versa. This is because $[I \equiv true]$.

The importance of the substitution axiom is twofold: First, it is necessary for the completeness of our proof system, and second, it allows us to abbreviate cumbersome notation.

6.11 On Program Composition

We use the same notions of program composition as in UNITY, namely, *union* and *superposition*.

6.11.1 Composition by Union

The *union* of two programs is defined if the component programs do not have any inconsistenices in the declarations and initializations of their variables. It is obtained by merging the declaration and initialization sections of the component programs, and by taking the union of the sets of statements in the **assign** sections of the two programs. The union of programs F and G is written as $F \parallel G$. Like set union, it is a symmetric and associative operator.

The study of program composition by union is facilitated by the union theorem. An important condition on all cases of the theorem is that any application of the substitution axiom in the proof of a property of either the component or the composite program can only use an invariant of the *composite* program.

Theorem 6.11.1 (Union Theorem for unless). *For state predicates X and Y and programs F and G,*

$$(X \text{ unless } Y \text{ in } F \ \wedge \ X \text{ unless } Y \text{ in } G) \ \equiv \ (X \text{ unless } Y \text{ in } F \parallel G).$$

Proof. The proof is exactly as in Chandy and Misra [1988].   □

Theorem 6.11.2 (Union Theorem for ensures). *For state predicates X and Y and programs F and G,*

$(X \text{ ensures } Y \text{ in } F \ \lor \ X \text{ ensures } Y \text{ in } G) \land (X \text{ unless } Y \text{ in } F \,[\!] \, G)$

Proof. The proof is exactly as in Chandy and Misra [1988].   □

Theorem 6.11.3 (Union Theorem for upto). *For state predicates X and Y and programs F and G,*

$$(X \text{ upto } Y \text{ in } F \land X \text{ upto } Y \text{ in } G) \ \equiv \ (X \text{ upto } Y \text{ in } F \,[\!] \, G).$$

Proof.

$\quad (X \text{ upto } Y \text{ in } F \land X \text{ upto } Y \text{ in } G)$
$= \ \{\text{definition of } \textbf{upto} \text{ twice}\}$
$\quad \langle \forall s : s \text{ in } F : [X \land \neg Y \Rightarrow \textbf{wp}.s.X \lor \textbf{wpp}.s.Y]\rangle \land$
$\quad \langle \forall s : s \text{ in } G : [X \land \neg Y \Rightarrow \textbf{wp}.s.X \lor \textbf{wpp}.s.Y]\rangle$
$= \ \{\text{predicate calculus}\}$
$\quad \langle \forall s : s \text{ in } F \lor s \text{ in } G : [X \land \neg Y \Rightarrow \textbf{wp}.s.X \lor \textbf{wpp}.s.Y]\rangle$
$= \ \{\text{definition of } [\!]\}$
$\quad \langle \forall s : s \text{ in } F \,[\!] \, G : [X \land \neg Y \Rightarrow \textbf{wp}.s.X \lor \textbf{wpp}.s.Y]\rangle$
$= \ \{\text{definition of } \textbf{upto}\}$
$\quad X \text{ upto } Y \text{ in } F \,[\!] \, G$

□

Theorem 6.11.4 (Union Theorem for entails). *For state predicates X and Y and programs F and G,*

$$(X \text{ entails } Y \text{ in } F \ \lor \ X \text{ entails } Y \text{ in } G) \land (X \text{ upto } Y \text{ in } F \,[\!] \, G)$$

$$\equiv \ (X \text{ entails } Y \text{ in } F \,[\!] \, G).$$

Proof.

$\quad X \text{ entails } Y \text{ in } F \,[\!] \, G$
$= \ \{\text{definition of } \textbf{entails}\}$
$\quad (X \text{ upto } Y \text{ in } F \,[\!] \, G) \land \langle \exists s : s \text{ in } F \,[\!] \, G : [X \land \neg Y \Rightarrow \textbf{wpp}.s.Y]\rangle$
$= \ \{\text{Union theorem for } \textbf{upto}\}$
$\quad (X \text{ upto } Y \text{ in } F) \land (X \text{ upto } Y \text{ in } G) \land$
$\quad\quad\quad \langle \exists s : s \text{ in } F \,[\!] \, G : [X \land \neg Y \Rightarrow \textbf{wpp}.s.Y]\rangle$
$= \ \{\text{predicate calculus}\}$
$\quad (X \text{ upto } Y \text{ in } F) \land (X \text{ upto } Y \text{ in } G) \land$
$\quad ((\exists s : s \text{ in } F : [X \land \neg Y \Rightarrow \textbf{wpp}.s.Y]) \lor$
$\quad\quad\quad\quad \langle \exists s : s \text{ in } G : [X \land \neg Y \Rightarrow \textbf{wpp}.s.Y]\rangle)$
$= \ \{\text{predicate calculus and definition of } \textbf{entails}\}$

$(X$ entails Y in $F \wedge X$ upto Y in $G) \vee$
$\qquad (X$ upto Y in $F \wedge X$ entails Y in $G)$

$\square$

Theorem 6.11.5 (Union Theorem for unless and entails). *For state predicates X and Y and programs F and G,*

$(X$ entails Y in $F \wedge X$ unless Y in $G) \vee (X$ unless Y in $F \wedge X$ entails Y in $G)$

$$\Rightarrow (X \text{ entails } Y \text{ in } F \parallel G)$$

Proof. The proof follows from the union theorem for **entails** and **upto** by strengthening the left side using Theorem 6.8.1. $\square$

The following corollaries follow from the union theorem:

1.

$$X \text{ stable in } F \parallel G \equiv (X \text{ stable in } F \wedge X \text{ stable in } G).$$

2.

$$\frac{X \text{ unless } Y \text{ in } F, \ X \text{ stable in } G}{X \text{ unless } Y \text{ in } F \parallel G}$$

3.

$$\frac{X \text{ invariant \ in } F, \ X \text{ stable in } G}{X \text{ invariant \ in } F \parallel G}$$

4.

$$\frac{X \text{ ensures } Y \text{ in } F, \ X \text{ stable in } G}{X \text{ ensures } Y \text{ in } F \parallel G}$$

5.

$$\frac{X \text{ upto } Y \text{ in } F, \ X \text{ stable in } G}{X \text{ upto } Y \text{ in } F \parallel G}$$

6.

$$\frac{X \text{ entails } Y \text{ in } F, \ X \text{ stable in } G}{X \text{ entails } Y \text{ in } F \parallel G}$$

6.11.2 Conditional Properties

The union theorem illustrates that basic progress properties compose; that is, the property holds for the composite program if its holds for the components. This is not the case with $\rightsquigarrow$, $\mapsto$, and $\Longmapsto$.

To address this shortcoming, we resort to *conditional* properties, as in UNITY. All program properties seen thus far have been expressed using one or more relations: **unless**, **ensures**, **upto**, and **entails**; these properties are called *unconditional* properties. A conditional property has two parts — *a hypothesis* and *a conclusion*, each of which is a set of unconditional properties. Both the hypothesis and the conclusion can be properties of the F, G, or $F \parallel G$, where G is a generic program. The meaning of a conditional property is as follows: Given the hypothesis as a premise, the conclusion can be proved from the text or specification of F. Thus, in proving properties, a conditional property is used as an inference rule. The interested reader is referred to Chandy and Misra [1988] for further elucidation.

6.11.3 Superposition

The second structuring operator that we employ in our proofs is the *superposition* operator. This is exactly the same operator as in UNITY. We recapitulate the salient details.

Unlike program union, program superposition is an *asymmetric* operator. Given an *underlying program* (whose variables will be called *underlying variables*), superposition allows it to be transformed by the application of the following two rules.

1. Augmentation rule: A statement s in the underlying program may be transformed to the statement $s\|r$, where r is a statement that does not assign to the underlying variables, and is executed *in synchrony* with s.
2. Restricted union rule: A statement r may be added to the underlying program, provided that r does not assign to the underlying variables.

By adhering to the discipline of superposition, it is ensured that every property of the underlying program is a property of the transformed program. This is also called the superposition theorem.

6.12 Comments on Soundness and Completeness

In Pnueli [1983], Amir Pnueli presented a theorem that shows that every property that holds for all extremely fair executions holds with probability 1 for the program. In our computational model, all executions are extremely fair. Any property that we prove in our computational model holds for all such executions and, thus, holds with probability 1.

In this section, we informally argue that our logic is complete for finite–state programs. By the results of Hart et al. [1983], if a progress property holds with probability 1 for a finite–state program, it induces a decomposition on the (finite) set of states that can be visited before the goal states are reached. Each partition of this decomposition satisfies certain conditions. These conditions guarantee that in any unconditionally fair and extremely fair computation the property is attained. This shows that our model is sound and complete for proving properties that hold with probability 1 of finite–state programs.

Let Σ be the set of states of the program. Let s be an initial state, and let $X (X \subset \Sigma)$ be the set of final states of the program, with $s \notin X$. Define $\hat{I}$ as the set of all states that can be reached (with a nonzero probability) from s before a state in X is reached, using any finite sequence of processes. $\hat{I}$ includes s and is disjoint from X. Furthermore, let K be the set of processes of the program, and let $P_{i,j}^k$ be the probability of process k taking the system from state i to any state in set J. One of the main results of Hart et al. [1983] is that by assuming s, X, Σ, and $\hat{I}$ as above and by assuming $\hat{I}$ is *finite*, the following two conditions are equivalent:

1. $\models s \Longrightarrow X$
2. There exists a decomposition of $\hat{I}$ into disjoint sets $I_1, I_2, \ldots, I_n$ such that, if we put $J_m = \cup_{r=0}^m I_r$, $m = 0, 1, \ldots, n$, with $I_0 = X$, then for each $m = 1, 2, \ldots, n$ we have the following:
   - For each $i \in I_m$, $k \in K$, if $P_{i,J_{m-1}}^k = 0$, then $P_{i,I_m}^k = 1$.
   - There exists $k \equiv k(m) \in K$ such that, for each $i \in I_m$, $P_{i,J_{m-1}}^k > 0$.

The first part of the second condition says that, if process k can transfer the system from a state in I_m to a state outside I_m, then some k–transitions (with nonzero probability) move the system "down" the chain $\{I_r\}$, toward the goal I_0; the second part of the second condition ensures the existence of at least one process that would do this for all states in I_m.

Thus, given that some progress property holds in a model with probability 1, we are guaranteed that the chain $\{I_r\}$ exists. Clearly, $\hat{I}$ **unless** I_0 holds by the definition of $\hat{I}$ and **unless**. For each element of the chain, we can show that I_r entails J_{r-1}. By using transitivity of $\leadsto$, we can show that, $I_r \leadsto I_0$. Using the finite disjunction property of $\leadsto$, we can conclude that $\hat{I} \leadsto I_0$. The proof follows from the **unless** property, the $\leadsto$ property, and the definition of $\Longrightarrow$.

6.13 Examples

Note that in all examples, if a common boolean guard applies to all of the modes of a probabilistic assignment, it has been pulled out and written once. This has been done in the interest of brevity.

Example 6.13.1. (An unintuitive example).

To show how unintuitive, reasoning about probabilistic algorithms can be, consider the following program:

```
declare      x, y : (heads, tails)
assign       x := heads | tails
       ‖  y := heads | tails
end
```

It can be shown that the property

$$true \implies (x = heads) \wedge (y = heads)$$

does not hold for the given program. This is because it is possible for the execution of the program to be unconditionally fair with respect to the selection of the coin to be tossed and to be extremely fair in the tossing of the coins, without reaching a state in which both coins turn up *heads*. Abbreviating *heads* by H and *tails* by T, consider the following segment σ of state transformations (the state is denoted by the ordered pair giving the values of x and y):

$$(H,T) \xrightarrow{x:=heads} (H,T) \xrightarrow{x:=tails} (T,T) \xrightarrow{y:=tails} (T,T) \xrightarrow{y:=heads} (T,H) \xrightarrow{y:=heads}$$

$$(T,H) \xrightarrow{y:=tails} (T,T) \xrightarrow{x:=tails} (T,T) \xrightarrow{x:=heads} (H,T).$$

The sequence σ iterated indefinitely gives an execution sequence which is *unconditionally fair* and *extremely fair*. One way of ensuring that a state satisfying $[(x = heads) \wedge (y = heads)]$ is reached is to use extreme fairness in the scheduling of the statements, rather than unconditional fairness, as illustrated by the program below. This also illustrates the power of extreme fairness over unconditional fairness:

```
declare      x, y : (H, T)
assign       x, y := H, H | H, T | T, H | T, T
end
```

Example 6.13.2. (from Pnueli [1983]).

Consider the UNITY program:

```
declare      b : integer
initially    b = 0
assign       b := b + 1  if  (b mod 3) ≤ 1
       ‖  b := b + 2  if  (b mod 3) ≤ 1
end
```

For this program, it is not the case that

$$true \mapsto (b \, mod \, 3 = 2).$$

We have already shown that this program does not satisfy the property

$$true \mapsto (b \, mod \, 3 = 2).$$

Now consider the probabilistic program:

```
declare     b : integer
initially   b = 0
assign      b := b + 1 | b + 2  if  (b mod 3) ≤ 1
end
```

We show that the required property is achieved with probability 1, that is,

$$true \Longmapsto (b \bmod 3 = 2).$$

By applying the definition of **wpp** .s, it can be shown that **wpp** .s.$((b \bmod 3) = 2)$ evaluates to true. Thus:

$\langle \exists s :: [true \land \neg(b \bmod 3 = 2) \Rightarrow \textbf{wpp} .s.((b \bmod 3) = 2)] \rangle$
= {predicate calculus}
$[\neg(b \bmod 3 = 2) \Rightarrow true]$
= {predicate calculus}
$true$

0. $\langle \exists s :: [true \land \neg(b \bmod 3 = 2) \Rightarrow \textbf{wpp} .s.(b \bmod 3 = 2)] \rangle$
      ,From above
1. $true$ **upto** $(b \bmod 3 = 2)$
      ,Tautology for **upto**
2. $true$ **entails** $(b \bmod 3 = 2)$
      ,From 0, 1, and the definition of **entails**
3. $true$ **unless** $(b \bmod 3 = 2)$
      ,Tautology for **unless**
4. $true \Longmapsto (b \bmod 3 = 2)$
      ,From 2, 3, and the definition of $\Longmapsto$

Example 6.13.3. (Random walk[6] problems).

At any instant of time, a particle inhabits one of the integer points of the real line. At time 0, it starts at the specified point, and at each subsequent "clock-tick", it moves from its current position to the new position according to the following rule: with probability p, it moves one step to the right, and with probability $q = 1 - p$, it moves one step to the left; the moves are independent of each other.

For the random walk problem with no barriers on the real line, it is possible to show that the particle returns to 0 with probability 1 only if $p = q$. This is also called the *symmetric random walk problem*. Although this property holds with probability 1, it is not possible to prove it in our proof system. This is because the property *depends* on the values of the probabilities of the transition, that is, $p = q$.

There is a class of random walk problems whose progress properties are independent of the values of the probabilities of the transition. As our first example, we consider random walk with two *absorbing* barriers at 0 and M.

---

[6] In general, random walks can be in many dimensions, and the step size can be arbitrary. For ease of exposition, we restrict ourselves to one dimension and a step size of 1.

This means that the instant the particle reaches a barrier, it is trapped. The movement of the particle is modeled by the following program.

$$\begin{array}{ll} \textbf{declare} & x : [0 \ldots M] \\ \textbf{assign} & x := x - 1 \mid x + 1 \ \ \textbf{if} \ \ (0 < x \wedge x < M) \\ \textbf{end} \end{array}$$

For this program we prove that

$$true \Longmapsto (x = 0) \vee (x = M).$$

We assume, without proof, that

$$\textbf{invariant} \ \ (0 \leq x) \wedge (x \leq M).$$

Assume that the range of k is given by $0 < k \wedge k < M$.

0. $\langle \forall k :: (x = k) \ \textbf{entails} \ (x = k - 1) \rangle$
    ,From the program text
1. $\langle \forall k :: (x = k) \leadsto (x = 0) \rangle$
    ,Transitivity of $\leadsto$
2. $\langle \exists k :: (x = k) \rangle \leadsto (x = 0)$
    ,Finite disjunction for $\leadsto$
3. $\langle \exists k :: (x = k) \rangle \leadsto (x = M)$
    ,Proof similiar to 2
4. $\langle \exists k :: (x = k) \rangle \leadsto (x = 0) \vee (x = M)$
    ,Finite disjunction using 2 and 3
5. $(x = 0) \vee (x = M) \leadsto (x = 0) \vee (x = M)$
    ,Implication for $\leadsto$
6. $\langle \exists k :: (x = k) \rangle \vee (x = 0) \vee (x = M) \leadsto (x = 0) \vee (x = M)$
    ,Disjunction of 4 and 5
7. $true \leadsto (x = 0) \vee (x = M)$
    ,predicate calculus and substitution axiom
    ,using invariant above
8. $true \ \textbf{unless} \ (x = 0) \vee (x = M)$
    ,Tautology for **unless**
9. $true \Longmapsto (x = 0) \vee (x = M)$
    ,From 7, 8, and the definition of $\Longmapsto$

As our second example illustrating random walk, consider two *reflecting* barriers to be placed at 0 and M. This means that when the particle reaches the barrier at 0 (or M) it bounces back to 1 (or $M - 1$) with probability 1. The movement of the particle is modeled by the following program.

$$\begin{array}{ll} \textbf{declare} & x : [0 \ldots M] \\ \textbf{assign} & x := x - 1 \mid x + 1 \ \ \textbf{if} \ \ (0 < x \wedge x < M) \\ & \| \ \ x := 1 \ \ \textbf{if} \ \ (x = 0) \\ & \| \ \ x := M - 1 \ \ \textbf{if} \ \ (x = M) \\ \textbf{end} \end{array}$$

For this program, it is easy to show that

$$\textbf{invariant } (0 \leq x) \wedge (x \leq M).$$

The range of k is assumed to be $0 \leq k \wedge k \leq M$. We show that

$$true \Longmapsto (x = 0).$$

0. $\langle \forall k :: (x = k) \textbf{ entails } (x = k - 1) \rangle$
    ,From program text
1. $\langle \forall k :: (x = k) \rightsquigarrow (x = 0) \rangle$
    ,Transitivity of $\rightsquigarrow$
2. $\langle \exists k :: (x = k) \rangle \rightsquigarrow (x = 0)$
    ,Finite disjunction of $\rightsquigarrow$
3. $true \rightsquigarrow (x = 0)$
    ,predicate calculus and substitution axiom
    ,using the invariant above
4. $true \textbf{ unless } (x = 0)$
    ,Tautology for **unless**
5. $true \Longmapsto (x = 0)$
    , From 3, 4, and the definition of $\Longmapsto$

Notice that this proof breaks down for the random walk without barriers, precisely because the relation $\rightsquigarrow$ is not universally disjunctive in its first argument.

As our third example, we consider the case of an *absorbing* barrier at 0 and a *reflecting* barrier at M. The movement of the particle would be modeled by the following program:

```
declare    x : [0 ... M]
assign     x := x - 1 | x + 1  if  (0 < x ∧ x < M)
        [  x := M - 1  if  (x = M)
end
```

For this program, we assume, without proof, that

$$\textbf{invariant } (0 \leq x) \wedge (x \leq M).$$

The range of k is assumed to be $0 < k \wedge k \leq M$. We show that

$$true \Longmapsto (x = 0).$$

0. $\langle \forall k :: (x = k) \textbf{ entails } (x = k - 1) \rangle$
    ,From program text
1. $\langle \forall k :: (x = k) \rightsquigarrow (x = 0) \rangle$
    ,Transitivity of $\rightsquigarrow$
2. $\langle \exists k :: (x = k) \rangle \rightsquigarrow (x = 0)$
    ,Finite disjunction of $\rightsquigarrow$
3. $(x = 0) \rightsquigarrow (x = 0)$
    ,Implication rule of $\rightsquigarrow$
4. $\langle \exists k :: (x = k) \rangle \vee (x = 0) \rightsquigarrow (x = 0)$

,Finite disjunction using 2 and 3
5. $true \rightsquigarrow (x = 0)$
        ,predicate calculus and substitution axiom
        ,using the invariant above
6. $true$ **unless** $(x = 0)$
        ,Tautology for **unless**
7. $true \Longmapsto (x = 0)$
        , From 5, 6, and the definition of $\Longmapsto$

Example 6.13.4. (Two–process mutual exclusion). In this example, we give a brief overview of specification refinement. The example is designed to give a flavor of proof machinery at work.

Specifically, we consider the problem of mutual exclusion between two processes, u and v. Each process u has a variable $u.dine$, which can take one of three values t, h, or e, corresponding to *thinking*, *hungry*, or *eating*, respectively. We abbreviate by $u.t$, $u.h$, and $u.e$ the expressions $u.dine = t$, $u.dine = h$, and $u.dine = e$ respectively. Note that *we make the assumption that every thinking process eventually becomes hungry.* A hungry process remains hungry till it eats. An eating process eats for a finite time and then transits to thinking.

Our initial specification is as follows: We use the anonymous process name x: when x refers to process u (v), $\overline{x}$ will refer to process v (u).

Specification of Program *mutex*:

(0a)   **invariant** $\neg(u.e \wedge v.e \wedge u \neq v)$
(0b) $x.h \Longmapsto x.e$

Property (0a) states that the two processes do not access the critical section at the same time. Property (0b) states that, with probability 1, every hungry process gets to eat.

Our first refinement consists of the introduction of a two-sided coin that can take on values u and v such that if the process u is eating then the coin has the value u.

Specification 1 :

(1a)   **invariant** $(x.e \Rightarrow coin = x)$
(1b) $(x.h \wedge (coin = x)) \Longmapsto x.e$
(1c) $(x.h \wedge (coin = \overline{x})) \Longmapsto (x.h \wedge (coin = x))$

Property (1a) states that $coin = x$ is a necessary condition for a process x to eat. It is easy to show that (1a) $\Rightarrow$ (0a). Property (1b) and (1c) refine property (0b), as shown by the following derivation:

0. $(x.h \wedge (coin = \overline{x})) \Longmapsto (x.h \wedge (coin = x))$
    ,property 1c
1. $(x.h \wedge (coin = x)) \Longmapsto x.e$
    ,property 1b
2. $(x.h \wedge (coin = \overline{x})) \Longmapsto x.e$
    ,transitivity of $\Longmapsto$ using 0 and 1
3. $x.h \Longmapsto x.e$
    ,disjunction on 1 and 2

Our next refinement is to ensure that the two progress properties (1b) and (1c) are met. We propose that if a process u is hungry and if the *coin* has value u then the process be allowed to enter the critical section. To avoid starvation, we need to ensure that the coin eventually takes the value of every process. Thus, our next specification follows:

Specification 2:

(2a)   **invariant** $(x.e \Rightarrow coin = x)$
(2b) $x.h \wedge (coin = x)$ **ensures** $x.e$
(2c) $x.h \wedge (coin = \overline{x}) \rightsquigarrow x.h \wedge (coin = x)$
(2d) $x.h \wedge (coin = \overline{x})$ **unless** $x.h \wedge (coin = x)$

We show that specification 2 implies specification 1. Property (2a) implies property (1a). The proof of property (1b) is straightforward and is given by the following derivation.

0. $x.h \wedge (coin = x)$ **ensures** $x.e$
    ,property (2b)
1. $x.h \wedge (coin = x) \longmapsto x.e$
    ,From 0 and definition of $\longmapsto$
2. $x.h \wedge (coin = x) \Longmapsto x.e$
    ,From 1 and Theorem 6.8.3

Property (1c) follows from properties (2c) and (2d) and the definition of $\Longmapsto$.
    Our final step is to refine property (2c). We propose the following specification.

Specification 3:

(3a)   **invariant** $(x.e \Rightarrow coin = x)$
(3b) $x.h \wedge (coin = x)$ **ensures** $x.e$
(3c) $\overline{x}.e$ **entails** $(coin = x)$
(3d) $x.t \longmapsto x.h$
(3e) $x.h \wedge (coin = \overline{x})$ **unless** $x.h \wedge (coin = x)$

Properties (2a), (2b), and (2d) follow from properties (3a), (3b), and (3e) respectively. The following derivation shows that specification 3 refines property (2c):

0. $\overline{x}.t \mapsto \overline{x}.h$
        ,property (3d) applied to $\overline{x}$
1. $(\overline{x}.t \wedge x.h \wedge (coin = \overline{x})) \mapsto (\overline{x}.h \wedge x.h \wedge (coin = \overline{x})) \vee (x.h \wedge (coin = x))$
        ,PSP theorem on 0 and property (3e)
2. $\overline{x}.h \wedge (coin = \overline{x})$ **ensures** $\overline{x}.e$
        ,property (3b) applied to $\overline{x}$
3. $\overline{x}.h \wedge x.h \wedge (coin = \overline{x}) \mapsto (\overline{x}.e \wedge x.h \wedge (coin = \overline{x})) \vee (x.h \wedge (coin = x))$
        ,PSP theorem on 3 and property (3e)
4. $\overline{x}.e$ **entails** $(coin = x)$
        ,property (3c)
5. $\overline{x}.e \wedge x.h \wedge (coin = \overline{x})$ **entails** $x.h \wedge (coin = x)$
        ,PSP theorem on 4 and property (3e)
6. $(\overline{x}.t \wedge x.h \wedge (coin = \overline{x})) \rightsquigarrow (\overline{x}.h \wedge x.h \wedge (coin = \overline{x})) \vee (x.h \wedge (coin = x))$
        ,1 and definition of $\rightsquigarrow$
7. $\overline{x}.h \wedge x.h \wedge (coin = \overline{x}) \rightsquigarrow (\overline{x}.e \wedge x.h \wedge (coin = \overline{x})) \vee (x.h \wedge (coin = x))$
        ,3 and definition of $\rightsquigarrow$
8. $\overline{x}.e \wedge x.h \wedge (coin = \overline{x}) \rightsquigarrow x.h \wedge (coin = x)$
        ,5 and definition of $\rightsquigarrow$
9. $x.h \wedge (coin = \overline{x}) \rightsquigarrow x.h \wedge (coin = x)$
        ,cancellation and disjunction on 6, 7, and 8

The final specification suggests the following program:

declare $coin$: (u, v)

initially $u.dine, v.dine := t, t$

assign

$\langle [\![\ x : x \in (u, v) :$
$\qquad\qquad x.dine := h$ **if** $x.t$
$\qquad [\![\qquad x.dine := e$ **if** $x.h \wedge (coin = x)$
$\qquad [\![\qquad x.dine, coin := t, x \mid t, \overline{x}$ **if** $x.e$
$\qquad \rangle$

end

The first statement follows from property (3d), the second statement from property (3b) and the third statement from property (3c). It is easy to verify that the safety properties (3a) and (3e) hold for this program.

An alternative derivation. In the above derivation, we had made the choice of a two–sided coin. Suppose instead that we had chosen a three–sided coin that takes on the values u, v, and 0. It is interesting to note that we can keep the same original specification 0 and the same specification 1. We modify specification 2 as follows: Instead of replacing property (1c) by two properties, we use the following useful theorem to replace it by three properties:

$$X \longmapsto Y \vee Z$$
$$Y \text{ entails } Z$$
$$\frac{X \vee Y \text{ unless } Z}{(X \vee Y) \Longmapsto Z}$$

Specification 2 :

(2a)	**invariant** $(x.e \Rightarrow coin = x)$
(2b)	$x.h \wedge (coin = x)$ **ensures** $x.e$
(2c)	$x.h \wedge (coin = \overline{x}) \longmapsto x.h \wedge (coin \neq x)$
(2d)	$x.h \wedge (coin = 0)$ **entails** $x.h \wedge (coin = x)$
(2e)	$x.h \wedge (coin \neq x)$ **unless** $x.h \wedge (coin = x)$

We now show that specification 2 implies specification 1. Property (2a) implies property (1a). The proof of property (1b) is straightforward and is the same as the one given before. Property (1c) follows from properties (2c), (2d), and (2e) by the meta-theorem stated above.

Our final step is to refine property (2c). We propose the following specification.

Specification 3 :

(3a)	**invariant** $(x.e \Rightarrow coin = x)$
(3b)	$x.h \wedge (coin = x)$ **ensures** $x.e$
(3c)	$x.h \wedge (coin = 0)$ **entails** $x.h \wedge (coin = x)$
(3d)	$x.h \wedge (coin \neq x)$ **unless** $x.h \wedge (coin = x)$
(3e)	$x.h \wedge (coin = \overline{x})$ **unless** $x.h \wedge (coin = 0)$
(3f)	$x.e$ **ensures** $x.t \wedge (coin = 0)$
(3g)	$x.t \longmapsto x.h$

The following derivation shows that specification 3 refines property (2c):

0. $\overline{x}.t \longmapsto \overline{x}.h$
    ,property (3g) applied to $\overline{x}$
1. $(\overline{x}.t \wedge x.h \wedge (coin = \overline{x})) \longmapsto (\overline{x}.h \wedge x.h \wedge (coin = \overline{x})) \vee (x.h \wedge (coin = 0))$
    ,PSP theorem on 0 and property (3e)
2. $\overline{x}.h \wedge (coin = \overline{x})$ **ensures** $\overline{x}.e$
    ,property (3b) applied to $\overline{x}$
3. $\overline{x}.h \wedge x.h \wedge (coin = \overline{x}) \longmapsto (\overline{x}.e \wedge x.h \wedge (coin = \overline{x})) \vee (x.h \wedge (coin = 0))$
    ,PSP theorem on 3 and property (3e)
4. $\overline{x}.e$ **ensures** $\overline{x}.h \wedge (coin = x)$
    ,property (3f)
5. $\overline{x}.e \wedge x.h \wedge (coin = \overline{x})$ **ensures** $x.h \wedge (coin = 0)$
    ,PSP theorem on 4 and property (3e)
6. $\overline{x}.h \wedge x.h \wedge (coin = \overline{x}) \longmapsto (x.h \wedge (coin = x))$
    ,Cancellation on 3 and 4
7. $(\overline{x}.t \wedge x.h \wedge (coin = \overline{x})) \longmapsto (x.h \wedge (coin = 0))$
    ,Cancellation on 1 and 6

8. $x.h \wedge (coin = \overline{x}) \longmapsto x.h \wedge (coin = 0)$
           ,disjunction on 5, 6, and 7

The final specification suggests the following program.

declare $coin$: $(0, u, v)$
initially $u.dine, v.dine = t, t \;\|$
           $coin = 0$
assign
    $\langle\![\, x : x \in (u, v) :$
           $x.dine := h$ **if** $x.t$
    $[\!]$ $coin := u \mid v$ **if** $x.h \wedge (coin = 0)$
    $[\!]$ $x.dine := e$ **if** $x.h \wedge (coin = x)$
    $[\!]$ $x.dine, coin := t, 0$ **if** $x.e \wedge (coin = x)$
    $\rangle$

end

The first statement follows from property (3g), the second statement from property (3c), the third statement from property (3b) and the fourth statement from property (3f). It is easy to verify that the safety properties (3a), (3d), and (3e) hold for this program.

7. Eventual Determinism: Using Probabilistic Means to Achieve Deteministic Ends

Ever since Michael Rabin's seminal paper (Rabin [1976]) on Probabilistic Algorithms , several algorithms employing randomization have appeared in the literature (see Gupta et al. [1994] for a survey). Often these algorithms are simpler and more efficient — in terms of space, time and communication complexity — than their deterministic[1] counterparts. It has also been recognized that for certain problems, especially in the areas of multi–processing and distributed computing, it is possible to construct a probabilistic solution where no deterministic one exists. One such problem is that of resolving symmetry in a parallel environment (Dijkstra [1974], Lehmann and Rabin [1981]).

In a parallel system consisting of a multitude of processes, it is possible to customize each process with a special starting state or program. However as the multitude grows, the cost of customizing increases and symmetry becomes an interesting and desirable feature. For our purposes, a system of processes is said to be *symmetric*, if all processes have identical starting states and execute identical programs. It has been shown in Dijkstra [1974] and Lehmann and Rabin [1981], that such a symmetric system can reach an asymmetric state only if the processes are allowed to make probabilistic transitions. It is not possible to break the symmetry of a parallel environment in a deterministic and deadlock–free manner.

Although probabilistic algorithms have several charms like simplicity, efficiency and solvability, trading determinacy for randomization has its price. As has been mentioned in the previous chapter, the traditional notion of absolute correctness of deterministic algorithms has to be generalized to a notion of correctness with a quantitative probability. This means that some probabilistic programs may take an inordinate amount of time to execute. Complexity measures for such algorithms are expected values. Specifically, it is not possible to bound the worst–case complexity. On the other hand, there is a large and growing body of literature of deterministic algorithms that have provably optimal upper bounds using varying complexity measures.

To bridge the gap between the capabilities of probabilistic and deterministic algorithms and to harness the advantages of both, we propose a new paradigm — *eventual determinism*. An *eventually–determinizing system* of processes is symmetric and all processes execute an algorithm with two parts (alternatively called *modes*) — *probabilistic* and *deterministic*. Each process begins execution from the

---

[1] We use the term *deterministic* to mean *non–probabilistic*.

same starting state in the probabilistic mode. When the system reaches a legal starting state for the deterministic part, each process, independently, switches to the deterministic mode. It is possible that a process may switch back to the probabilistic mode but it is required that eventually the process switch to the deterministic mode and remain in that mode thereafter. In many applications, the legal starting state for the deterministic algorithm is simply an asymmetric state. It is required that the decision to switch modes be made *locally*. Further, each process that begins execution, switches mode with probability one. An *eventually–determinizing* algorithm should satisfy the following criteria.

- *Symmetry*: All processes execute identical programs from identical starting states.
- *Locality*: Each process begins execution in a probabilistic mode and *independently* switches to a deterministic mode. Thus a process can execute in a deterministic mode while another process is executing in the probabilistic mode. This switch is made by each process with probability 1.
- *Transparency*: The mode of a process is transparent to the processes it synchronizes with.
- *Uniformity*: Since probabilistic and deterministic processes co–exist in the system and transparency is required, a uniform and clean interface is needed between the probabilistic and deterministic modes.
- *Eventual Determinacy* : While a process may switch back to the probabilistic mode, it is required that eventually, each process switch to the deterministic mode and remain in that mode thereafter.

Note that in an eventually–determinizing algorithm, it is sufficient for the probabilistic mode to establish a legal starting state for the deterministic mode. Thus the specification of the probabilistic mode can be much weaker than the specification of the algorithm. Also, existing proofs of the probabilistic and deterministic modes can be used along with a proof of correctness of their interaction to construct a proof of the eventually–determinizing algorithm.

In this chapter, we illustrate the idea of eventual determinacy by two examples — fair conflict–resolution for distributed systems and self–stabilization for token rings. In the first example, a process changes its mode at most once. That is, determinacy is a stable property. In the second example, if the token ring contains more than one token, a deterministic process can become probabilistic. However, after the ring stabilizes to one token, each process independently becomes deterministic and remains so, provided that no new tokens are created in the ring.

The problem of eventual determinism was first formulated by Jayadev Misra. Eliezer Levy (Levy [1988]) was the first to apply it to the dining philosophers problem. Though our basic idea is the same as his, he makes stronger assumptions about the Lehmann–Rabin algorithm than we do. Our development has been aided by the proof techniques for reasoning about composition of probabilistic programs.

In Goldreich and Petrank [1990], the authors present a combination of a probabilistic and a deterministic algorithm for the Byzantine Agreement Problem. In their algorithm, the probabilistic solution is run for a predetermined number of rounds k. While it is conceivable that the algorithm terminates before k rounds, after k rounds every process becomes deterministic. An alternate method of integrating probabilistic and deterministic algorithms is suggested by Lipton and Park [1990]. The authors present a probabilistic algorithm for assigning unique process identifiers. It is conceivable that this could be integrated with a deterministic algorithm that uses such unique identifiers. In the both of the above approaches, the switchover point constitutes a bottleneck for the system. Thus, their integration is not seamless as ours.

7.1 The Symmetric Dining Philosophers Problem

Processes, called *philosophers* are placed at the vertices of a ring, with one philosopher at every vertex. A philosopher can be in one of three states : *thinking*, *hungry* or *eating*. Associated with each edge of the ring is a *fork*. A philosopher can eat only if it possesses the forks corresponding to both its incident edges. A thinking philosopher may become hungry. A hungry philosopher remains hungry until it gets its incident forks, when it begins to eat. On entering the eating state, a philosopher eats for a finite period and then transits to the thinking state. A philosopher may think for an arbitrary period of time.

The problem is to design an eventually–determinizing algorithm that is starvation–free. That is, no philosopher remains hungry indefinitely.

7.1.1 Notation and Variable Declarations

In this section, we define the variables used by the eventually determinizing algorithm. The philosophers are assumed to be numbered from 0 through $N-1$. Associated with each philosopher u are the following variables.

- $u.dine$: This can take values t, h or e corresponding to *thinking*, *hungry* or *eating* respectively. For convenience, we abbreviate by a boolean variable $u.t$, the boolean predicate $(u.dine = t)$. The boolean variables $u.h$ and $u.e$ are similiarly defined.
- $u.mode$: This can take values p or d corresponding to *probabilistic* or *deterministic* respectively. For convenience, we abbreviate by a boolean variable $u.p$, the boolean predicate $(u.mode = p)$. The boolean variable $u.d$ can be similiarly defined.
- $draw.u$: This can take values $u-1$, $u+1$ or N. This variable is intended to contain the value of a random choice made by a process. It will be used in the Lehmann–Rabin Algorithm.

An edge between philosophers u and v is denoted by (u, v) (or equivalently (v, u)). Two philosophers are said to be *neighbors* if and only if there is an edge between them. For convenience, the ring is assumed to be represented by a boolean matrix E, where $E[u, v]$ holds if and only if there is an edge between vertices u and v. Associated with each edge (u, v) of the ring, are the following variables.

- $fork[u, v]$: The *fork* is shared by neighboring philosophers u and v and can take values u or v indicating the identity of the philosopher in possession of the fork.
- $clean[u, v]$: This boolean variable is an attribute of the fork and indicates whether the corresponding fork is *clean* or *dirty*.
- $rf[u, v]$: The *request token* is shared by neighboring philosophers u and v and can take values u or v indicating the identity of the philosopher in possession of the request token.
- $rfclean[u, v]$: This boolean variable is an attribute of the request token and indicates whether the corresponding request token is *clean* or *dirty*.
- $rffirst[u, v]$: This boolean variable is an attribute of the request token.

For an edge (u, v), the reflection function $R(u, v)$ denotes the second neighbor of v.

7.1.2 The Lehmann–Rabin Algorithm

In Lehmann and Rabin [1981], the authors describe two probabilistic algorithms to solve the problems of deadlock–freedom (the Free Philosopher's Algorithm) and starvation–freedom (The Courteous Philosopher's Algorithm) for a finite number of dining philosophers arranged around a circular table. In the sequel, we shall be concerned only with the Free Philosopher's Algorithm.

We give an informal description of the original Free Philosopher's Algorithm. In the starting state, all forks are down and all philosophers are thinking. When a philosopher becomes hungry, it makes a random choice between its left and right neighbor. If the neighbor of choice is holding the common fork, the philosopher waits for the fork to be put down. Once the common fork is down, the philosopher picks it up and then inspects the status of the second fork it needs. If the second fork is being used by its neighbor, it puts down the first fork and repeats the whole process by making another random choice. If the second fork is down, the philosopher picks it up and starts eating. On leaving the eating state, it puts down both forks (in any order) and starts thinking.

It is important to note the subtle distinction between the first and second forks. While a philosopher waits for the first fork to be put down, it does not wait for the second one. Clearly, a fork being up or down is determined by whether the neighbor is using it or not. How are "up" and "down" implemented in a distributed environment? How does a philosopher request a fork? Under what conditions can a philosopher release a fork? More importantly, when can a philosopher assume that a neighbor is using a fork and stop waiting ?

To tailor the Free Philosopher's algorithm to execute in a distributed environment, we reformulate it using the variables introduced in Section 7.1.1. The variable $draw.u$ reflects the random choice by philosopher u. It has the values N, $u - 1$ or $u + 1$ to denote repectively that it has not drawn, drawn the left neighbor or drawn the right neighbor respectively.

Having made a random choice, a philosopher uses the request tokens it possesses to requisition the forks it doesn't have. If philospher u is hungry and needs $fork[u, v]$, it sends request token $rf[u, v]$ to the neighbor v who is currently holding the fork. The $rffirst[u, v]$ attribute of the request token is set to inform philosopher v of the random choice of philosopher u. That is, $rffirst[u, v]$ is set to true if $(draw.u = v)$ and it is set to false if $(draw.u = R(v, u))$. This information helps philosopher v decide, whether an immediate response to philosopher u is necessary or not. A true value for $rffirst[u, v]$ indicates that philosopher u will wait for v to put the fork "down", whereas a false indicates it is enough to inform philosopher u that the fork is "in use".

To inform philosopher u that $fork[u, v]$ is "in use", philosopher v "dirties" the request token and sends it to philosopher u. That is, the request token $rf[u, v]$ is returned to u with a false value for the $rfclean[u, v]$ attribute. On receipt of a dirty request token, philosopher u stops waiting, cleans the request token and makes another random choice.

The starting state of the algorithm is the same for each philosopher and is given as follows.

- All philosophers are thinking.
- No philosopher has made a random choice.
- For a given edge, the fork and request token are held by different philosophers.
- All request tokens are clean.
- The $rffirst$ attribute of each request token is set to true.

The Lehmann–Rabin algorithm is shown in Figure 7.1. Pnueli and Zuck [1986] contains an alternate exposition of the same algorithm.

The proof obligation of the distributed version of the Lehmann–Rabin algorithm is twofold.

- *Mutual Exclusion*: Neighboring philosophers do not eat simultaneously.
- *Deadlock Freedom*: If a philosopher is hungry, then it is guaranteed, with probability one, that *some* philosopher will eat.

The proof is similiar to one given in Pnueli and Zuck [1986] for the original Free Philosopher's algorithm.

7.1.3 The Chandy–Misra Algorithm

In Chandy and Misra [1984], the authors present a deterministic solution to the dining philosphers problem. Although their solution is applicable to an arbitrary network of philosophers, we are interested in applying their solution to a ring of philosophers.

The key idea of the algorithm is to maintain asymmetry as an invariant. This necessitates an asymmetric starting state. In the algorithm, asymmetry is represented by the *acyclicity* of a precedence graph of philosophers. This precedence graph is identical to the interconnection graph of the philosophers (a ring, in our case) except that each edge of the precedence graph is directed from a philosopher having higher precedence to a philosopher having lower precedence.

always

$\langle \, [\!] \, u \, ::$

	$u.mayeat$	$=$	$u.h \wedge (draw.u \neq N) \wedge (fork[u, u-1] = u)$ $\wedge (fork[u, u+1] = u)$
$[\!]$	$u.retry$	$=$	$u.h \wedge (draw.u \neq N) \wedge (fork[u, draw.u] = u) \wedge$ $(fork[u, R(draw.u, u)] \neq u) \wedge$ $(rf[u, R(draw.u, u)] = u) \wedge$ $\neg rfclean[u, R(draw.u, u)]$

$\rangle$
$[\!]$ $\langle \, [\!] \, (u, v) : E[u, v] :$

	$sendreq[u, v]$	$=$	$u.h \wedge (draw.u \neq N) \wedge (fork[u, v] = v) \wedge$ $(rf[u, v] = u) \wedge rfclean[u, v]$
$[\!]$	$sendfork[u, v]$	$=$	$(fork[u, v] = u) \wedge (rf[u, v] = u) \wedge$ $(u.t \vee (u.h \wedge (draw.u = N)) \vee$ $(u.h \wedge draw.u = R(v, u)$ $\wedge fork[u, draw.u] \neq u))$
$[\!]$	$forkinuse[u, v]$	$=$	$(fork[u, v] = u) \wedge (rf[u, v] = u) \wedge$ $(u.e \vee (u.h \wedge (draw.u = v)) \vee$ $(u.h \wedge draw.u = R(v, u) \wedge fork[u, draw.u] = u))$

$\rangle$

initially

$\langle \, [\!] \, u \, ::$

$\quad u.dine, draw.u \ = \ t, N$
$[\!] \quad fork[u, u+1] \ = \ u$
$[\!] \quad rf[u, u+1], rfclean[u, u+1], rffirst[u, u+1] \ = \ (u+1), true, true$
$\rangle$

assign

$\quad draw.u \ := \ u-1 \, | \, u+1 \ \ \textbf{if} \ \ u.h \wedge (draw.u = N)$

$[\!]$

$\quad rf[u, draw.u], rffirst[u, draw.u] \ := \ draw.u, true \ \ \textbf{if} \ sendreq[u, draw.u]$

$[\!]$

$\quad rf[u, R(draw.u, u)], rffirst[u, R(draw.u, u)] \ :=$
$\quad R(draw.u, u), false \ \textbf{if} \ sendreq[u, R(draw.u, u)] \wedge (fork[u, draw.u] = u)$

$[\!]$

$\quad u.dine := e \ \ \textbf{if} \ \ u.mayeat$

$[\!]$

$\quad draw.u, rfclean[u, R(draw.u, u)] := N, true \ \ \textbf{if} \ \ u.retry$

$[\!]$

$\quad \langle \, [\!] \, v : E[u, v] :$
$\qquad fork[u, v], rf[u, v], rfclean[u, v]$
$\qquad := fork[u, v], v, false \ \ \textbf{if} \ \ forkinuse[u, v] \wedge \neg rffirst[u, v] \sim$
$\qquad v, rf[u, v], rfclean[u, v] \ \ \textbf{if} \ \ sendfork[u, v]$
$\quad \rangle$

end

Fig. 7.1. The Lehmann–Rabin algorithm

A hungry philosopher having higher precedence than all its neighbors is allowed to eat. The algorithm manipulates the acyclicity of the precedence graph so that every hungry philospher eventually takes precedence over all its neighbors and eats.

The algorithm describes a way to implement the precedence graph in a distributed manner so that all changes to the edge directions can be made locally. To this end, all forks are assumed to be either *clean* or *dirty*. A clean fork remains clean until it is used for eating. The act of eating with a fork dirties it. A philosopher cleans a fork only when sending it to its neighbor. The direction of an edge between two neighboring philosophers u and v is directed from u to v if and only if

- u holds the common fork and the fork is clean or,
- v holds the common fork and the fork is dirty.

Note that only eating can change the orientation of the edges of the precedence graph. Since eating dirties the forks used, an eating philosopher has *all* its incident edges directed towards it. Redirecting *all* the edges of a vertex of a graph to point towards it cannot create any new cycles involving that vertex. So if the precedence graph was acyclic before the philosopher ate, it continues to remain so. Initially all forks are dirty and are located at philosophers such that the precedence graph is acyclic. Hence acyclicity is an invariant.

A hungry philosopher requisitions the forks it needs by sending out request tokens to the philosophers that hold the forks. A philosopher holding both the fork and the corresponding request token, releases the fork only if the requisitioning philosopher has higher precedence than it. It can be shown that every hungry philosopher receives the forks it has requested and eventually eats.

The starting state of the algorithm is as follows.

- All philosophers are thinking.
- For each edge, the fork and request token are held by different philosophers.
- All forks are dirty.
- The forks are placed in such a manner that the precedence graph is acyclic.

The deterministic Chandy–Misra algorithm is shown in Figure 7.2.

For the purposes of our development, we note that the algorithm has the following properties.

- *Mutual Exclusion*: Neighboring philosophers do not eat simultaneously.
- *Starvation Freedom*: Every hungry philosopher eats eventually.

The interested reader is referred to Chandy and Misra [1988] for an excellent exposition and proof of this algorithm.

7.1.4 The Eventually–Determinizing Algorithm

Now we show how to merge the algorithms of Sections 7.1.2 and 7.1.3 to obtain an eventually–determinizing algorithm for the dining philosophers problem.

always

$$\langle [\!] \; u :: \quad u.mayeat \quad = \quad \langle \wedge v : E[u,v] : (fork[u,v] = u) \wedge$$
$$(clean[u,v] \vee (rf[u,v] = v))\rangle$$

$$\rangle$$
$$[\!]$$
$$\langle [\!] \; u, v : E[u,v] ::$$
$$sendreq[u,v] \quad = \quad (fork[u,v] = v) \wedge (rf[u,v] = u) \wedge u.h$$
$$[\!] \quad sendfork[u,v] \quad = \quad (fork[u,v] = u) \wedge \neg clean[u,v] \wedge (rf[u,v] = u)$$
$$\wedge \neg u.e$$

$$\rangle$$

initially

$$\langle [\!] \; u :: u.dine = t \rangle$$
$$[\!] \quad \langle [\!] \; (u,v) :: clean[u,v] = false \rangle$$
$$[\!] \quad \langle [\!] \; (u,v) : u < v :: fork[u,v], rf[u,v] = u,v \rangle$$

assign

$$\langle [\!] \; u :: \quad u.dine := e \qquad\qquad\qquad \textbf{if} \quad u.h \wedge u.mayeat$$
$$\|\langle \| v : E[u,v] :: clean[u,v] := false \quad \textbf{if} \quad u.h \wedge u.mayeat\rangle$$

$$\rangle$$
$$[\!] \quad \langle [\!] \; (u,v) ::$$

$$rf[u,v] := v \qquad\qquad\qquad \textbf{if} \quad sendreq[u,v]$$
$$[\!] \quad fork[u,v], clean[u,v] := v, true \quad \textbf{if} \quad sendfork[u,v]$$
$$\rangle$$

end

Fig. 7.2. The Chandy–Misra algorithm

The eventually–determinizing algorithm is shown in Figures 7.3 and 7.4. It is obtained by merging the UNITY–like notations of the modified Lehmann–Rabin and the Chandy–Misra algorithms.

It is required that the starting state of the algorithm be identical for all philosophers. Except for the positioning of the dirty forks, there is no conflict in the starting states of the probabilistic and deterministic algorithms. Thus they can be consistently merged.

- All philosophers are thinking.
- No philosopher has made a random choice.
- For each edge, the fork and the request token are with different philosophers. In particular, a philosopher holds the fork it shares with its right neighbor and the request token it shares with its left neighbor.
- All forks are dirty.
- All request tokens are clean.
- The $rffirst$ attribute of the request token is true.

During the execution of an eventually–determinizing algorithm, it is possible to have a mix of probabilistic and deterministic philosphers. Since a philosopher executing in a particular mode expects certain responses from its environment it is necessary that the interface between the modes be carefully designed. For

always

$\langle\mathbb{I}\; u ::$

$$
\begin{aligned}
u.mayeatp \quad &= \quad u.h \wedge u.p \wedge (draw.u \neq N) \\
&\quad \wedge (fork[u, u-1] = u) \\
&\quad \wedge (fork[u, u+1] = u)
\end{aligned}
$$

$\mathbb{I} \qquad u.retry \quad = \quad u.h \wedge u.p \wedge (draw.u \neq N)$
$$
\begin{aligned}
&\quad \wedge (fork[u, draw.u] = u) \\
&\quad \wedge (fork[u, R(draw.u, u)] \neq u) \\
&\quad \wedge (rf[u, R(draw.u, u)] = u) \\
&\quad \wedge \neg rfclean[u, R(draw.u, u)]
\end{aligned}
$$

$u.mayswitch \quad = \quad \langle \vee v : E[u, v] : (fork[u, v] = u) \wedge clean[u, v])$

$\rangle$

$\mathbb{I} \qquad \langle \mathbb{I}\; (u, v) : E[u, v] :$
$$
\begin{aligned}
psendreq[u, v] \quad &= \quad u.h \wedge u.p \wedge (draw.u \neq N) \wedge (fork[u, v] = v) \wedge \\
&\quad (rf[u, v] = u) \wedge rfclean[u, v]
\end{aligned}
$$

$\mathbb{I} \qquad psendfork[u, v] \quad = \quad (fork[u, v] = u) \wedge (rf[u, v] = u)wedgeu.p \wedge$
$$
\begin{aligned}
&\quad (u.t \vee (u.h \wedge (draw.u = N)) \\
&\quad \vee (u.h \wedge draw.u = R(v, u) \\
&\quad \wedge fork[u, draw.u] \neq u))
\end{aligned}
$$

$\mathbb{I} \qquad forkinuse[u, v] \quad = \quad (fork[u, v] = u) \wedge (rf[u, v] = u) \wedge u.p \wedge$
$$
\begin{aligned}
&\quad (u.e \vee (u.h \wedge (draw.u = v))) \vee \\
&\quad u.h \wedge draw.u = R(v, u) \wedge fork[u, draw.u] = u))
\end{aligned}
$$

$\rangle$

$\langle \mathbb{I}\; u :: \quad u.mayeatd \quad = \quad u.d \wedge \langle \wedge v : E[u, v] : (fork[u, v] = u) \wedge$
$$
(clean[u, v] \vee (rf[u, v] = v)))
$$

$\rangle$

$\mathbb{I} \qquad \langle \mathbb{I}\; u, v : E[u, v] ::$
$$
\begin{aligned}
dsendreq[u, v] \quad &= \quad (fork[u, v] = v) \wedge (rf[u, v] = u) \wedge u.h \wedge u.d \\
dsendfork[u, v] \quad &= \quad (fork[u, v] = u) \wedge \neg clean[u, v] \wedge (rf[u, v] = u) \\
&\quad \wedge \neg u.e \wedge u.d
\end{aligned}
$$

$\rangle$

Fig. 7.3. The Eventually–determinizing algorithm: **always** section

example, a philosopher executing in a probabilistic mode should not have to wait, if the second fork is "in use". Similiarly, a philosopher in the deterministic mode should not have the dirty request token returned to it. It waits for all the forks that it requests.

A close inspection of the variables defined and their occurrence in the algorithms helps us solve the problem. Notice that the attributes of the request token ($rfclean[u, v]$ and $rffirst[u, v]$) are only of relevance to the probabilistic algorithm while the attribute of the fork ($clean[u, v]$) is only used in the deterministic algorithm. We propose the following two rules.

– Before sending a request token to philosopher v, a deterministic philosopher u sets the $rffirst[u, v]$ attribute to true.
– A probabilistic philosopher u dirties a fork when sending it to philospher v.

The first rule ensures that if v is a probabilistic philospher, it will interpret the *true* value $rffirst[u, v]$ attribute to mean that u will wait for the fork. Thus the

initially

$\langle \lbrack\!\lbrack\ u\ ::$
$$\qquad u.dine, u.mode, draw.u\ =\ t, p, N$$
$\lbrack\!\lbrack \qquad fork[u, u+1], clean[u, u+1]\ =\ u, false$
$\lbrack\!\lbrack \qquad rf[u, u+1], rfclean[u, u+1], rffirst[u, u+1]\ =\ u+1, true, true$
$\rangle$

assign

$$draw.u\ :=\ u-1\ |\ u+1\quad \text{if}\ \ u.h \wedge u.p \wedge (draw.u = N)$$

$\lbrack\!\lbrack$

$$rf[u, draw.u], rffirst[u, draw.u]\ :=\ draw.u, true\quad \text{if } psendreq[u, draw.u]$$

$\lbrack\!\lbrack$

$$rf[u, R(draw.u, u)], rffirst[u, R(draw.u, u)]\ :=$$
$$R(draw.u, u), false\quad \text{if } psendreq[u, R(draw.u, u)] \wedge (fork[u, draw.u] = u)$$

$\lbrack\!\lbrack$

$$u.dine, u.mode, clean[u, u-1], clean[u, u+1]\ :=$$
$$e, p, false, false\quad \text{if } u.mayeatp$$

$\lbrack\!\lbrack$

$$draw.u, rfclean[u, R(draw.u, u)], u.mode\ :=$$
$$N, true, d\quad \text{if}\ \ u.retry \wedge u.mayswitch \sim$$
$$N, true, u.mode\quad \text{if}\ \ u.retry \wedge \neg u.mayswitch$$

$\lbrack\!\lbrack$

$\qquad \langle \lbrack\!\lbrack\ v : E[u, v] :$
$$\qquad\quad fork[u, v], rf[u, v], rfclean[u, v], clean[u, v]$$
$$\qquad\qquad := fork[u, v], v, false, clean[u, v]$$
$$\qquad\qquad\quad \text{if}\ \ forkinuse[u, v] \wedge \neg rffirst[u, v] \sim$$
$$\qquad\qquad v, rf[u, v], rfclean[u, v], false\quad \text{if}\ \ psendfork[u, v]$$
$\qquad \rangle$

$\lbrack\!\lbrack \qquad \langle \lbrack\!\lbrack\ u\ :: \qquad u.dine := e \qquad\qquad\qquad \text{if}\ \ u.h \wedge u.mayeatd$
$\qquad\qquad\qquad \| \langle \| v : E[u, v] :: clean[u, v] := false\ \ \text{if}\ \ u.h \wedge u.mayeatd \rangle$
$\qquad\qquad \rangle$
$\lbrack\!\lbrack \qquad \langle \lbrack\!\lbrack\ (u, v)\ ::$
$$\qquad\qquad\qquad rf[u, v], rffirst[u, v] := v, true \qquad \text{if}\ \ dsendreq[u, v]$$
$\qquad\qquad \lbrack\!\lbrack \qquad fork[u, v], clean[u, v] := v, true \qquad \text{if}\ \ dsendfork[u, v]$
$\qquad\qquad \rangle$

end

Fig. 7.4. The Eventually–determinizing algorithm

v does not send a dirty request token to u. The case where the v is a deterministic philosopher is easily ruled out as the $rffirst$ attribute has no relevance for such a philosopher.

The second rule is more subtle. It is designed to ensure that if a probabilistic philosopher ever has higher precedence than a deterministic philosopher then it will continue to do so until it becomes deterministic. That is, by the rules of precedence of the Chandy–Misra algorithm, philosopher u will have higher precedence than v. Suppose v is a deterministic philosopher. From the rules of the deterministic algorithm, if u ever requests the fork from v, it will get it back immediately. This is particularly useful when $(draw.u = R(v, u))$. In such a case, u will not have to wait for its second fork. The problem of a deterministic philosopher having to send a dirty request token to a probabilistic philosopher has vanished ! The case where v is a probabilistic philosopher is easily ruled out as the *clean* attribute has no relevance for such a philosopher.

The above two rules allow a uniform interface to be constructed between two philosophers executing in different modes. We now present the conditions under which a philosopher can switch its mode from probabilistic to deterministic. The rules are

- A probabilistic philosopher who eats, dirties his forks and becomes deterministic.
- Upon receipt of a clean fork, a probabilistic philospher becomes deterministic.

We informally argue about the soundness of these rules. Given the starting state of the algorithm, by the rules of the Chandy–Misra algorithm, the precedence graph is a cycle. If a philosopher becomes hungry, by the Lehmann–Rabin algorithm some other philosopher eats. By the first rule, he dirties his forks and becomes deterministic. Since both the incident edges now point towards it, the precedence graph is acyclic. At this point, there exists a deterministic philosopher whose precedence is lower than that of its neighbors. We claim that this condition is stable.

The only way that the direction of an edge can be changed is if a philosopher eats or if a probabilistic philosopher sends a dirty fork to its neighbor. In the first case, the philosopher who eats, dirties his forks and becomes deterministic. This only validates the claim further. In the second case, suppose that the probabilistic philosopher sends a dirty fork to a deterministic neighbor. The direction of an edge between a probabilistic and deterministic philosopher has been changed to point towards the deterministic philosopher. This does not invalidate the claim. The case of a probabilistic philosopher sending a dirty fork to another probabilistic philosopher can be ignored. Thus the precedence graph continues to be acyclic.

Note that the forks are initially dirty and can only be cleaned by deterministic philosophers. Thus the receipt of a clean fork assures a philosopher that determinism has been achieved in the ring. This alongwith the above stable condition guarantees that the precedence graph is acyclic. It is safe for the receiving philosopher to switch modes.

We sketch an argument to show that every hungry philospher eventually eats.

Lemma 7.1.1. *If a hungry probabilistic philosopher u chooses to wait for a fork$[u, v]$, then, with probability one, either u gets the fork or philosopher v eats.*

Lemma 7.1.2. *Let u be a probabilistic philosopher and let v be a neighboring deterministic philosopher. If the common fork is at v then the fork is dirty.*

Lemma 7.1.3. *If a hungry probabilistic philospher u has a deterministic neighbor, then either u eats or becomes hungry in the deterministic mode.*

Proof Sketch: Let t, u and v be three consecutive philosophers. Let u be the hungry, probabilistic philosopher and let v be its deterministic neighbor. If $draw.u = v$ and v possess fork$[u, v]$, then due to Lemma 7.1.2, u will succeed in getting a clean fork from v. If it fails in getting fork$[t, u]$, it will become hungry in the deterministic mode.

If $draw.u = v$ and u possesses fork$[u, v]$ then with probability one, philosopher u's random choice will become t. Thus philosopher u will wait for fork$[t, u]$ and by Lemma 7.1.1 will either get the fork$[t, u]$ or t will eat. In the latter case, t becomes deterministic and by the rules of the deterministic algorithm, t will send fork fork$[t, u]$ to u. Recall, that a probabilistic philosopher dirties its forks when sending them to its neighbor. Thus a probabilistic philosopher u always has precedence over deterministic philosopher v, and will succeed in getting fork$[u, v]$ and eating. (End of Proof Sketch)

Lemma 7.1.4. *Let u, v and w be three consecutive probabilistic philosophers. Let v be hungry and w be thinking. Then, with probability one, either one of u or v will eat or w will become hungry.*

Lemma 7.1.5. *Every philosopher who is hungry in the probabilistic mode, either eats or becomes hungry in the deterministic mode.*

Proof Sketch: Let u, v and w be three consecutive philosophers. Let v be the hungry probabilistic philosopher. By the Lehmann–Rabin proof, some philosopher z eats and becomes deterministic. Assume that none of v's neighbors is deterministic and one neighbor (say, w) is thinking. Then Lemma 7.1.4, either u eats or v eats or w becomes hungry in the probabilistic mode. By a simple induction argument, a chain of hungry probabilistic philosophers is set up until a deterministic philosopher is encountered. By Lemma 7.1.3, either the last hungry probabilistic philosopher on the chain (who has z for a neighbor) eats or becomes hungry in the deterministic mode. In either case, it becomes deterministic and the contagion of determinism flows back along the chain. Eventually v eats or becomes hungry in the deterministic mode. (End of Proof Sketch)

Lemma 7.1.6. *Every philosopher who is hungry in the deterministic mode eats.*

Proof Sketch: Let v be a hungry, deterministic philosopher. If there are no probabilistic philosophers in the ring, since the precedence graph is acyclic, the starvation–freedom proof of Chandy–Misra is applicable and eventually v eats. Otherwise, let M be the number of probabilistic philosophers in the ring, N the number of deterministic ancestors of u in the precedence graph and L the number of thinking deterministic ancestors of u in the precedence graph. By an induction argument, we show that the metric (M, N, L) decreases until u eats. (End of Proof Sketch)

Theorem 7.1.1. *No philosopher is hungry forever.*

We have proved the eventually determinizing algorithm in our probabilistic generalization of UNITY. We are omitting the full proofs in the interests of brevity.

7.2 The Self–Stabilization Problem

The problem of self–stabilization was introduced in Dijkstra [1974]. To date, most known deterministic algorithms for the problem introduce asymmetry in one form or another. More importantly, Tcheunte [1981] has shown that a minimum number of three states per process are needed for any deterministic solution to the self–stabilizing token ring problem. There have been two symmetric probabilistic solutions proposed for the problem (Israeli and Jalfon [1990], Herman [1990]). While these solutions are interesting in their own right, the processes continue to use randomization even after the system has stabilized. So in Herman [1990], for example, there is no bound on the worst–case time that it might take for a given process to get a token. In this section, we describe an elegant and simple probabilistic algorithm for a ring containing an odd number of processes. Using this, we show how to construct an eventually–determinizing algorithm for a ring with an odd number of processes. The algorithm has the pleasing property that after a point in the computation, all transitions are deterministic. Thus each process uses only one bit (two values) of shared state and at worst, a process receives the token in time proportional to the number of processes in the ring.

7.2.1 Notation and Variable Declarations

Assume that we have a ring of odd number, N, of processes. The processes are completely symmetric; in particular, a process does not possess a unique identifier. Associated with a process i are the following variables.

- x_i: This can take values 0 or 1. It is used to denote the state of the process.
- $x_i.count$: This is an integer variable and can take values between 1 and N (inclusive).

A process is said to possess a *token*, if its state is the same as the state of its left neighbor, that is, $x_i = x_{i-1}$. We assume that, in a single step, a process can read the state of its left neighbor and set its own state. The goal is to design an algorithm that stabilizes to a state in which there is only one token in the network.

7.2.2 A Probabilistic Algorithm

Each process in the ring executes the following algorithm *synchronously*.

$$x_i = x_{i-1} \rightarrow x_i := 0 \mid 1$$

The expression on the right hand side of the assignment is based on notation introduced in Chapter 6 and is intended to denote probabilistic choice between 0 and 1. The correctness of the algorithm is proved by showing

Theorem 7.2.1 (Safety). *The number of tokens in the ring does not increase.*

Theorem 7.2.2 (Progress). *The token circulates in the ring and with probability 1, every process receives the token.*

Theorem 7.2.3 (Convergence). *If there is more than one token in the ring, then, with probability 1, the system converges to a state in which there is exactly one token.*

7.2.3 The Eventually–Determinizing Algorithm

The probabilistic algorithm presented above has one drawback — even after the system has converged to a state in which there is only one token, randomization is used to pass the token. There is no bound on the number of steps that it would take for a process to receive a token. Even the expected time for a process to receive the token in the probabilistic scheme is twice the expected time of the deterministic scheme.

A simple–minded solution to this problem is for the process holding the token to pass it by negating its state. While this would succeed in moving the token in one step, it is based on the assumption that there is only one token in the network. This assumption is untenable as in most self–stabilizing solutions, a process has no way of knowing that the system has reached a stable state (that is, one having a single token).

We demonstrate a way to circumvent this problem, for a ring that executes synchronously. That is, all the processes in the ring work in lock–step. The program executed by a process constitutes of the following set of actions.

$$
\begin{array}{rcl}
1 < x_i.count \leq N, \ x_i = x_{i-1} & \rightarrow & x_i := 0 \mid 1 \\
x_i.count = 1, \ x_i = x_{i-1} & \rightarrow & x_i, x_i.count := \neg x_i, N \\
1 < x_i.count \leq N, \ x_i \neq x_{i-1} & \rightarrow & x_i.count := x_i.count - 1 \\
\neg(1 \leq x_i.count \leq N) & \rightarrow & x_i.count := N
\end{array}
$$

The following points are noteworthy.

- At a given time, only one of the actions is enabled at any of the processes.
- It is possible for the count $x_i.count$ to become corrupted. It is this fact coupled with the lack of global information that contributes most to the complexity of the problem.
- A process *cannot* infer from its state that the system has stabilized to one token. It is possible for a process to be deterministic when there are several tokens in the network. Thus, our solution does not solve the *detection* problem for self–stabilizing systems.

We have proved that, in addition to the usual requirements of self–stabilizing systems, the above system becomes eventually deterministic. That is, in any infinite execution, in which there are no faults after a point, the system uses only deterministic transitions.

8. Epilogue

8.1 Conclusions

In this book, we have attempted to explore and understand the limitations of UNITY's approach to program verification in four different ways. First, we have used the UNITY methodology to formulate and tackle existing problems of parallelism. Second, we have changed the assumptions underlying the UNITY computational model in an effort to understand the effects it has on UNITY logic. In particular, we have tried to develop a unified framework for reasoning with the various fairness abstractions that have been used to reason about parallelism. Third, we have tried to generalize the UNITY programming notation and logic to reason about the important class of probabilistic parallel programs. Finally, we have proposed a useful paradigm for combining probabilistic and deterministic algorithms and have tried to use our probabilistic generalization of UNITY to reason about it in a compositional manner. The time has come to assess the lessons of our research.

Our investigations reaffirm our feeling that, in some sense, the choices that UNITY has made in its economy of notation, its operators and the format of the proof rules are fundamental. Our success in tackling three different problems of parallelism can be traced to the use of the machinery of UNITY in formulating the problem.

1. In developing a compositional theory of progress, we were able to define and exploit properties of concepts such as the closure of a program, decoupling and weak decoupling in a simple and straightforward way. Our definitions of commutativity – dec_{safe} and $wdec_{safe}$ – were *formally derived*, by inducting on the UNITY proof system for progress. In fact, the intuitive significance of our definitions dawned upon us *after* we had derived them.

2. We were able to develop a framework for *systematically* designing UNITY style proof systems for progress for a variety of fairness assumptions. The soundness and relative completeness of the proof rules was guaranteed by simple, ordinal–free arguments, the most complicated of which required showing that a given predicate was the extremal solution of an equation. In the process we were able to bring together work in the previously disparate fields of predicate transformer theory, temporal logic and μ–calculus, to create a *unified* theory of fairness.

3. By generalizing the deterministic transitions and operators of UNITY to corresponding probabilistic versions, we were able to reason effectively about a class of properties of probabilistic parallel programs.

These observations seem to vindicate UNITY's approach to parallelism.

8.2 Topics for Future Research

That said and done, we would be at fault, if we didn't point out that the jury on UNITY is still out and that our results have merely scraped the tip of the iceberg. One of the complaints about proposals for program verification is that they don't scale up. While researchers have applied UNITY to specify and verify "industrial strength" programs (Staskauskas [1992]) with varying degrees of success, it is our belief that a number of problems need to be solved before the elegance and simplicity of program derivations in UNITY can be achieved in large–scale programs.

Our work on a compositional theory for progress tried to make a beginning. At the end of Chapter 4, we had given a rigorous semantic justification for including logic variables in a parallel programming language. It is natural to wonder if any other features qualify for inclusion in programming languages on these grounds? In his doctoral dissertation, Ernie Cohen (Cohen [1993]) has taken a different and more promising approach: he has used decoupling and weak decoupling to vastly simplify reasoning about distributed programs ranging from communication protocols to transaction management.

In a similiar vein, our work on designing proof rules for fairness can be extended in two ways. First, our treatment had assumed a uniform notion of fairness for all the statements of the program. Suppose, the different statements had different notions of fairness attached to them. How would one prove the progress properties of such a system? A second variation is to consider each statement of a program to be a program with its own uniform notion of fairness. Note that this means that a program would have a tree–like structure. How would one prove progress for such a program?

We can also extend our work on probabilistic parallel programs. Our treatment had not made any assumption about the probability values attached to each of the modes of a probabilistic statement. We had done this intentionally to keep our treatment simple. Suppose, we make our treatment slightly more quantitative: for instance, we could assume that all the modes have an equal probability of occurrence. This is an interesting concept as the random walk on the infinite line returns to its starting point with probability one, only if the probabilities of taking a left and right step are equal. What useful programs could be designed with such an assumption? How would our probabilistic generalization of UNITY have to be modified to prove properties of such programs?

The paradigm of eventual determinism opens up several interesting problems in the theory and practice of algorithm design. A first question is to generalize the paradigm further. Can the idea of mode switching be applied to other properties, like asynchrony and synchrony? Our detailed proofs of the algorithms are long and tedious. We would like to develop a theory of eventually–determinizing algorithms that would shorten these proofs. Such a theory would suggest conditions under which a probabilistic algorithm and a deterministic algorithm could be put together to produce an eventually determinizing algorithm. It would help in answering questions such as: What is the weakest specification that a probabilistic mode has to satisfy for its combination with a given deterministic mode to be eventually determinizing? In our example of conflict resolution, we have assumed the probabilistic mode to satisfy deadlock-freedom. Would something weaker have done the job? Another question relates to other applications of eventual determinism. Currently the author is working on applying the paradigm to mutual exclusion and network routing.

Bibliography

Krzysztof Apt and E.-R. Olderog. Proof rules and transformations dealing with fairness. *Science of Computer Programming*, 3:65–100, 1983.

Krzysztof Apt and Gordon Plotkin. Countable nondeterminism and random assignment. *Journal of the ACM*, 33(4):724–767, 1986.

Krzysztof Apt, Amir Pnueli, and J. Stavi. Fair termination revisited with delay. *Theoretical Computer Science*, 33:65–84, 1984.

Krzysztof Apt. Ten years of Hoare logic – part 1. *ACM Transactions on Programming Languages and Systems*, 3(4):431–483, 1981.

Bowen Alpern and Fred Schneider. Defining liveness. *Inf. Process. Lett.*, 24(4):181–185, October 1985.

Michael Ben-Or. Another advantage of free choice: completely asynchronous agreement protocols. In *Proceedings of the 2nd Annual ACM SIGACT-SIGOPS Symposium on the Principles of Distributed Computing, Quebec City, Canada, August 1983*, pages 27–30. ACM, New York, August 1983.

S. Cohen, Daniel Lehmann, and Amir Pnueli. Symmetric and economic solution to the mutual exclusion problem in distributed systems. *Theor. Computer. Sci.*, 34(1–2):215–226, November 1984.

K. Mani Chandy and Jayadev Misra. The drinking philosophers problem. *ACM Transactions on Programming Languages and Systems*, 6:632–646, October 1984.

K. Mani Chandy and Jayadev Misra. *Parallel Program Design: A Foundation.* Addison-Wesley, Reading, Massachusetts, 1988.

Ernie Cohen. Modular progress proofs of asynchronous programs. Ph.D. Dissertation, Department of Computer Sciences, The University of Texas at Austin, Austin, Texas, may 1993.

Stephen Cook. Soundness and completeness of an axiom system for program verification. *SIAM Journal of Computing*, 7(1):70–90, 1978.

K. Mani Chandy and Stephen Taylor. A primer for program composition notation. Technical Report, Department of Computer Sciences, California Institute of Technology, Pasadena, CA, 1990.

Edsger W. Dijkstra. Position paper on fairness. EWD 1013, Department of Computer Sciences, The University of Texas at Austin, Austin, Texas, 1987.

Edsger W. Dijkstra. Self-stabilizing systems in spite of distributed control. *Communications of the ACM*, 17:643–644, November 1974.

Edsger W. Dijkstra. Guarded commands, nondeterminacy and the formal derivation of programs. *Commun. of the ACM*, 18(8):453–457, August 1975.

Edsger W. Dijkstra. *A Discipline of Programming.* Prentice-Hall, 1976.

Edsger W. Dijkstra and Carel S. Scholten. *Predicate Calculus and Program Semantics.* Springer-Verlag, New York, 1990.

E. Allen Emerson and Ed Clarke. Characterizing correctness properties of parallel programs using fixpoints. In Jaco de Bakker and Jan van Leeuwen, editors, *Lecture Notes in Computer Science 85 : Proceedings of the Seventh ICALP.* Springer-Verlag, New York, 1981.

E. Allen Emerson and Charanjit S. Jutla. Complexity of tree automata and modal logics of programs. In *Proceedings of the 29th Annual IEEE Transactions on the Foundations of Computer Science*, 1988.

E. Allen Emerson and D. L. Lei. Modalities for model checking: Branching time strikes back. In *Proceedings of the 12th Annual ACM Symposium on the Principles of Programming Languages*, New Orleans, LA, January 1985.

Robert W. Floyd. Assigning meanings to programs. In *Proceedings of the American Mathematical Society's Symposia in Applied Mathematics*, volume 19, pages 19–31, 1967.

Nissim Francez and M. Rodeh. A distributed data type implemented by a probabilistic communication scheme. In *Proceedings of the 21st IEEE Symposium on the Foundations of Computer Science*, San Diego, California, pages 373–379, 1980.

Nissim Francez. *Fairness*. Springer-Verlag, New York, 1986.

O. Grumberg, N. Francez, J. A. Makowsky, and W-P. De Roever. A proof rule for the fair termination of guarded commands. In *Proceedings of the International Symposium on Algorithmic Languages*, Amsterdam, The Netherlands, October 1981.

A. Giacalone, C. Jou, and S. A. Smolka. Algebraic reasoning for probabilistic concurrent systems. In *Proceedings of the IFIP Working Group 2.2/2.3 Conference on Programming Concepts and Methods, Sea of Gallilee, Israel, April 1990*, pages 453–458, April 1990.

Robert Gerth and Amir Pnueli. Rooting UNITY. In *Proceedings of the Fifth International Workshop on Software Specification and Design*, May 1988.

Oded Goldreich and Erez Petrank. The best of both worlds: Guaranteeing termination in fast randomized byzantine agreement algorithms. *Information Processing Letters*, 36(1):45–49, 1990.

D. Gabbay, Amir Pnueli, S. Shelah, and J. Stavi. On the temporal analysis of fairness. In *Proceedings of the Seventh Annual ACM Symposium on the Principles of Programming Languages*, Las Vegas, Nevada, January 1980.

David Gries. *The Science of Programming*. Springer–Verlag, 1981.

Rajive Gupta, Scott Smolka, and Shaji Bhaskar. On randomization in sequential and distributed algorithms. *ACM Computing Surveys*, 26(1), March 1994.

Ted Herman. Probabilistic self-stabilization. *Information Processing Letters*, 35(2):63–67, June 1990.

C. A. R. Hoare. An axiomatic basis for computer programming. *Communications of the ACM*, 12(10):576–580,583, 1969.

Sergiu Hart and Micha Sharir. Probabilistic propositional temporal logics. In *Proceedings of the 16th Annual ACM Symposium on Theory of Computing, Washington, DC, USA, April 1984*, pages 1–13. ACM, New York, April 1984.

Sergiu Hart and Micha Sharir. Concurrent probabilistic programs, or: How to schedule if you must. *Siam J. of Comput.*, 14(4):991–1012, November 1985.

Sergiu Hart, Micha Sharir, and Amir Pnueli. Termination of probabilistic concurrent programs. *ACM Trans. on Program. Lang. Syst.*, 5(3):356–380, July 1983.

John E. Hopcroft and Jeffrey D. Ullman. *Intoduction to Automata Theory, Languages and Computation*. Addison-Wesley, 1979.

Amos Israeli and Marc Jalfon. Token management schemes and random walks yield self-stabilizing mutual exclusion. In *Proceedings of the 9th Annual ACM SIGACT-SIGOPS Symposium on the Principles of Distributed Computing, Quebec City, Quebec, Canada, August 1990*. ACM, New York, August 1990.

A. Itai and M. Rodeh. The lord of the ring or probabilistic methods for breaking symmetry in distributive networks. Technical Report RJ 3110, IBM, San Jose, Calif., 1981.

Charanjit S. Jutla, Edgar Knapp, and Josyula R. Rao. A predicate transformer approach to the semantics of parallel programs. In *Proceedings of the Eighth Annual ACM Symposium on the Principles of Distributed Computing*, pages 249–263, 1989.

C. Jones and G. D. Plotkin. A probabilistic powerdomain of evaluations. In *Proceedings of the 4th IEEE Annual Symposium on Logic in Computer Science, Cambridge, Massachusetts, March 1989*, pages 186–195. IEEE Computer Society, Washington DC, March 1989.

Thomas W. Doeppner Jr. Parallel program correctness through refinement. In *Proceedings of the 4th Annual ACM Symposium on the Principles of Programming Languages*, January 1977.

Charanjit S. Jutla and Josyula R. Rao. On a fixpoint semantics and the design of proof rules for fair parallel programs. Technical Report TR-92-23, The University of Texas at Austin, Department of Computer Sciences, 1992.

C. Jou and S. A. Smolka. Equivalences, congruences and complete axiomatizations for probabilistic processes. In *Lecture Notes in Computer Science 458: Proceedings of CONCUR '90, Theories of Concurrency: Unification and Extension, Amsterdam, the Netherlands, August 1990*, pages 367–383. Springer Verlag, New York, August 1990.

R. M. Keller. Formal verification of parallel programs. *Communications of the ACM*, 19(7):371–384, 1976.

Edgar Knapp. A comparison of the *led-from* and *leads-to*. Technical Report TR-88-35, The University of Texas at Austin, Department of Computer Sciences, 1988.

Edgar R. Knapp. Soundness and relative completeness of UNITY. Submitted to Journal of the ACM, 1990.

Leslie Lamport. Proving the correctness of multiprocess programs. *IEEE Transactions on Software Engineering*, 3(2):125–143, 1977.

Eliezer Levy. A probabilistic-deterministic algorithm, or an exercise in program composition. Private Communication, 1988.

Richard J. Lipton. Reduction: A method of proving properties of parallel programs. *Communications of the ACM*, 18(12):717–721, December 1975.

Richard J. Lipton and Arvin Park. The processor identity problem. *Information Processing Letters*, 36(2):91–94, 1990.

Daniel Lehmann, Amir Pnueli, and J. Stavi. Impartiality, justice and fairness : The ethics of concurrent termination. In O. Kariv and S. Even, editors, *Lecture Notes in Computer Science 115 : Proceedings of the Eighth ICALP*. Springer-Verlag, New York, 1981.

Daniel Lehmann and Michael O. Rabin. On the advantages of free choice: A symmetric and fully distributed solution to the dining philosophers problem (extended abstract). In *Conference Record of the 8th Annual ACM Symposium on Principles of Programming Languages, Williamsburg, Virginia, 1981*, pages 133–138. ACM, New York, 1981.

Daniel Lehmann and S. Shelah. Reasoning with time and chance. *Inf. Control*, 53(3):165–198, June 1982.

Leslie Lamport and Fred B. Schneider. Pretending atomicity. Technical Report 44, DEC Systems Research Center, May 1989.

Robin Milner. Calculi for synchrony and asynchrony. *Theor. Comput. Sci.*, 25(3):267–310, July 1983.

Jayadev Misra. Soundness of the substitution axiom. Notes on UNITY 14-90, Dept. of Computer Science, Univ. of Texas at Austin, Austin, Texas, 1990.

Jayadev Misra. Loosely coupled processes. In *Proceedings of PARLE '91, Parallel Architectures and Languages Europe, Eindhoven, The Netherlands, LNCS 506*, pages 1–26, June 1991.

Zohar Manna and Amir Pnueli. Adequate proof principles for invariance and liveness properties of concurrent programs. *Science of Computer Programming*, 4:257–289, 1984.

Damien Niwinski. Fixed points versus infinite generation. In *Proceedings of the Third Annual IEEE Symposium on Logic in Computer Science*, pages 402–409, 1988.

E.-R. Olderog and Krzysztof Apt. Proof rules and transformations dealing with fairness. Technical Report LIENS-86-1, Laboratoire d'Informatique de l'Ecole Normale Supérieure, November 1986.

Susan Owicki and David Gries. An axiomatic proof technique for parallel programs. *Acta Informatica*, 5:319–339, 1976.

Susan Owicki and David Gries. Verifying properties of parallel programs : An axiomatic approach. *Communications of the ACM*, 19(5):279–286, 1976.

Susan Owicki and Leslie Lamport. Proving liveness properties of concurrent programs. *ACM Transactions on Programming Languages and Systems*, 4(3):455–495, July 1982.

Jan Pachl. Three definitions of *leads-to* for UNITY. Notes on UNITY 23–90, Department of Computer Sciences, The University of Texas at Austin, Austin, Texas, 1990.

David Park. On the semantics of fair parallelism. In D. Biorner, editor, *Lecture Notes in Computer Science 86 : Proceedings of the Winter School on Formal Software Specification*. Springer-Verlag, 1980.

David Park. A predicate transformer for weak fair iteration. In *Proceedings of the Sixth IBM Symposium on Mathematical Foundations of Computer Science (Hakone)*, IBM, New York, 1981.

Amir Pnueli. On the extremely fair treatment of probabilistic algorithms. In *Proceedings of the 15th Annual ACM Symposium on the Theory of Computing, Boston, Mass., 1983*, pages 278–290. ACM, New York, 1983.

Amir Pnueli and Lenore Zuck. Verification of multiprocess probabilistic protocols. In *Proceedings of the 3rd Annual ACM Symposium on Principles of Distributed Computing, Vancouver, B.C., Canada, August 1984*, pages 12–27. ACM, New York, August 1984.

Amir Pnueli and Lenore Zuck. Verification of multiprocess protocols. *Distributed Computing*, 1(1):53–72, January 1986.

J. P. Queille and J. Sifakis. Fairness and related properties in transition systems – a temporal logic to deal with fairness. *Acta Informatica*, 19:195–220, 1983.

Michael O. Rabin. *Algorithms and Complexity*, chapter Probabilistic Algorithms, pages 21–40. Academic Press, New York, 1976.

Michael O. Rabin. The choice coordination problem. *Acta Inf.*, 17(2):121–134, June 1982.

Michael O. Rabin. N process synchronization with a 4 log_2 n-valued shared variable. *J. Comput. Syst. Sci.*, 25(1):66–75, August 1982.

Josyula R. Rao. Eventual determinism: Using probabilistic means to achieve deterministic ends. Technical Report TR-90-08, Dept. of Computer Sciences, Univ. of Texas at Austin, Austin, Texas, 1990.

Beverly Sanders. Eliminating the substitution axiom from UNITY. Technical Report 128, Departement Informatik Institut für Computersysteme, Eidgenössische Technische Hochschule, Zürich, Switzerland, 1990.

F. A. Stomp, W-P. de Roever, and R. T. Gerth. The μ-calculus as an assertion language for fairness arguments. *Information and Computation*, 82(3):278–322, September 1989.

Mark Staskauskas. Specification and verification of large–scale reactive programs. Ph.D. Dissertation, Department of Computer Sciences, The University of Texas at Austin, Austin, Texas, 1992.

M. Tchuente. Sur l'auto–stabilisation dans un reseau d'ordinateurs. *RAIRO Inf. Theor.*, 15:47–66, 1981.

Moshe Vardi. Automatic verification of concurrent probabilistic finite state programs. In *Proceedings of the 26th IEEE Symposium on the Foundations of Computer Science*, pages 327–338, Portland, Oregon, 1985.

Mitchell Wand. A new incompleteness result for Hoare's system. *Journal of the ACM*, 25(1):168–175, 1978.

Lenore Zuck. *Past Temporal Logic*. PhD thesis, The Weizmann Institute of Science, Rehovot, Israel, 1986.

Index

Lecture Notes in Computer Science

For information about Vols. 1–831
please contact your bookseller or Springer-Verlag

Vol 867: L. Steels, G. Schreiber, W. Van de Velde (Eds.), A Future for Knowledge Acquisition. Proceedings, 1994. XII, 414 pages. 1994. (Subseries LNAI).

Vol. 868: R. Steinmetz (Ed.), Multimedia: Advanced Teleservices and High-Speed Communication Architectures. Proceedings, 1994. IX, 451 pages. 1994.

Vol. 869: Z. W. Raś, Zemankova (Eds.), Methodologies for Intelligent Systems. Proceedings, 1994. X, 613 pages. 1994. (Subseries LNAI).

Vol. 870: J. S. Greenfield, Distributed Programming Paradigms with Cryptography Applications. XI, 182 pages. 1994.

Vol. 871: J. P. Lee, G. G. Grinstein (Eds.), Database Issues for Data Visualization. Proceedings, 1993. XIV, 229 pages. 1994.

Vol. 872: S Arikawa, K. P. Jantke (Eds.), Algorithmic Learning Theory. Proceedings, 1994. XIV, 575 pages. 1994.

Vol. 873: M. Naftalin, T. Denvir, M. Bertran (Eds.), FME '94: Industrial Benefit of Formal Methods. Proceedings, 1994. XI, 723 pages. 1994.

Vol. 874: A. Borning (Ed.), Principles and Practice of Constraint Programming. Proceedings, 1994. IX, 361 pages. 1994.

Vol. 875: D. Gollmann (Ed.), Computer Security – ESORICS 94. Proceedings, 1994. XI, 469 pages. 1994.

Vol. 876: B. Blumenthal, J. Gornostaev, C. Unger (Eds.), Human-Computer Interaction. Proceedings, 1994. IX, 239 pages. 1994.

Vol. 877: L. M. Adleman, M.-D. Huang (Eds.), Algorithmic Number Theory. Proceedings, 1994. IX, 323 pages. 1994.

Vol. 878: T. Ishida; Parallel, Distributed and Multiagent Production Systems. XVII, 166 pages. 1994. (Subseries LNAI).

Vol. 879: J. Dongarra, J. Waśniewski (Eds.), Parallel Scientific Computing. Proceedings, 1994. XI, 566 pages. 1994.

Vol. 880: P. S. Thiagarajan (Ed.), Foundations of Software Technology and Theoretical Computer Science. Proceedings, 1994. XI, 451 pages. 1994.

Vol. 881: P. Loucopoulos (Ed.), Entity-Relationship Approach – ER'94. Proceedings, 1994. XIII, 579 pages. 1994.

Vol. 882: D. Hutchison, A. Danthine, H. Leopold, G. Coulson (Eds.), Multimedia Transport and Teleservices. Proceedings, 1994. XI, 380 pages. 1994.

Vol. 883: L. Fribourg, F. Turini (Eds.), Logic Program Synthesis and Transformation – Meta-Programming in Logic. Proceedings, 1994. IX, 451 pages. 1994.

Vol. 884: J. Nievergelt, T. Roos, H.-J. Schek, P. Widmayer (Eds.), IGIS '94: Geographic Information Systems. Proceedings, 1994. VIII, 292 pages. 19944.

Vol. 885: R. C. Veltkamp, Closed Objects Boundaries from Scattered Points. VIII, 144 pages. 1994.

Vol. 886: M. M. Veloso, Planning and Learning by Analogical Reasoning. XIII, 181 pages. 1994. (Subseries LNAI).

Vol. 887: M. Toussaint (Ed.), Ada in Europe. Proceedings, 1994. XII, 521 pages. 1994.

Vol. 888: S. A. Andersson (Ed.), Analysis of Dynamical and Cognitive Systems. Proceedings, 1993. VII, 260 pages. 1995.

Vol. 889: H. P. Lubich, Towards a CSCW Framework for Scientific Cooperation in Europe. X, 268 pages. 1995.

Vol. 890: M. J. Wooldridge, N. R. Jennings (Eds.), Intelligent Agents. Proceedings, 1994. VIII, 407 pages. 1995. (Subseries LNAI).

Vol. 891: C. Lewerentz, T. Lindner (Eds.), Formal Development of Reactive Systems. XI, 394 pages. 1995.

Vol. 892: K. Pingali, U. Banerjee, D. Gelernter, A. Nicolau, D. Padua (Eds.), Languages and Compilers for Parallel Computing. Proceedings, 1994. XI, 496 pages. 1995.

Vol. 893: G. Gottlob, M. Y. Vardi (Eds.), Database Theory – ICDT '95. Proceedings, 1995. XI, 454 pages. 1995.

Vol. 894: R. Tamassia, I. G. Tollis (Eds.), Graph Drawing. Proceedings, 1994. X, 471 pages. 1995.

Vol. 895: R. L. Ibrahim (Ed.), Software Engineering Education. Proceedings, 1995. XII, 449 pages. 1995.

Vol. 896: R. N. Taylor, J. Coutaz (Eds.), Software Engineering and Human-Computer Interaction. Proceedings, 1994. X, 281 pages. 1995.

Vol. 897: M. Fisher, R. Owens (Eds.), Executable Modal and Temporal Logics. Proceedings, 1993. VII, 180 pages. 1995. (Subseries LNAI).

Vol. 898: P. Steffens (Ed.), Machine Translation and the Lexicon. Proceedings, 1993. X, 251 pages. 1995. (Subseries LNAI).

Vol. 899: W. Banzhaf, F. H. Eeckman (Eds.), Evolution and Biocomputation. VII, 277 pages. 1995.

Vol. 900: E. W. Mayr, C. Puech (Eds.), STACS 95. Proceedings, 1995. XIII, 654 pages. 1995.

Vol. 901: R. Kumar, T. Kropf (Eds.), Theorem Provers in Circuit Design. Proceedings, 1994. VIII, 303 pages. 1995.

Vol. 902: M. Dezani-Ciancaglini, G. Plotkin (Eds.), Typed Lambda Calculi and Applications. Proceedings, 1995. VIII, 443 pages. 1995.

Vol. 903: E. W. Mayr, G. Schmidt, G. Tinhofer (Eds.), Graph-Theoretic Concepts in Computer Science. Proceedings, 1994. IX, 414 pages. 1995.

Vol. 904: P. Vitányi (Ed.), Computational Learning Theory. EuroCOLT'95. Proceedings, 1995. XVII, 415 pages. 1995. (Subseries LNAI).

Vol. 905: N. Ayache (Ed.), Computer Vision, Virtual Reality and Robotics in Medicine. Proceedings, 1995. XIV, 567 pages. 1995.

Vol. 906: E. Astesiano, G. Reggio, A. Tarlecki (Eds.), Recent Trends in Data Type Specification. Proceedings, 1995. VIII, 523 pages. 1995.

Vol. 907: T. Ito, A. Yonezawa (Eds.), Theory and Practice of Parallel Programming. Proceedings, 1995. VIII, 485 pages. 1995.

Vol. 908: J. R. Rao Extensions of the UNITY Methodology: Compositionality, Fairness and Probability in Parallelism. XI, 178 pages. 1995.

Vol. 910: A. Podelski (Ed.), Constraint Programming: Basics and Trends. Proceedings, 1995. XI, 315 pages. 1995.